In the Shadow of the Art Work

Michelangelo Merisi da Caravaggio, *David with the Head of Goliath* (intersecting diagonals), 1609, p. 78

Michelangelo Merisi da Caravaggio, *David with the Head of Goliath* (horizontal axis), 1609, p. 58

Michelangelo Merisi da Caravaggio, *David with the Head of Goliath* (planar division in circles), 1609, p. 80

Michelangelo Merisi da Caravaggio, *David with the Head of Goliath* (vertical axis), 1609, p. 54

Michelangelo Merisi da Caravaggio, *David with the Head of Goliath* (circle), 1609, p. 60

Michelangelo Merisi da Caravaggio, *David with the Head of Goliath* (perspective lines), 1609, p. 92

Jeroen Lutters

VIS-À-VIS

Valiz

In the Shadow of the Art Work

Art-Based Learning in Practice

Contents

Foreword

This book is the translation of the Dutch thesis *In de schaduw van het kunstwerk: Art-based learning in de praktijk* published in 2012 by Garant Uitgevers. Since first appearing, Art-Based Learning (ABL) has resonated highly among Dutch-speaking readers. It has proved to strike a note with/impact on a wide audience wishing to find a way of looking at art, with art as a source of information. The ABL approach spread rapidly into formal and informal sectors of art and cultural education, and is currently applied in vocational training, in primary, secondary and advanced education.

In view of the focus on the visual arts, ABL has also proved to be useful tool within museum-related education. Several Dutch museums have meanwhile adopted the method as a unique means of acquainting their public with art works, and thus stimulating creative thinking, with and through art. The dissemination of ABL in the Dutch-speaking world is largely thanks to the efforts of the ABL Centre, in collaboration with ArtEZ University of the Arts. In particular, the Jan Cunen Museum in Oss has become an active centre for ABL in regions where Dutch is spoken.

Growing interest abroad for ABL has not gone unheeded—thanks in part to three of my books on Art-Based Learning published in English by ArtEZ Press. All three can be obtained individually, but are published in a deluxe box set, practically simultaneously with this translation. The works in question are: *Teaching Objects: Studies in Art-Based Learning* (2015): a series of essays on well-known art works, *Ema: Nude on a Staircase* (2017): a highly autobiographical text, and *Cy Twombly's Quattro Stagioni: Studies in Art-Based Learning* (2018) which has the structure of an art novella.

An English version of my thesis was necessary, considering the international interest in ABL. My book on Mieke Bal, my thesis supervisor, led to collaboration with Valiz publishers. It resulted in *The Trade of the Teacher: Visual Thinking with Mieke Bal* (2018) which, like the present work, is published in the vis-à-vis series. The next step was to have the Dutch thesis translated into an English version, which has now materialised, thanks to the enthusiasm of the publisher, Astrid Vorstermans.

With respect to the realisation of the present publication, Wendy van Os-Thompson deserves special mention for her fantastic translating endeavours. She has given the work a sparkle I had never dared to hope for or expect. English possesses a poetic potency that is highly appropriate to ABL as a form of thinking. Wendy understands, as no other, its inherent possibilities. An excellent translator, she has succeeded in 'reinventing' the work. The original art works this study addresses and the beauty of the English language coincide in way that seems almost predestined.

Another person I cannot fail to mention is the designer Sam de Groot, who, yet again, has deployed his graphic talents to help create this book. A book is a carrier of information, but also an artistic object. I know Sam from his beautiful designs in the vis-à-vis series. In this new publication, he has succeeded in creating a design with his customary flair, as well as a feeling for balance—one that does justice to Paul Scheulderman's original design of the Dutch publication. I am exceedingly pleased with the outcome.

You now have the result of all these efforts before you. A book that, for me, is certainly as good as the Dutch original of 2012. I wish to dedicate it to the students, lecturers and researchers in Liberal Arts Colleges, Art Universities, and faculties of Humanities throughout the world who, I have discovered in recent years, are extremely interested in ABL, since this approach links essential questions, expressive art works, possible worlds and forms of storytelling. I also hope the book will find its way to curators and museum educators in museums, large and small, in Europe and farther afield, and thus contribute to the continued development of 'the museum of the future' where exhibiting and learning through and for the arts increasingly coincide.

Jeroen Lutters
June 2019

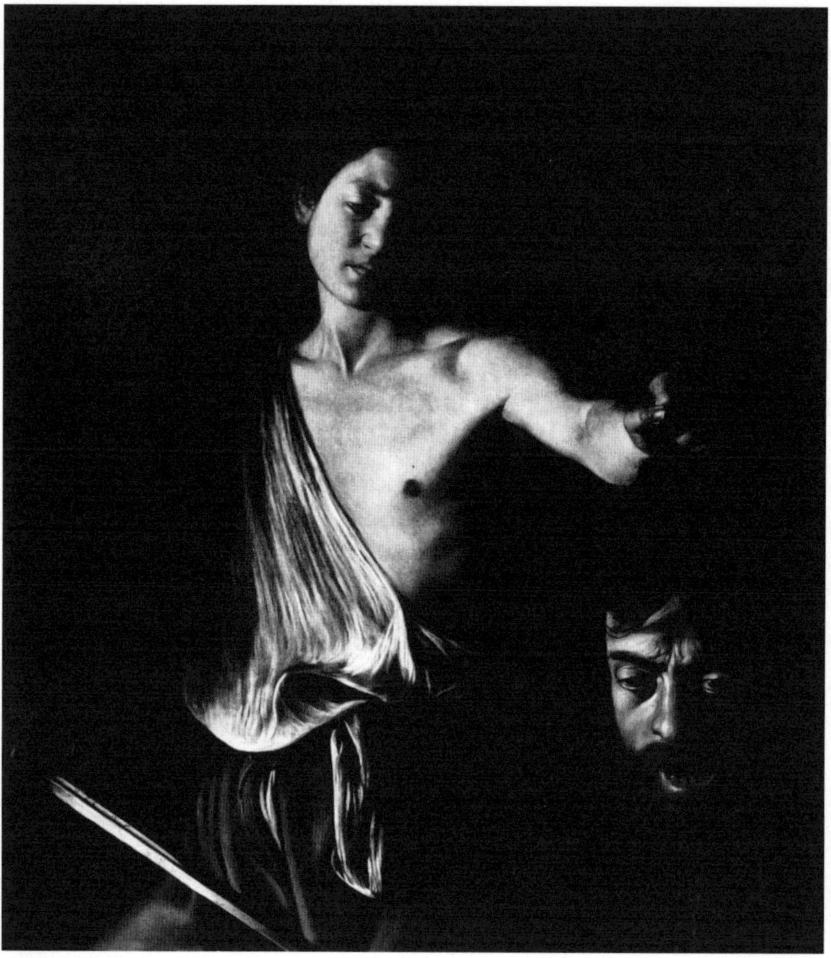

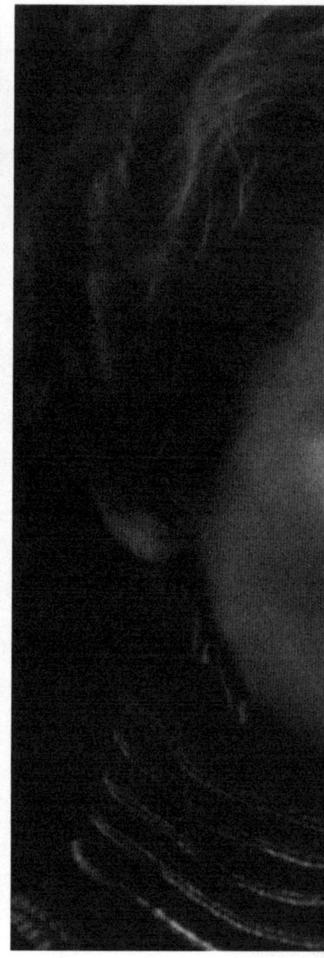

I.1.1 Triptych Caravaggio—Woolf—Ray

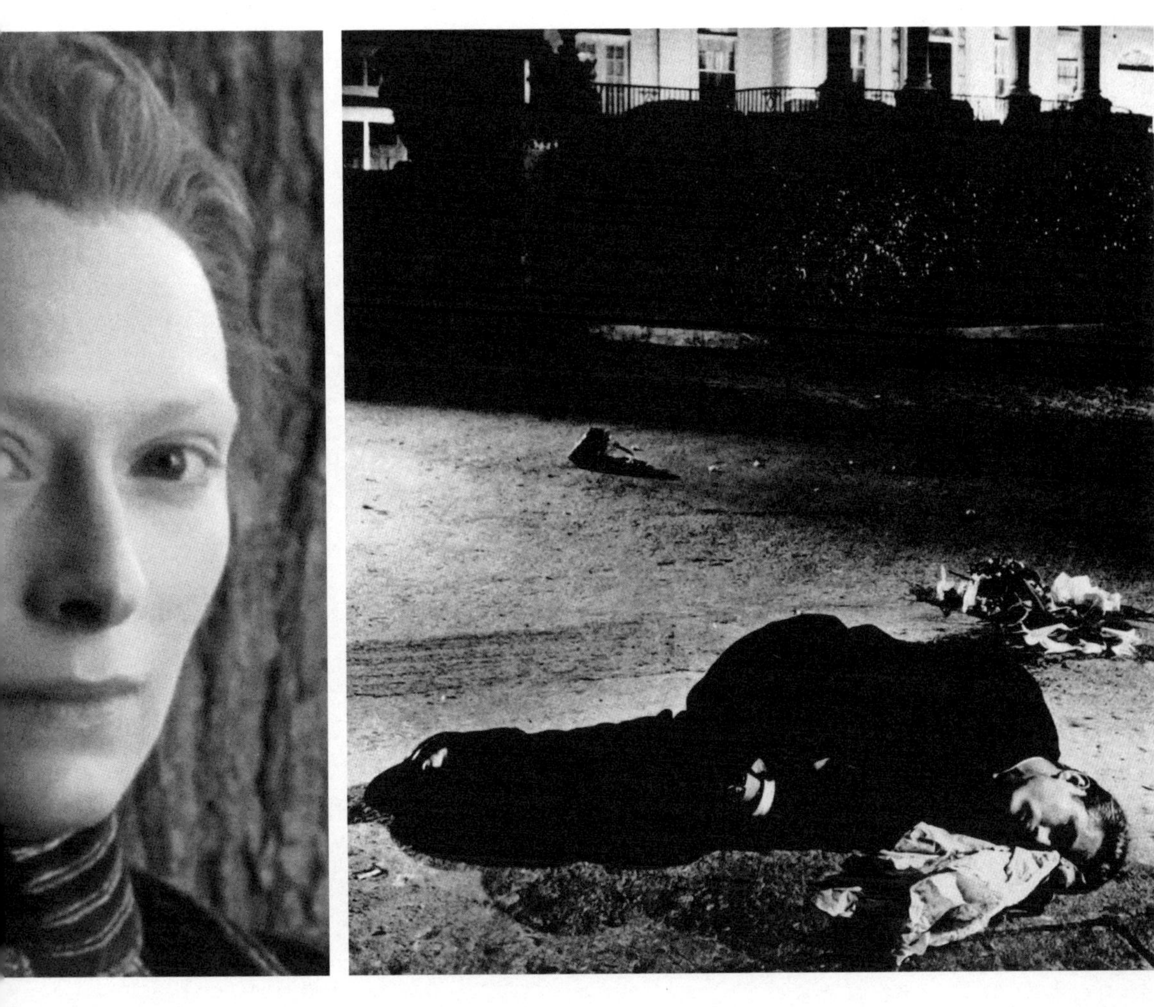

I

Introduction

Art is a mode of telling.
—Ernst van Alphen (2005, 84)

This publication is a about a method for learning not *about* art, but *from* art. I call this Art-Based Learning, ABL for short. The method has been developed in a practical setting: on the one hand, by me myself, in which I see myself as a pupil in a process of "life-long learning", and on the other hand, as a lecturer, based on experience with groups of students at colleges, art academies and universities. In line with *learning from art* I developed a methodical/didactic tool that translates the more liberal, intellectual approach to art found in the work of Mieke Bal, Ernst van Alphen and Hubert Damisch, into pedagogical practice. So ABL constitutes added value within interdisciplinary fields. I will be concentrating here on studies of adolescence.

A Dialogical Method

The term Art-Based Learning is derived from the term Art-Based Education—a somewhat hybrid word that can refer both to learning about art as a source and learning about art as a means. Within the latter, art is primarily a source of knowledge, with no attention being paid to the way art can generate insight, or to the significance of learning itself. However, that is actually what ABL does do.

The diagnostic method that has been developed in the context of the book can be applied concretely for students and lecturers, particularly in higher education, but it is in fact suitable for any form of interdisciplinary art education. The method described was inspired by the work of the psychoanalyst Christopher Bollas, who in turn based his method on Donald Winnicott's work. Bollas' most important publications are *The Shadow of the Object: Psychoanalysis of the Unknown Thought* (1987) and *Being a Character: Psychoanalysis and Self Experience* (2003). The distinctive feature of the method is its poetic and dialogical character.[1]

In practice, ABL can be divided into four steps. It is an open, non-coercive process with many variations which need not necessarily be followed in the sequence given below. The method offers the possibility to seek fresh correlations in

1 Christopher Bollas maintains that the psyche is poetically structured. He sees human development as a process from simplicity to complexity. The process is partially conscious, partially unconscious, like "dream-work". He calls the process of identity development a "dialectics of self experiencing" (2003, 31). He describes in the novella *Dark at the End of the Tunnel* (2004) the process of identity development as something that takes place in the client, but also in the psychoanalyst. Every human being "forms his own culture" (Bollas, 1987, 48). According to Bollas, the process of identity formation has much in common with a "dream script" (1987, 47).

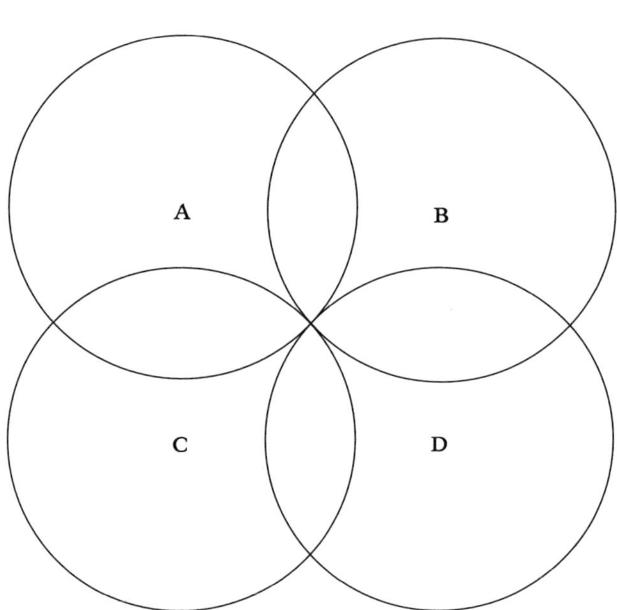

a dialogue with the art work. It is a linguistic game with the character of ongoing co-creation: with varying interlocutors, in an open space.

The four steps of ABL:

- A Ask a personally relevant question.
- B Listen to a speaking object.
- C Enter a possible world.
- D Tell one's own story.

The A-form of thinking, associative, free thinking has a prominent place in this approach. A new reality is born. It is not a traditional representation of a tangible reality, but a story—a story that approaches what Barend van Heusden describes as an "artistic mimesis" (1998). Van Heusden uses that term to indicate an imitable, new, personal creation resulting from personal investigation. It amounts to setting foot in what Bertrand Russell terms "the pace of perspectives" (Banfield 2000, 74). In that context, Bal refers to "a perpetual adjustment of images passing before the subject who makes them into a whole" (1997, 5).[2]

2 In *The Mottled Screen: Reading Proust Visually* (1997) Mieke Bal draws attention to the importance of literature as a form of knowledge that heralds this new, possible world. She states: "Proust's work offers, represents and constitutes a theory of knowledge" (1997, 239).

Step One: A Relevant Question

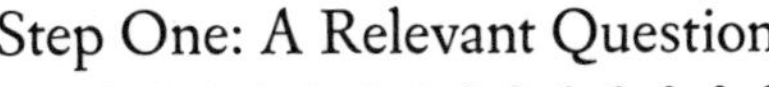

Art-Based Learning starts by asking a personally relevant question. The question is the outcome of a dialectic process of self-experience. It is important to ask a good question that is appropriate to you. It can be anything. Why am I frightened of dying? How can I enjoy the moment more? The question greatly affects the answer. The choice of subject is often far more subjective than we are prepared to admit.

The next step entails the choice of the art work. Bollas says: "When I pick up a book, go to a concert, telephone a friend, I select the object of my choice" (2003, 31). The choice takes place during a process of daydreaming: the ultimate choice is largely determined by an unnoticed dialogue with (unconscious) desires, needs and fears. The question and the resultant choice of an object are partly thought out, partly intuitive. They present themselves. As Bollas writes: "[W]e are not free to only use objects in this manner; sometimes they use us" (2003, 30). So choosing not only requires the ability to appropriate something, but, in particular, the ability to let yourself be appropriated.[3]

3 Sigmund Freud's *The Interpretation of Dreams* (originally published 1900) is an important source of inspiration here. Freud bases this on the dream-work, i.e. the ensemble of processes by which dream material is turned into a dream. It covers condensation, displacement, 'figurability' and secondary revision. Interpretation of dreams might be seen as undoing that dream-work: it is a realisation process in which the latent meaning of a dream (the hidden wish) is revealed. In this publication, choice processes are seen as a form of dream-work. It requires a construal process in order to discover how and why the choice came about.

In 2010 I went with a group of students to the Edvard Munch exhibition in the Kunsthal in Rotterdam. One student stood in front of the *Fisherboy from Nice* (1891), a small painting. Beforehand he had already asked himself: "What shall I do with my future?" The choice of this simple composition, with dominant light and the innocent lad's confrontational gaze, gave him insights he had not previously had. He concluded, thanks to the painting, that we live in a complex, hectic world. We ask ourselves questions which are perhaps totally irrelevant. The painting emitted quietness and simplicity. Munch's fisherboy offered this student another way.

Step Two: The Speaking Object

The second step allows the art work to speak. The object, the painting, the book or the film speaks. The spectator becomes a listener. The art work is the speaking subject, the 'I' at the centre. The spectator becomes the 'You', the listening subject on the periphery. The art work has its say, using its own grammar. As a spectator, you are engaged in a kind of *close reading*: attentively observing what is different, focused especially on noting aesthetic details as they reveal themselves. It is a kind of poetic observation in which you allow the object to speak, or you focus on the music or film, and are alert to special moments. Bollas in *Dark at the End of the Tunnel* refers to "A form of meditation and a sort of openness to the possibility of inspiration" (Bollas 2004, 4).

The art work is the protagonist. It is permitted to step outside its frame. The painting, play or film resembles an individual with an opinion. It tells a story through text, image or sound. At this stage the spectator is not intended to indicate what he sees or hears. He takes the art work seriously, while what he himself thinks about what the art work has to tell is irrelevant.

The spectator is "manipulated" by the object, to use Bollas' words. The person with the most daring, the one who permits himself to be manipulated the most, has the most valuable experience. As Bollas says: "At the moment of my use, the particularity specific to the object—its integrity—transforms me, whether it is Bruckner's *Eighth Symphony* moving me, a novel evoking associations, or a friend persuading me" (2003, 31). However, a rich inner experience is not all. The experience has an effect—something changes in the observer. The sensation results in transformation, in the process of which a fictive reality comes about. Moreover, the difference between fiction and psychosis entails a *willing suspension of disbelief*. The first case involves free will, in the second case the experience is part of the unfreedom of madness.[4]

In this second step it is important to allow the object to speak for as long as possible. The biggest danger is to start too quickly with the analysis. There must first be enough information for the person concerned to ponder on. Close reading is not so much a process of seeking, but especially a process of receiving, registering and allowing transformation.

4 The term 'suspension of disbelief' stems from Samuel Taylor Coleridge (1772–1834). Together with Wordsworth, Byron, Keats and Shelley, Coleridge counts as one of the 'greats' of the English romantic movement. Art-Based Learning is a romantic approach to education. It requires a basic attitude that is both empathetic and intellectual in which the recipient is willing to enter fully into the story, the experiences and the thoughts before giving them meaning. In *Biographia Literaria* (1817) Coleridge uses the formula 'a willing suspension of disbelief' to describe this attitude. Here the suspension is temporary. Only in that way—by suspending judgement—is it possible to enjoy, enter into and ultimately also learn from art.

You follow the object for analysis and intervene as little as possible. In that context, the psychoanalyst Donald Winnicott stresses the importance of an open third area, a space between the subject and the object for analysis where play can take place. This concept is crucial for the process of Art-Based Learning.[5]

5 In Winnicott's approach, the art of listening is the key focus and the 'transitional object' plays an important part. He believes that transitional phenomena form a play experience in a third area that lays the foundations in (and thus also derives its inspiration from) art, science and religion. Winnicott's contention in *Playing and Reality* (originally published 1971) could be the motto for Art-Based Learning that I support: "[I]t is only in being creative that the individual discovers the self " (73).

Step Three: Possible Worlds

The third step is a pre-eminently dialectic moment—one that can result in the spectator losing himself in a self-experience. It calls for willpower and daring from the spectator, to break free and move through an intertextual space. Following naturally from Coleridge's appeal for 'temporary suspension of disbelief', this dialogue with the source triggers a process of visualisation. The subject (spectator) enters into a dialogue/ conversation with the object. It is important that the subject dares to move with the object, yet itself continues to occupy space.

The subject and the object move together in a space where countless elements are linked together associatively. The researcher and the object of research are constantly changing places. There is no need to press for meaning; it is more important to traverse all manner of paths and side-paths.

The spectator/listener, who keeps on adding new dimensions or episodes to the story, is, in Doležel's words, in a "possible world". Winnicott refers to a "third area". That interim space, in which it is particularly important to play, withdraws from containable forms. Action and reaction follow in succession. Actuality, memory and idea merge in a sensitive way. You must dare to play the game. Metonyms and metaphors are useful aids in that respect. They help you to discover new lines, ask new questions. Bollas notes that the subject in its "prior self state" and the object in its "simple integrity" come to an end. They are "destroyed in the experiential synthesis of mutual effect" (Bollas 2003, 31).[6]

We are now in the area where the spectator can say: "I am lost in self experiencing" (Bollas 2003, 31). When you enter that terra incognita must have the courage to let go of the reins completely, after having loosened them somewhat in step two when you listened to the object. You are entering an area of associative, adjacent experiences when you let in all the images, ideas and memories that present themselves. More and more things reveal themselves that are no longer directly connected with the world of the speaking object. So a possible world transpires that is far greater and comprises numerous adjacent art works and other sources. The spectator or researcher changes more and more. The art work loses its previous 'simple' state. When he analyses this, in step four, the researcher seeks to understand by degrees something of the cohesion of this possible world.

6 The term 'possible world' is found in Lubomír Doležel. He states that the distinction between fact and fiction is gradual rather than a matter of principal and that reality consists of a series of stories which, following Leibniz's monads, function as possible worlds in which the reader can move—if he is prepared to do so. See for example *Heterocosmica: Fiction and Possible Worlds* (1998).

Step Four: Telling a Story

The fourth and last step is the rhetoric moment in which reflection, understanding and assignment of meaning transform into a story of their own. So the assignment of meaning proves to be a performative linguistic act. ABL is a narrative approach and leads to a new story, new knowledge, and a tentative answer to the original question.

Bollas typifies this final stage as follows: "I observe the self as an object" (2003, 31). The researcher leaves the process of 'self experiencing proper' and pauses to consider his own experiences. "This is the place of the complex self", according to Bollas. In *The Shadow of the Object* he devotes an entire chapter to the self as an object. He describes how there is evidence of what Freud calls an intrasubjective process involving both ego and superego.

As Bollas puts it, this intrasubjective process is a form of self-management in which the researcher steers certain aspects of himself, as a mother or father would do with a child (1987, 42). It is not always clear who is speaking. The complex individual, with the first and third person coinciding, is an "ironic position". The simple self is permanently seeking experiences. The complex self reflects on those experiences.

The ironic position is characterised by simultaneity. The individual is both the "arranged" (simple) and the "arranger of his life" (complex). In other words, we are both the "initiated" and the "initiators of our existence" (Bollas, 2003, 28).[7]

ABL, which starts with asking a question and goes on to develop into a dialogue with the art work, now changes into liberal practice. It creates the possibility for independent liberal thought: an open fundamental attitude in which, ultimately, the narrative is based on fiction (Barrett 2003, 15). Liberal thought is a creative, innovative, liberating form of thinking deriving inspiration from the work of philosophers like Roland Barthes, Michel Foucault and Richard Rorty.

Roland Barthes would say: the reader has become a writer. The recipient has embarked on the path of choosing, allowing to speak, losing and ascribing meaning. A new text reveals itself. Or, in more concrete terms: the spectator has not only learned something new about himself. He has received answers to his initial question and created fresh knowledge of a cultural phenomenon. The author is dead. A new story has developed.[8]

7 The historian Frank Ankersmit makes a comparable distinction between research and narration. He describes the moment when the research-related process changes into a creative process. An important publication in that context is *Narrative Logic: A Semantic Analysis of the Historian's Language* (1983). In 2005 Ankersmit published *Sublime Historical Experience* in which he emphasises that it is important to reach an aesthetic experience: there must be a brief break in the clouds, as it were, if one is to achieve a unique, intense and complex experience. I discern in this a connection with the method of Art-Based Learning as described. Modern psychology is regularly the cloud cover that stops us from obtaining fresh insights into the individual. Art-Based Learning stands for aesthetic politics that are not hampered by normative impediments and can thus lead to new insights into "possible worlds".

8 The well-known phrase "the death of the author" originates from Roland Barthes. His post-structuralist work is of great importance for the method of Art-Based Learning. In works like *S/Z* he demonstrates that, as he puts it, "rereading is no longer consumption but play" (1974, 16). He elaborates further on what he already wrote in the essay "The Death of the Author" (1977, originally published 1967) and posits that it is not the author, but the reader who ascribes meaning to the text within this type of semiotics.

Permanent Education

ABL is a method of permanent education with resemblances concepts such as liberal education and continuing education. It is a process of life-long learning—an in principal infinite process of acquisition and sharing of knowledge. It is a way of learning "through which individuals recreate themselves" (Eisner 2002, 240). In addition, a position is explicitly taken against exclusive, market-orientated thinking, for instance as revealed in such phrases as "training for X". In the latter case, the focus is solely on the (economic) goal of the training: it loses sight of the student's personal development. ABL is a way of thinking that takes time (as does psychoanalysis) and ties in more with the tradition of Liberal Arts, in which learning and living go together, and the subsequent practise of one's profession is not all that counts.

There are two schools of thought in the Liberal Arts—a traditional and a progressive. I personally have a pronounced preference for the latter. The traditional European school is rooted in the idea of *Bildung* (formation) and reaches back to eighteenth- and nineteenth-century philosophers like Wilhelm von Humboldt. The Anglo-Saxon variant of Liberal Arts has its roots in a Catholic tradition and is inspired by the ideas of cardinal John Henry Newman. That school ties in to a large extent with the Core Curriculum movement, with considerable focus on what are classified as *Great Works*. Martha Nussbaum is a prominent American proponent.

A more progressive variant of learning for life which ties in better with the ABL model I advocate, is found in Gayatri Chakravorty Spivak's 'Live theory'. In *Death of a Discipline* (2003) Spivak argues in favour of using the imagination as a form of knowledge. This type of knowledge occurs in literature, among other things. She presses for education with a "role of teaching literature as training the imagination" (2003, 13). Literature can teach us to stimulate the imagination, seeks to achieve heterogeneity and wants to escape the system. It is a form of learning that pays more attention to a "politics of friendship" (28).[9]

The Netherlands also has a long tradition in the area of *Bildung* and Liberal Arts. Erasmus' and Comenius' works are the foremost examples. It is with good reason that their names are given to two of the European Commission's programmes for lifelong learning. Desiderius Erasmus was a passionate advocate of the permanent practice of the liberal sciences. Jan Amos Comenius, with his attention to mathetics rather than didactics—the art of learning versus the art of teaching—is another source of inspiration for ABL.

In contemporary Dutch literature the Liberal Arts can be found in the work of the economist Arjo Klamer, the founder of the Academia Vitae, the sociologist Hans Adriaanse, the founder of the University College Utrecht and the Roosevelt College Middelburg, the theologian Rob Riemen, the founder of the Nexus Instituut in Tilburg. All are advocates of lifelong learning. This active lobby affirms that there is considerable interest in the Liberal Arts, but also that this alternative approach to learning has to be secured because it is not run of the mill.[10]

Art as a Form of Thinking

The structure of ABL as described here is a method in which the subject of ABL is interlinked with a process of lifelong learning, and the object of research—art—"thinks" in its own medium. The imagination renders in a subtle and complex

9 On the back flap of *Death of a Discipline* Judith Butler posits that Spivak "maps a new way of reading not only the future of literary studies but its past as well." And accordingly, Spivak's work is an example of how ABL can work. In this case it is about how "literature teach[es] us that there are no certainties" (Spivak 2003, 26). When we enter the area of the imagination—as art does—we are following in Walter Benjamin's footsteps and entering the area "outside the law" (Spivak 2003, 33). This is an area of unprecedented educative strength. Art (literature in particular) represents thinking outside the law. It provides knowledge of matters which would otherwise remain hidden. All of which indicates the importance of ABL for the total accumulation of knowledge within the humanities. Specifically, this method allows all possible scope for alternative perceptions of reality.

10 Klamer describes in *In hemelsnaam!* (2011) the restructuring of universities as an example of economic thinking that's gone overboard. He states: "I dream of a university in the Liberal Arts. For people with experience who want to reflect on all manner of questions and problems, and to do so in a dialogue with the classics (i.e. renowned texts, scholars and artists)" (2011, 144). This is not training aiming at the practice of a profession, but a lifelong process of study.

way what young people/students generally face. Consequently, it is important to enter into a dialogue with images. That intellectual view on art is, as we have found, directly related to the work of Mieke Bal, Hubert Damisch and Ernst van Alphen.

Mieke Bal is a cultural theoretician with an impressive oeuvre, which includes such works as *Verf en Verderf: Lezen in Rembrandt* (1990), *Quoting Caravaggio: Contemporary Art, Preposterous History* (1999), and *Louise Bourgeois' Spider: The Architecture of Art-Writing* (2001b). Bal describes her method as "culture analysis", a concept in which art and the ascribing of meaning to art within the humanities are constantly interconnected. In this approach, art is a complex way of thinking. The protagonist is the researcher, who questions art, in order to gain greater insight in relevant cultural themes.[11]

In his descriptions of the work of Francis Bacon and Armando, Van Alphen shows how art thinks. He is also of significance for this study in view of his focus on form; his poetic attitude to reading. In *Op poëtische wijze: Handleiding voor het lezen van poëzie* (1996) he describes the attitude to reading poetry as reading with attention to what is divergent. It is of great importance to recognise, analyse and question details as characteristics of a way of thinking that is inspired by culture. In *Art in Mind* (2005) he primarily addresses the process of observation: the learning from art itself.

Hubert Damisch also sees art as a form of thinking. In this context he reaches back to the work of Leonardo da Vinci who, according to Damisch, was primarily a researcher and only after that an artist (2007, 4). Damisch also refers to the Italian philosopher and historian, Benedetto Croce, who sees art as intuitive knowledge that is comparable to dreams (9).[12]

11 A short, succinct description of Bal's approach can be found in the essay 'Art and Intersubjectivity', the introduction to Mieke Bal's *Looking In: The Art of Viewing* (2001a). Norman Bryson describes how semantically mobile Bal's method is, it is characterised by what he calls a quest for details, sees things from a rhetorical perspective and considers an image as a visual narrative in which the narrator of the image differs from the (human) author. Bal is an example for me in "doing theory", not only as an author but also in her work with her numerous students. Bal's culture analysis forms the theoretical framework of this study.

12 Damisch has published several works which have been of importance for ABL, one being *A Childhood Memory by Piero della Francesca* (2007), in which he examines the work of the fifteenth-century painter Piero della Francesca and addresses the importance of linear perspective in Renaissance thought. Another well-known book is *A Theory of Cloud: Towards a History of Painting* (2002). Here he considers a new way of shaping, experiencing space in art starting in the Baroque in which clouds play an important part. He refers to the "concept of a 'Baroque' or 'pictorial' or 'painterly' (malerisch) style, whose most striking feature is possibly its 'antipathy to any form with a clear contour'" (4). In *Skyline: The Narcissistic City* (2001) he examines the design of space as evidenced in contemporary architecture. Damisch's work is a source of inspiration for the present study with respect to method. With his aesthetic approach he mainly explores the dynamic of the design of an art work, analysed as a form of thinking—a language with its own logic.

The idea that art "thinks" legitimises the use of art as a source of knowledge. Accordingly, art is constantly around us. When people enter into a more dialogical relationship with the world, and especially the images in it, as a way of thinking more acutely, it means they learn to deal more actively or interactively with what culture and art can offer. The dialogue with art challenges you to undertake an intelligent dialogue with yourself and the culture in which you live—with art not restricting itself to Great Works. I shall show that Art-Based Learning can constitute both big and small stories at the same time.

An Interdisciplinary Result

Christopher Winch and John Gingell define in *Philosophy of Education* (2004) "learning" as a process and a result. In that respect, studies of adolescence form an interdisciplinary field of activity. It is important for educationalists, development psychologists, cultural anthropologists, philosophers and historians.

ABL in the form featured here is geared to philosophy, specifically to those who are intrigued by Julia Kristeva's approach to adolescence—regardless of age. In that context, adolescence is a frame of mind, an experience, a memory or a desire. The defining feature is the basic attitude in which little is set in stone. This age-unrelated approach as set out in the essay "The Adolescent Novel" in *New Maladies of the Soul* (1995), breaks through every biological demarcation.

Kristeva's approach ties in with Judith Butler's views. Butler sees human identity as separate from every form of biological and psychological definition. Identity is a performative linguistic act, a "regulation of attributes along culturally established lines of coherence" (2007, 33). Adolescence is a form of fiction: an idea that results in a style and, with constant repetition, becomes reality.[13]

I also elaborate on the work of historians and anthropologists—historians like John Neubauer, for example, who deals extensively with the phenomenon of adolescence in his *The Fin-de-Siècle Culture of Adolescence* (1992). However, I have mainly drawn from the work of Dick Hebdige, an author originating from the semiotically orientated Birmingham School of Stuart Hall. His foremost works, for me, are *Subculture: The Meaning of Style* (2007, originally published 1979) and *Hiding in the Light* (1998, originally published 1988). His approach is both aesthetic and political, arguing as he does for adolescence in its 'otherness'. His studies can be read as examples of historical anthropology.[14]

I also focus on developmental psychologists and educationalists who are curious about the phenomenon of adolescence after having read the work of the psychoanalyst Peter Blos. In his work on adolescence, Blos analyses, for instance in *On Adolescence: A Psychoanalytic Interpretation* (1966, originally published 1962) and *Son and Father* (1985), the solipsistic process of separation and individuation.

13 Butler's identity concept features in *Gender Trouble* (2007, originally published 1990). The deconstructivist, non-essentialist conception of identity that she proposes forms the foundations for my study of adolescence. Butler's poststructuralist approach assumes that identity is a fictive construction, a physical style, a performative production, a consciously chosen masquerade and a fantasmatic structure. Butler's conception of identity also has a political dimension. She propagates a fiction that complies with the deed. She sees gender politics as a narrative strategy that can break through every exclusive discourse. Accordingly, she has developed a view on a third gender. *In Bodies That Matter: On the Discursive Limits of "Sex"* (1993) she refines the theme broached in *Gender Trouble*. Her key term "performativity" can easily be translated into a theory about biographical phases such as adolescence. Adolescence becomes a fictive construction. You become a child through repetition, you become an adolescent through repetition and you become an adult through repetition. So adolescent is not what you are, but what you become by doing it.

14 In various essays he has highlighted divergent forms of youth culture: from English punkers in the nineteen-eighties to Japanese Lolitas of recent years. In his best-known work *Subculture* he emphasises that youth styles are "signifying practices". His work contains variants on the themes 'youth and death', 'youth and beauty' and 'the game of youth'. These are the three language games which will be dealt with later in the case studies.

Tools for ABL

ABL has its own 'language', which (in line with Jos de Mul's work) I would like to describe as learning 2.0. 'Homo digitalis' affects the set-up of the framework of the notes (as a system of hyperlinks), the structure of virtual triptychs and the analogy with the sketchiness of a blog. It is the transition that Gilles Deleuze develops in *Cinema 1* (1986, originally published 1983) and *Cinema 2* (1989, originally published 1985)—the transition from "everything is cinema" to "everything is digital".[15]

ABL is a way of thinking in time and space. The cloud escapes the static space of the visual arts. It provides an answer to the linear thinking of the expressive artist. It affects the multidimensional world of dance.[16]

A good example of the blog-character of this study is the creation of the triptych featured here, comprising three different preliminary studies which I published at an earlier date. It is a process of framing and re-framing in which facts are continuously grouping and regrouping. The three preliminary studies are, in chronological order:

1. *The lost paradise of the adolescent* (1999). In this study I look at one of the greatest post-war icons of adolescence: James Dean as Jim Stark. I shall go into it in more detail in Chapter 4, as the perspective of the ironic adolescent.
2. *Adolescence in fiction: Caravaggio's portrayal of adolescence* (2006). There I address the "otherness" of the adolescent from the perspective of the tragic adolescent. That topic is explored further in Chapter 2, in particular.
3. *The Poetic language of the adolescent: On the beauty of otherness* (2009). The aspect of adolescent aesthetics featured there, is the story of the poetic adolescent as presented in Chapter 3.

15 Gilles Deleuze is one of the first to refer to *cinematographic thinking*. Between 1983 and 1985 he wrote *Cinema 1* and *2*, a two-volume study that plays an important part in the context of Art-Based Learning as a kind of cinematographic thinking and researching. It centres on a philosophy in flux which—in Deleuze's words—is geared to "posing the question of the 'new' instead of eternity" (1986, 3). In such space the 'whole' will never, of course, be found. Deleuze refers to Bergson, who states that "nature is to change constantly, or to give rise to something new" (9). From that vantage point, an impressive philosophy develops, with thinking being considered as a creative process in which we are constantly searching for something new. This process begins in the world of shots, cuts and frames, and results, via a process of montage, in "crystals of time" and "peaks of present and sheets of past". It goes so far that film—for example in Godard's work—"ceases to be images in a chain" (Deleuze 1989, 180). Instead of compelling mechanical thinking, a more poetic method of "free indirect vision" comes about that elaborates on Aristotelian syllogism, making it difficult to work in a world of possibilities and paradoxes (185).

16 The philosopher Jos de Mul studies the new digital reality. He published *Het romantische verlangen in (post)moderne kunst en filosofie* (1990), among other works. And more recently *De domesticatie van het noodlot: De wedergeboorte van de tragedie uit de geest van de technologie* (2006). De Mul is well known for his interest in cyberspace: post-geographical space and post-historical time. In *Cyberspace Odyssey* (2002) he discusses how the discovery of cyberspace has affected our cultural identity. He approaches identity as the "free play of identities", as a homepage identity, a hypertextual reality that is a work in progress (199). This idea largely coincides with the interpretation of identity and adolescence in the present study. Adolescence is a narrative, virtual, creative and fictive product of our imagination. It creates a reality rather than representing one. De Mul's work is not only very useful for the ABL process as regards content, but also as regards method. In his description of digital space, in which ABL is situated, he refers to the work of Leibniz, who does not interpret space as something absolute but as a relational concept between things. "Space is merely the totality of these interrelationships. Without things, no space would exist" (25). Cyberspace as a research area can be seen as a space in which objects occupy their places and interconnect as subjects in varying relationships. This results in a permanent dynamic and an infinite number of virtual configurations. And therefore cyberspace is the equivalent of Winnicott's 'third area'.

Conclusion

The research is threefold in character:

1. *The level of the content*: With respect to content, the adolescent's story is the primary focus, and especially the adolescent's thinking in a postmodern period. Adolescence has various specific characteristics, which I group under one denominator—adolescent aesthetics.
2. *The level of the method*: I aim to develop a method for the ABL form of learning I propose. The method is based on Christopher Bollas' "dialectics of self-experiencing".
3. *The level of didactics*: Lastly, I have developed an educative approach with the name Art-Based Learning. It is geared to creating the right conditions with which to support the method of Art-Based Learning.[17]

17 Consistent with Bal, I must emphasise that in ABL the reader can be either a spectator (painting) or visitor (museum).

Here it is relevant to tell a short story. Briefly it is a story in three parts: about youth when confronted with death for the first time and the efforts to overcome that tragedy in one's life. The first part, 'Youth and Death', concerns David and Goliath. The second part relates to 'Youth and Beauty', in which the adolescent seeks to escape the tragic aspects in a form of poetic sublimation (Orlando). The third, 'The Game of Youth', features the adolescent who discovers that poetry cannot provide a definite answer to the tragedy of life, reaching, as a last resort, for irony as a form of hope (Jim Stark).

This story is the outcome of an encounter with art works as speaking objects—images that provide insight into contemporary culture and which can thus be 'excavated' as archaeological finds. In *About Looking* (2009, originally published 1992) John Berger describes the methods of the photographer Paul Strand, who randomly sets up his camera somewhere where "something is about to happen". It is quite likely that his "subjects" almost automatically turn into narrators (47).

I present this change from a silent object to a speaking narrator in the pages that follow.[18]

18 In *The Moment of Cubism* (1969, orig. published 1967, 20) John Berger refers to the metaphorical model of the diagram as the foundation of our thinking—an idea that will recur frequently. He pays special attention to the power of images as sources of knowledge. In *Ways of Seeing* he states: "If the new language of images were used differently, it would, through its use, confer a new kind of power. Within it we could begin to define our experiences more precisely in areas where words are inadequate. (Seeing comes before words.) Not only personal experience, but also the essential historical experience of our relation to the past: that is to say the experience of seeking to give meaning to our lives, of trying to understand the history of which we can become the active agents. The art of the past no longer exists as it once did. Its authority is lost. In its place there is a language of images" (Berger 1972, 33).

II

Youth and Death

Concerning the Visual Arts

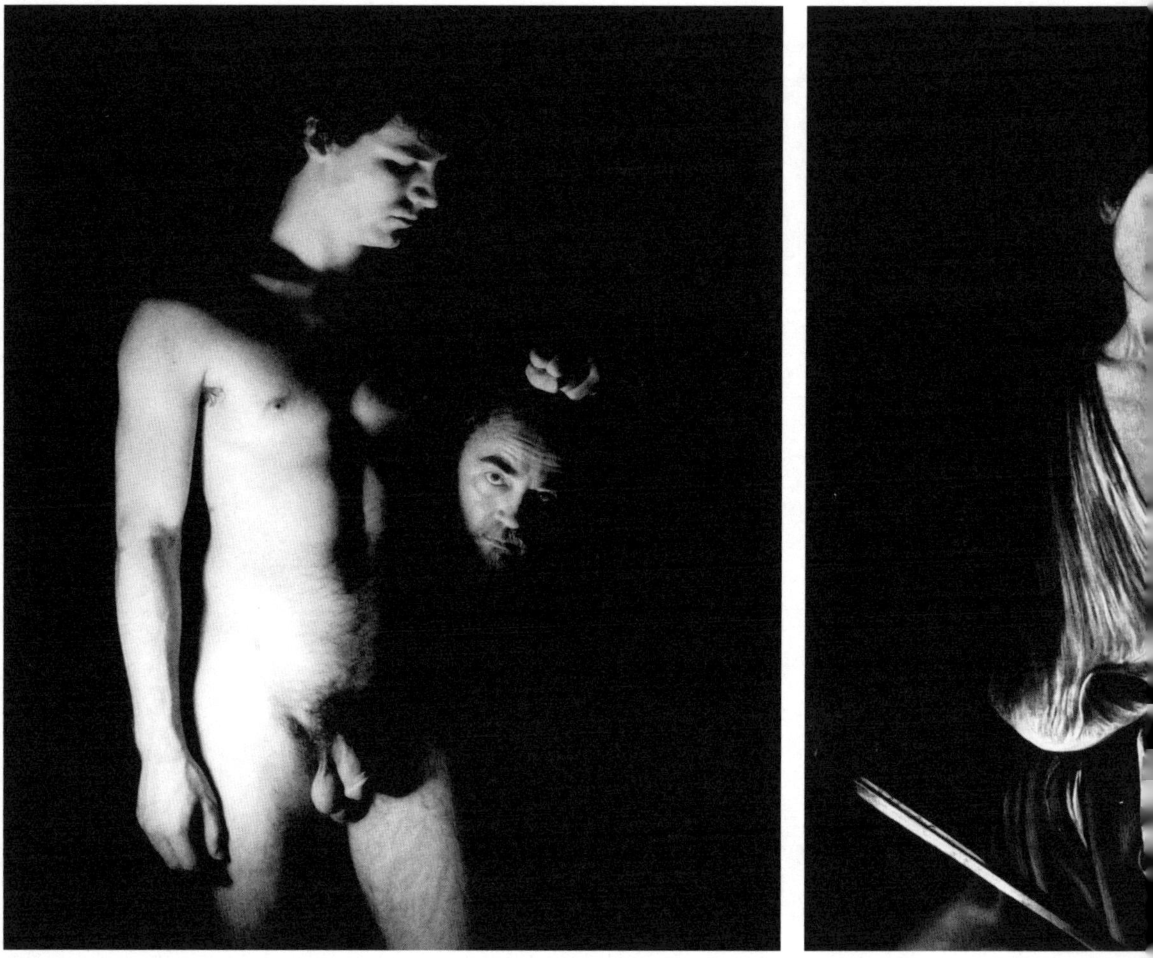

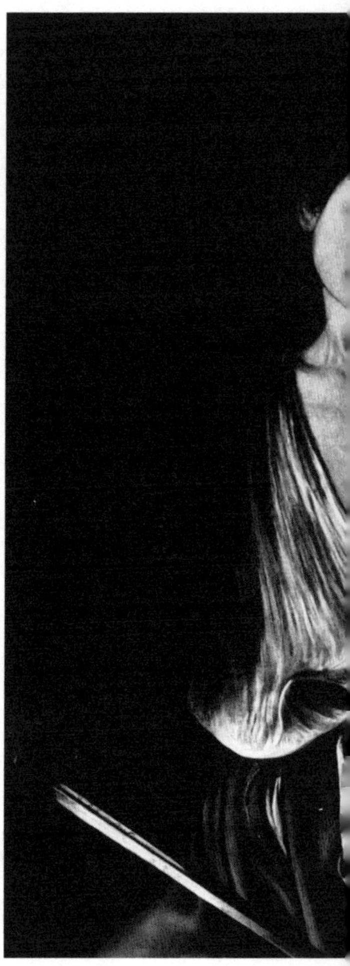

II.1.1 Triptych Pedriali—Caravaggio—Kassovitz

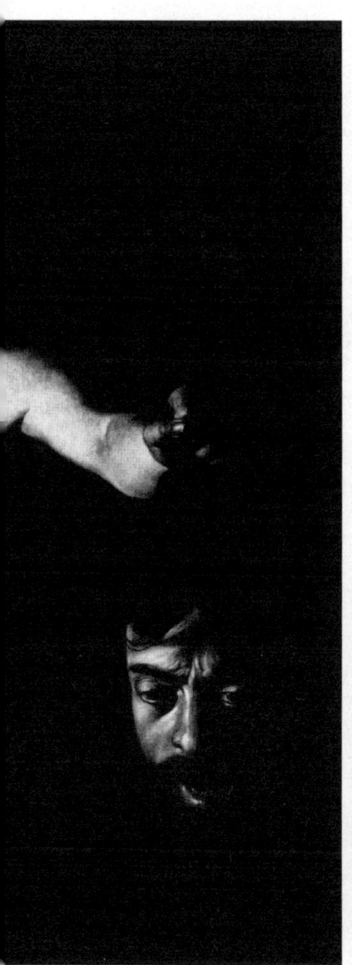

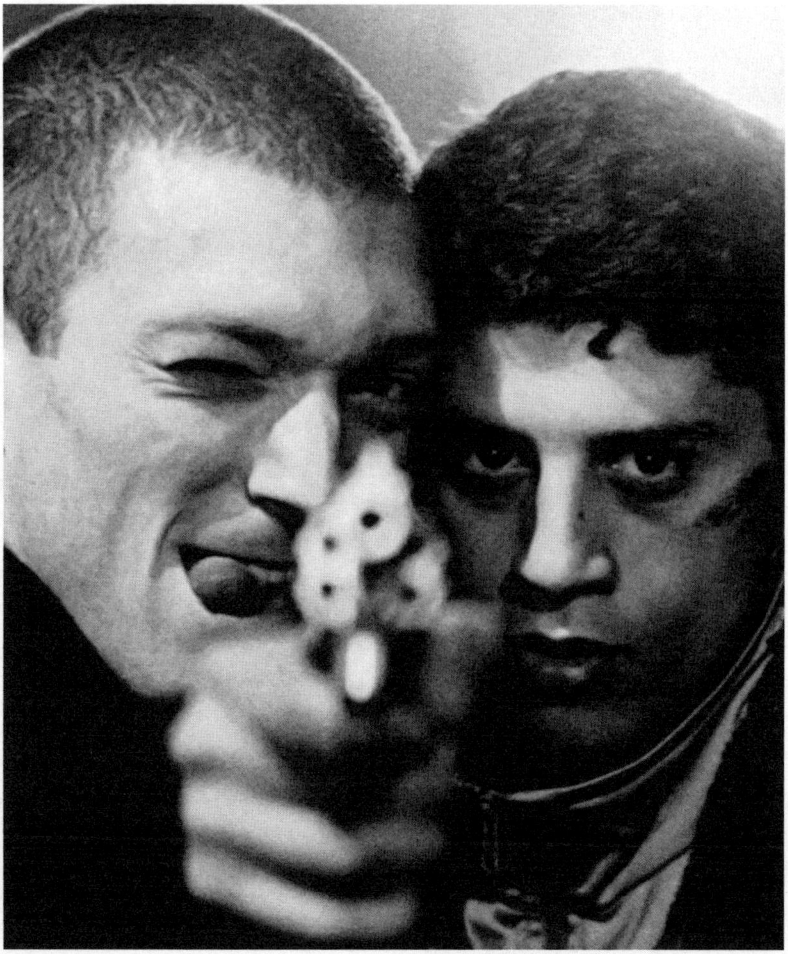

Thinking in *chiaroscuro*

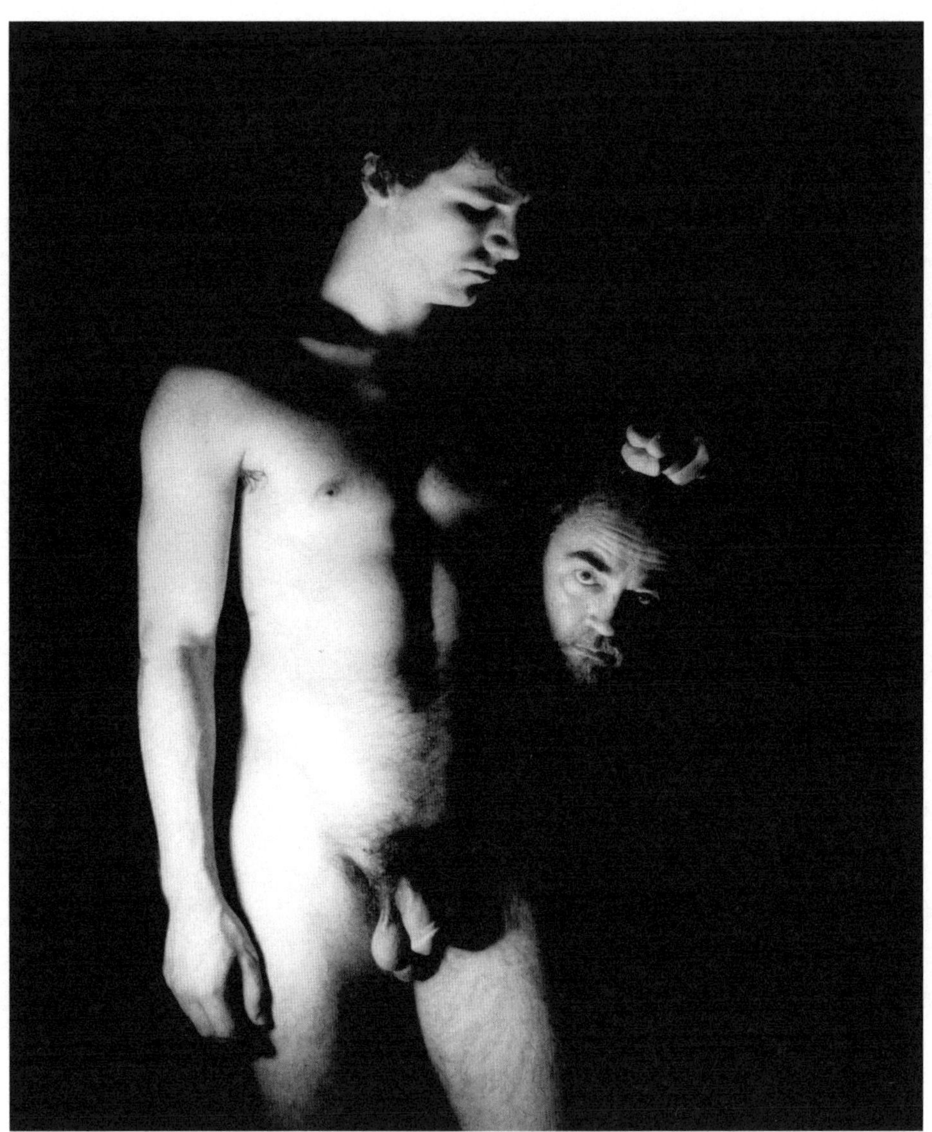

1
Exposition: Dino Pedriali

Introduction

Stories of adolescence in art and in fiction are linguistic games providing us with fresh insights into the possible worlds of adolescence and thus of our culture. Leibniz was the first to point to the existence of those possible worlds. Kripke (1980), Doležel (1998) and Pavel (1986) summarised their importance in a possible world theory.

The first possible world that will now come about is the 'caravaggesque' world of youth. It is the tragic world of the adolescent that I outlined briefly in a preliminary study. In the words of the art historian Barth David Schwartz it is "a giant arena constructed of baroque façades and peopled from paintings of Caravaggio and Guido Reni, where cherubs walked the streets and were willing to talk, or something more, just for the fun of it" (1995, 271).

In this chapter 'Youth and Death', I report again, more systematically and extensively, on this process of "free association that evokes a theatre of multiple selves and others"

II.1.2 Dino Pedriali,
Autoritratto immaginario, 1989

(Bollas 2009, 17). Caravaggio's story forms the middle panel in a triptych of three art works: a photo by Pedriali, a painting by Caravaggio and a film by Kassovitz (fig. II.1.1). With it, I want to show that we live in a world dominated by baroque aesthetics: a caravaggesque world that still determines our thoughts and deeds.

I start with the self-portrait of the photographer Dino Pedriali: *Autoritratto immaginario* (1989), the first image in the triptych. The self-portrait is like a monad. It is the reflection of a first, tragic allegory of youth: a picture of youth in its tragic guise, as we encounter it daily, in literature, film and the visual arts.[19]

PEDRIALI AND PASOLINI One day I walked into a modern second-hand bookshop in my home town of Arnhem and came across a book of photos featuring the theme of youth in photography. It related to the work of Dino Pedriali (b. 1950). His use of light immediately reminded me of Caravaggio. These associations formed a stepping stone to a neighbouring possible world. I leafed through the book and saw photos of boys on scooters in Rome. They looked as if they had just ridden out of a film by Pier Paolo Pasolini. Looking back, the association was not surprising. Pedriali is the one who took the notorious series of nude photos of Pasolini in the final weeks before his violent death in 1975.[20]

Pedriali's work is closely akin to that of Pasolini in terms of theme and style. Pier Paolo Pasolini's work is characterised primarily by stark realism. His fundamentally tragic thinking reflects the painful struggle between life and death, packaged in a play of light and darkness, expressing itself in a combination of tragedy, poetry and irony. His realism has something harsh about it, something unconventional; reality

19 The theory of monads comes from Gottfried Wilhelm Leibniz (1646–1716), a mathematician and physicist. The monad can be compared to an atom, singular and indivisible. Leibniz sees such monads as non-material entities and preconditions for the origin of material substances. Material substances are made up of compound substances and are brought about by aggregation (accumulation of monads). The reality of matter is essentially plural. The indivisible state is reserved for monads. With division, material reality always has an infinite number of new compositions. He compares this with the division of an object in pleats rather than grains: "[The division of an object] must not be considered to be like the division of sand into grains, but as … a drapery that dissolves in pleats; there will be an infinite number of pleats, some of which are smaller than others; and for this reason a body will never be dissolved into points or minima" (quoted in Mugnai 2005, originally published 2002, 82). Leibniz' ideas form the basis of thinking in possible worlds. You can see the tragic possible world as the singular monad, from which art works are a derivative. The theory of Art-Based Learning put forward here considers art to be a form of thinking and thinking as a form of art. This means that thinking is an infinite process of pleating. New variations are always possible.

20 For the photographic work, see Pedriali, *Pier Paolo Pasolini: 'Testamento del Corpo'* (1989).

is often presented, unpolished, in a filmic and literary idiom filled with extreme contrasts.

Pasolini sketches reality as something he loves, yet also curses. In an interview for the magazine *Rinascita* (1967), later included in the compilation *Heretical Empiricism* (1988, originally published 1972), he says: "Oh, I don't have any regrets: whoever loves reality too much, as I do, eventually hates it, rebels against it, and tells it to go to hell." The flight from reality described by Pasolini eventually takes him to poetry and a concomitant ironic reality, three themes that anticipate my great triptych of youth.[21]

In his monograph *Dino Pedriali* (1994), Peter Weiermair examines Pedriali's world in more depth. The monograph contains several interesting essays, including one by Maurizio Marini entitled "Dino Pedriali: Rappresentazione di anima e di corpo." Three themes soon emerge that are typical for Pedriali's work: light and dark, striking details and the underworld. These three would seem to relate directly to death and recur time and again in the following ABL exercise:

1. *Light and dark*: Pedriali makes considerable use of light effects. The characters are almost at odds with the sharp contrasts between light and darkness. In that way it resembles Caravaggio's *chiaroscuro*.
2. *Eye for detail*: Marini praises Pedriali's "camera eye", his "anthropomorphic empiricism" (Weiermair 1994, 109). Accordingly, Pedriali fits into a long tradition that developed in West-European art from the sixteenth century onwards. The art works attest to a cult of the body: the beauty of life and the horrors of death.
3. *Underworld*: Pedriali's work is about the street, eroticism, the young male nude as found in Rome's red-light district. He depicts street kids. It is the world of

21 Subjective reality can, according to Pasolini, be shaped with a "free indirect subjective camera focus" (1988, originally published 1972) which he illustrates by way of Godard's work. Important elements in this approach are attention to personal details, rhythm, a perceptible camera and the author who expresses himself in direct speech. Laura Rascaroli posits in *The Personal Camera: Subjective Cinema and the Essay Film* (2009) that this subjective method of working can be found in Pasolini's notebook films, which resemble travelogues, and in which the author specifically takes part, not only on the sound track (as voice-over) but also visually (as a narrator). Pasolini's work is interesting as regards both content and method for this exercise in Art-Based Learning.

Method-wise the notebooks have an essayist character that fits in with Art-Based Learning. Content-wise he describes the incongruence between the tragedy and romance of youth.

Pasolini's neo-realistic work: a world characterised by a "sense of evil (the negotiation of love)" (108).

A few months later I dropped into the same bookshop and again came across a book by Pedriali: the famous series of photos he took of Pasolini: *Testamento del Corpo*. It proved to be a catalogue that accompanied the 1989 exhibition in the municipal museum in Arnhem (today's Museum Arnhem). Beauty, love, sexuality, commitment and perversity were already defining for Pedriali's *Claudio* (1987), in which his subject was youth, and for his *Umberto* (1983) in which transience was the main theme.

Those themes now coincide in Pasolini's portraits, which are accompanied by such poetic captions as "I close my eye to dream on".

THE TRAGIC ADOLESCENT A first portrayal, a first personification, of today's adolescent emerges. It is the first step towards the tragic story of the adolescent—a story of light and dark, of the cult of the body and the underworld, as translated into the contemporary hip-hop scene, for instance. The prime focus is the transience of existence, and youth that is confronted time and again with its mortality.

Harsh Light

THE LIGHT The first thing that strikes me in the *Autoritratto immaginario* depicted earlier is the sharp contrast. The adolescent (arm, chest, averted face) appears in the light. Details are prominent: the genitals, hair, veins that make the arm stand out like a sculpted form. The light adds to the body the character of a sculpted figure, reminiscent of

Michelangelo's work. The light seems to enable the adolescent to brazenly say: here I am.

DINO PEDRIALI *Hiding in the light*: I am familiar with the world of the youth and light from Pedriali's early years—the seventies. The importance of light is very conspicuous in *Al Buco* (1976). This is a reportage with three photos in which the first depicts a naked boy on a scooter on the beach (fig. II.1.3). The photo tells more than a story: it also tells

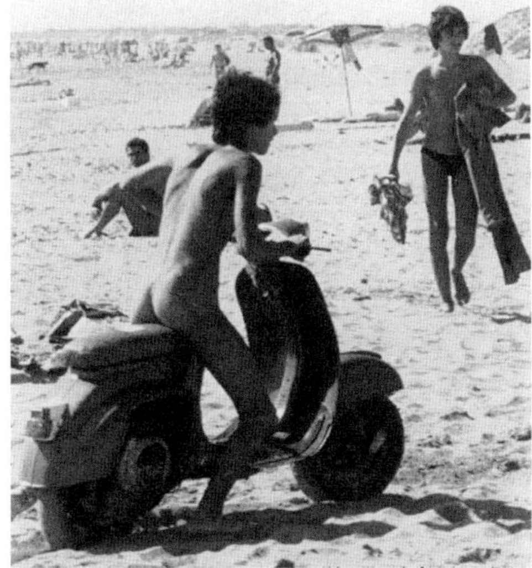

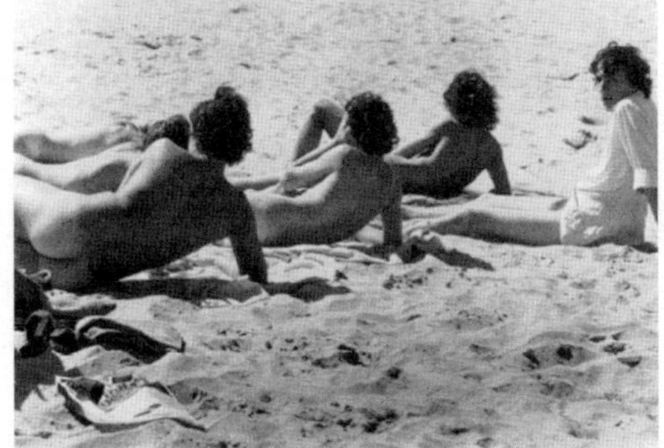

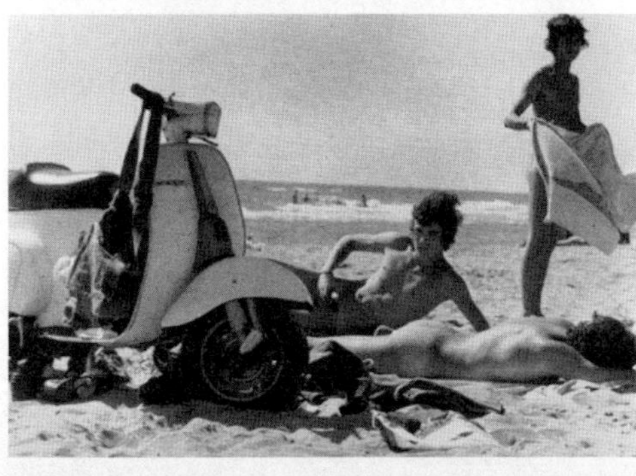

II.1.3 Dino Pedriali, *Al Buco* (photo series), 1976

about the personal narrative style that closely interconnects young people and light. Pedriali was twenty-six years of age when he took this photo, a late adolescent. It is a double exposure: an exposure of an art work, but also an "exposure of the self" (Bal 1996, 2). Is this image of the young adolescent the conclusion of that stage in his own life?

The title of the triptych guides us towards a possible world: *buco* means cavity, pit, hollow, hole or opening. It is the hole in which the boy gets stuck with his scooter. He is standing in bright sunlight in which everything is visible. The boy is not alone. An older man sits in the background. He is looking at the boy with his scooter stuck in a hollow. The second photo in the *Al Buco* series shows a next stage: five naked boys lying on the beach. They are all looking towards the sea. The boy in the white shirt, looking directly at the spectator, seemingly wanting to say: "Can you see it?" The spectator in the first photo—the older man in the background—is now the recipient.

The third, and last, photo, goes a step further. The first photo heralds the start of a trip, the second an intervening moment, but the third marks the climax of the series. A boy holding his penis in his hand raises himself above the boy lazing on the sand, holding his genitals. The gesture is perhaps a demonstratively provocative reaction to the spectator's voyeuristic gaze.

In the light of *Al Buco,* everything is visible. The dominant light, the lack of any contrast ensures that a dreamlike, unreal mood is evoked—the dreamlike world of youth, which Pasolini calls amoral, not immoral.[22]

THE LIBERATED ADOLESCENT In this photo series the adolescent appears as a heroic buccaneer. Pasolini remarks that 'cinema, lacking a conceptual, abstract vocabulary, is

22 Pedriali's work seeks to situate itself in the same "third space" as that of Caravaggio. Marini describes how Pedriali's work recalls Caravaggio's. "On a figurative level Dino Pedriali's message thus articulates itself in the perennial contest between light and shadows, which generate and extinguish each other in alternation in order to emphasize the coexistence of good and evil, of the spoken and the unspoken word, which finds its implicit parallel (and indeed its confirmation) in the tragic painting of Caravaggio. Pedriali does not, however, intend to revive Caravaggio in photography, nor does he mean to step beyond the limits of the image by means of a clever use of chiaroscuro. His originality pushes him to make use of light as an inexhaustible means of discovering the emotions associated with the most hidden elements of the universal being. One may also say that this is an artistic language that follows the path of a kind of anthropomorphic empiricism in which both the positive and the negative gain new values" (1994, 109).

powerfully metaphoric ...' (1988, 174). The adolescent is a shameless figure, posing without swimming trunks or a shirt. He is licentious and stands out from his surroundings. Like Riccetto, the protagonist in Pasolini's novel *The Street Kids* (originally published 1955) he is not concerned about conventions. He is cheeky, sometimes tough, sometimes brazen. He leaps off the photo paper.

Darkness as Absent Light

DARKNESS In *Autoritratto immaginario* darkness is more emphatically in evidence than light. The older man is a character in the dark. He seems to be saying: 'I'm here too'. If we look along the diagonal line, from below right to top left, the boy is somewhat further back. He would appear almost to disappear, rather than step forward. Is he losing ground? Who is the adolescent here? Is the adolescent someone who comes off worst—a light that, as life passes, gradually gets swallowed up in the darkness? Vitality that falls prey to mortality?

YOUTH AND OLD AGE Schwartz sketches in *Pasolini Requiem* a comparable, dark world: a 'giant arena of baroque facades' (1995, 271). It is the world of street urchins, dark alleyways and constant menace. We find ourselves in the rough world of Rome's street life.

This Pasolini-like shady world is repeated in Pedriali's *Davide e Golia* (1985). The standing David looks straight into the lens with one eye. The effect of this indirect look is that the character has something provoking, shameless and brazen. The young man appears to be playing with the spectator, with me, and so I—avoiding his look—almost automatically drop my eyes from the top to the bottom of the photo, and from left to right.

In *Davide e Golia*, Goliath is a young man with curly hair. David has him in a stranglehold with his right arm and he, Goliath, is sinking into the darkness, with eyes cast down. The look on his face is decidedly milder than that of the standing boy. The grip looks far from comfortable. He undergoes it submissively. The young man standing beside him pays him no attention. His eye is telling the spectator: "You may have a problem with this, I don't." He is casual, patronising, to his victim and the audience alike. The head of the young Goliath, gripped so casually, could also symbolise that of the spectator. This portrayal becomes even more gruesome when we realise that it is a head without a body—the body belonging with that head is not visible.

The Pasolini-like darkness into which young people disappear becomes even harsher when we look at Pedriali's picture of the vagrant, Umberto (fig. II.1.4). The harrowing illusion of youth is revealed. The empty look of the inward-looking, introvert young man is pushed aside by Umberto's

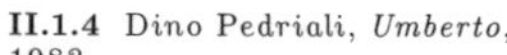

II.1.4 Dino Pedriali, *Umberto*, 1983

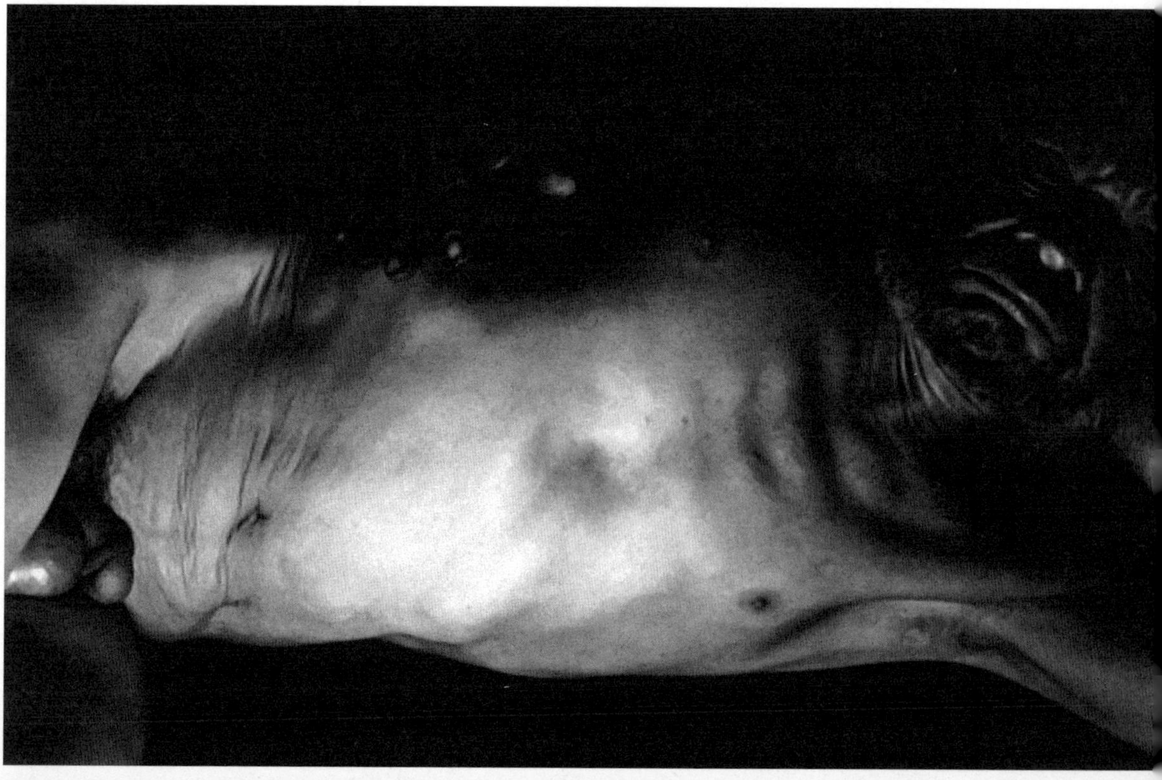

deathly look, his grimace. Youth is transformed into old age: a condition without progression and without hope.

THE VULNERABLE ADOLESCENT The liberated adolescent in *Autoritratto immaginario* changes, spurred on by the force of darkness, into a vulnerable young adult. Umberto, decay, turns youth into an illusion. The young man may appear powerful, but, ultimately, his pose is a form of over-compensation for an actual powerlessness. When one 'rereads' these photos, the fact that the character is a product of his environment is confirmed. It is the environment that is the true protagonist and makes of the character an unimportant, powerless and vulnerable subject.

The Importance of the Gaze

GAZE Finally, I would like to consider for a moment a single detail: the direction of the older man's gaze. Significantly, he is looking directly, head-on, animatedly and with some irritation into the camera. The composition radiates complete autonomy, independent of the surroundings. He displays contempt. The older man confronts me, as a spectator, with my own vulnerable, affective and searching insignificance which I see reflected in the attitude of the young man. The wrinkles on the older man's head allude to thoughts. I do not know what they are, but they seem negative. However, there is more than negative disdain. The direction of the gaze also invites a romantic desire. The older man not only repels. He also seems to be seeking rapprochement.

LEOPOLD VON SACHER-MASOCH The work of Pedriali and Pasolini deals with youth between pain and pleasure, and, from the victim's position, has a bearing on the work of Leopold von Sacher-Masoch. In *Coldness and Cruelty* (1991, originally published 1989)—an essay about Sacher-Masoch's novel *Venus im Pelz* (1870)—Deleuze addresses themes such as vitality and mortality, life and death, pleasure and pain. Having explored the work of Freud, Sacher-Masoch and De Sade, he comes to the conclusion that it is wrong to see masochism purely as pleasure that arises from pain. Rather, it is a process of desexualisation in order to facilitate a process of resexualisation, a sexual continuum. Deleuze writes:

> In sadism and masochism there is no mysterious link between pain and pleasure; the mystery lies in the desexualisation process which consolidates repetition at the opposite pole to pleasure, and in subsequent resexualisation which makes the pleasure of repetition seemingly proceed from pain. In sadism no less than in masochism, there is no direct relation to pain: pain should be regarded as an effect only (1991, 121).

The interplay between pain and pleasure is a form of mysticism. The greater the abstinence, the greater the pleasure.

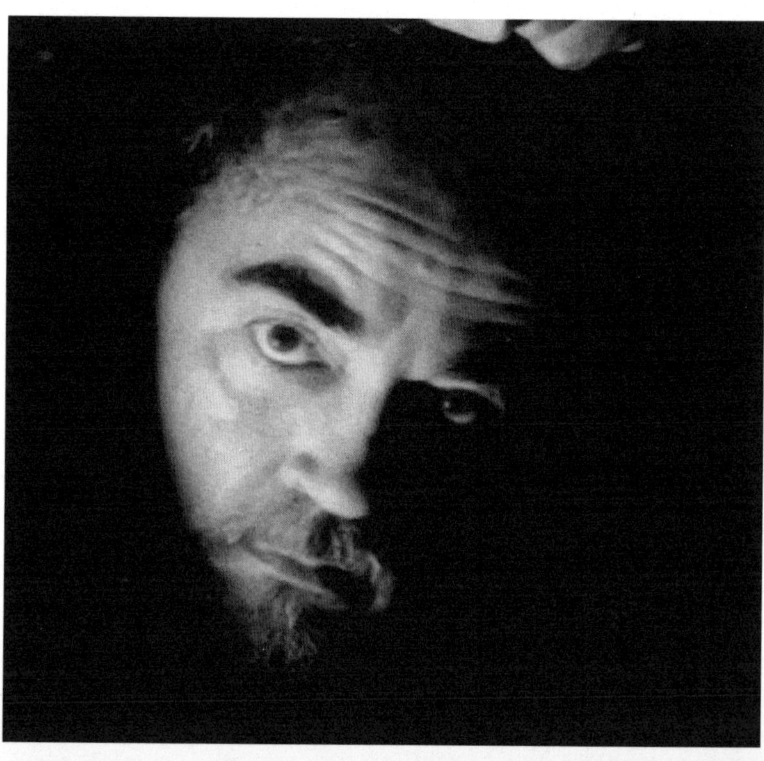

II.1.5 Dino Pedriali, *Autoritratto immaginario* (detail), 1989

That form of mysticism is clearly identifiable in Pedriali's photos and Pasolini's films. Darkness increasingly gains the upper hand. A tragically romantic world emerges. Is this the paradox of beauty and decay, of *coldness and cruelty*? Is this Deleuze's 'pornology'? He speaks of 'mysticism in perversion', referring to the interaction between Eros and Thanatos, the exchange between coldness and comfort, i.e. "the coldness of desexualisation and the comfort of resexualisation" (1991, 120)—a borderland where pain and pleasure touch.

The worlds of Pedriali and Sacher-Masoch do have substantial differences. Dino Pedriali's work is situated in a neorealistic tradition. The boys in his work are street kids, whereas the romantic Sacher-Masoch's characters belong to the aristocracy and bourgeoisie. Pedriali's adolescents live in hard-boiled reality. Their facial expressions are resigned, bored, sometimes tormented. Their skin shows signs of sickness, violence and addiction. Sacher-Masoch's individuals live in a lavish, decadent world of pleasure.

However, despite these difference, there is a kindred undercurrent: that of decay, of a world where there is no hope left. Light in Christian—and so Western—symbolism is identified with good, dark with evil. Both Pedriali and Sacher-Masoch reveal the material world that is subject to decay, where darkness prevails.

THE SUBSERVIENT ADOLESCENT What does this tell me about the world of the adolescent? The heroic adolescent would appear to have vanished and been replaced by his opposite. He has changed from a liberated boy into a subservient slave, a paladin who acts on behalf of an older master. He is not a ruler, but a servant—an attribute even, that the older man is free to set aside if it is no longer required to serve.

The direction of the gaze implies that the seemingly dominant position—the boy above, the older man below—is revoked. The downcast eyes, together with the stooping posture confirm the actual balance of power. The adolescent has lost his self-assurance. The man is powerful, severe and superior: a tyrant. The young man is subservient.

Much of Pedriali's work, as also in *Autoritratto immaginario,* contains an ironic clue. In this case, the irony lies in the fact that Pedriali is making a self-portrait (just like Caravaggio). The picture is ambiguous. It contains a tragic, as well as a comically ironic story line. Is the author a beheaded character? Or is he alive? Is the picture sad or amusing? Is it realistic? Or is it totally illusory?

Conclusion

What does adolescence mean now? Dino Pedriali's photo makes it clear that art is a form of thinking. Working with Art-Based Learning shows how much information photos like this can contain, and what they produce, if you allow them to speak. In this first case study I wanted to give a glimpse into the underworld: a world that is not a nice place to be, in which darkness takes the place of light, and in which the adolescent falls from his pedestal.

Pedriali's possible world ties in with the neorealistic underworld in post-war Italy, filled with individuals who have been picked up off the street and put in front of the camera. In the words of Weiermair: "Pedriali takes them from the streets, undresses them and creates them" (1994, 8). In addition, Pedriali's work also shows a world with romantic and ironic aspects. Transience is a tragic given. The unmistakable, hedonist elements seem romantic. And lastly, the hint to the spectator is the ironic component. The reality of the liberated, vulnerable slave is, as Pedriali explains it for me, both painful and appealing.

The possible world is inhabited by individuals: adolescents who appear out of Rome's dark alleyways of their own accord, to expose themselves to the eye of my hypothetical camera.

In fact, the spectator only has to do one thing to move along in this process of Art-Based Learning: he must ask himself a question and then surrender to "unconscious mental activity", in a state of "evenly suspended attention" (Bollas 2009, 10). He looks and associates. Worlds meet. The spectator abstains from a final judgement, and descends automatically into the depths. By means of art-as-a-way-of-thinking he gains insight into both the adolescent himself and into the complex network of cultural contexts in which the idea of adolescence is shaped.

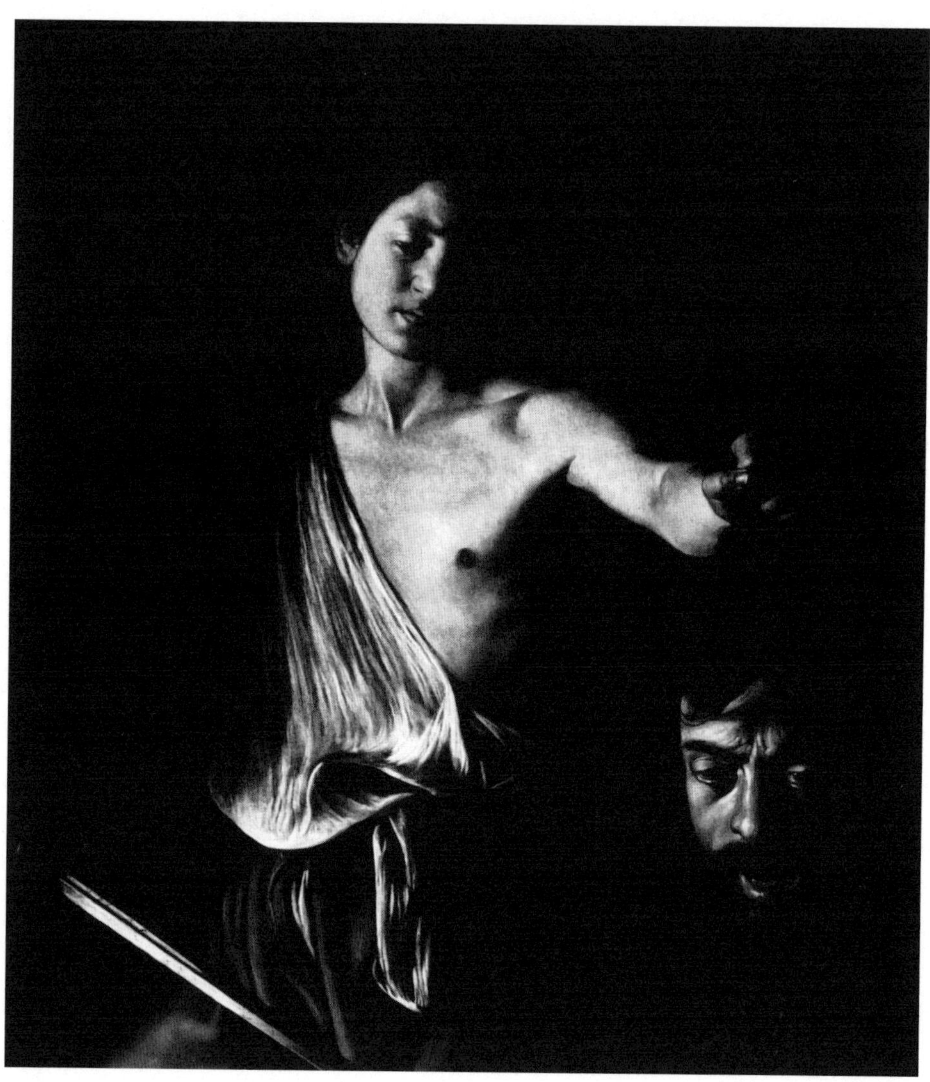

2

Continuing Impact: Caravaggio

When it appeared, this was the most dramatic and moving representation of David ever painted.
—Silvia Cassani (2005, 137)

Introduction

The Baroque was the embryo of the merciless realism encountered in the previous chapter. For the middle panel of the triptych I chose Caravaggio's *David with the Head of Goliath* (1609; fig. II.2.1). Why that work? Caravaggio marks the start of the modern time: the rudimentary depth, the continuing impact of a possible world. The photo and the painting also have a directly intertextual connection. Pedriali's late-modern photo is in fact a remake, a footnote to this early-modern, dramatic shot of the tragic adolescent. That is why I have linked Pedriali and Caravaggio.

I refer to a 'shot' because Caravaggio is, to my mind, a cinematographic thinker. Long before the Lumière brothers held their first film 'show' in Paris, Caravaggio was an

II.2.1 Michelangelo Merisi da Caravaggio, *David with the Head of Goliath*, 1609

ingenious thinker in consecutive images. For me, his cinematographic mentality is evidenced in the way he generates and assembles several series of pictures. Each sequence of 'shots' is actually a separate scene. In this way Caravaggio composes a complex, simultaneous reality.

Caravaggio's *David with the Head of Goliath* was painted in Naples, 380 years before Pedriali took his photo. I first saw the painting when I visited Villa Borghese in Rome. It belonged in the collection of Cardinal Borghese, who acquired it round 1613. David is the character who stands out most, owing to the planar division, the effect of light and composition. In the Baroque, the biblical figure of David was portrayed frequently, for instance by Guido Reni (1605), Orazio Gentileschi (1610), Enrico Haffner (1620), Bernardo Strozzi (1635) and Carlo Dolci (1670). The Bible story tells of the shepherd, David, who kills Goliath, an almost three-metre tall giant, on the battlefield. The biblical background, the iconological explanation are not the aspects I primarily wish to examine. I read Caravaggio as a philosopher and consult his work as theoretical study. I approach him as a thinker in *chiaroscuro*. Caravaggio's work is the testimonial to thinking in light (Eros), shadow (Chronos) and darkness (Thanatos). In the caravaggesque plot David, Goliath and an indiscernible figure are embroiled in a dramatic struggle. These three individuals together tell me the tragic story of youth. It is a film plot in light and dark. David, as Eros, initially plays the leading role. Then Chronos takes over. In the third part Thanatos becomes the protagonist.[23]

One of the best works about Caravaggio is Mieke Bal's *Quoting Caravaggio: Contemporary Art, Preposterous History* (1999). It clearly demonstrates that we are still living in a caravaggesque culture. She describes Caravaggio's

23 Youth is a recurring theme in the work of Caravaggio (1571–1610): often men, sometimes women. Seen from that perspective, his work can be divided into three periods. They reflect the arrangement found in *David with the Head of Goliath*, in which the three themes of youth, old age and death converge. The first period is marked by a strong emphasis on the classical Graeco-Roman portrayal of youth and runs from 1593 to 1598. The chief work from that period is *Boy with a Basket of Fruit* (1593/94), followed by *Young Sick Bacchus* (1593/94), *The Lute Player* (1595/96), *The Musicians* (1595/96), *Boy Bitten by a Lizard* (1596/97) and *Bacchus* (1597). The second period is typified by dramatic biblical stories and lasted from 1598 to 1605, starting with *Judith Beheading Holofernes* (1598); it also includes works like *The Calling of St Matthew* (1599–1600) and *The Entombment* (1602–04). For me, the pinnacle of this period is *John the Baptist* (1605). The second period is characterised by the clear contrast between youth and old age. The third period starts round 1605 and ends in 1610; it focuses on youth and death. The chief works from this tragic period in the light of this study are *David with the Head of Goliath* (1609), *Burial of St Lucy* (1608/09) and *The Raising of Lazarus* (1609).

paintings as a form of cultural awareness in which intellectual, aesthetic, political assumptions and thoughts are expressed in material objects. She typifies the space in which a painting is situated as "baroque aesthetics" (1999, 69). For Bal, Baroque is more than a historical style period. It is

> a perspective, a way of thinking which first flourished during a specific period and which now functions as a meeting point whose traffic lights make us halt and stop to think about (the culture of) the present and (some elements) of the past (16).

Bal's approach to art as a way of thinking coincides with the methods of Art-Based Learning. She outlines a conceptual time and space in which the works of Pedriali and Caravaggio can meet up and achieve an intertextual relationship. The work of the two artists is separated historically by a period of almost 500 years. Caravaggio is "the past", Pedriali is a "recasting of past images" (Bal 1999, 7). The third space bridges geographical and historical boundaries. The relations between artist and art work, art work and art work, and art work and spectator acquire a new dimension. We find ourselves in a possible world where everything is possible. The spectator is now a participant and can emerge better off than when he entered (22–25).

TRAVELOGUE In 2002 Joni Mitchell issued a jazz album called *Travelogue*. That term is an apt metaphor for this study. The cinematographic narrator is a traveller. He arrives in a space, the "unthought known", where dark and light, crooked and straight, foreground and background are constantly alternating. It is a third space: the research object and the researching subject meet. Freud uses the metaphor of the train journey with good reason when he addresses such subject-object relations. He says: "Act as though, for instance, you were a traveller sitting next to the window of a railway carriage and describing to someone inside the carriage the changing views which you see outside" (quoted in Bollas 2009, 6). In *Metaphors We Live By* (1980) and *Philosophy in the Flesh* (1999), George Lakoff and Mark Johnson contend that abstract concepts are often conveyed as metaphors. Metaphors are visual themes, images that unite dissimilar notions and produce new meaning. Youth, old age and death are metaphorical concepts. They serve as a temporary reality in the fictive world in which we have landed.[24]

24 Lakoff and Johnson's premise is that our thoughts and deeds are fundamentally metaphorical. They state that: "The essence of metaphor is understanding and experiencing one kind of thing in terms of another" (1980, 5). Working with metaphors provides on the one hand insight into cultural matters (among other things). On the other hand, metaphors are also sources of creativity: "metaphors are capable of giving us a new understanding of our experience" (139). The overlap with the methods of Art-Based Learning lies in these two functions. Art works relating to adolescents refer to underlying metaphors. They are speaking objects. The possible worlds correspond to three metaphors concerning the adolescent: death, beauty and play. The stories and pictures that give us fresh insight also use metaphors.

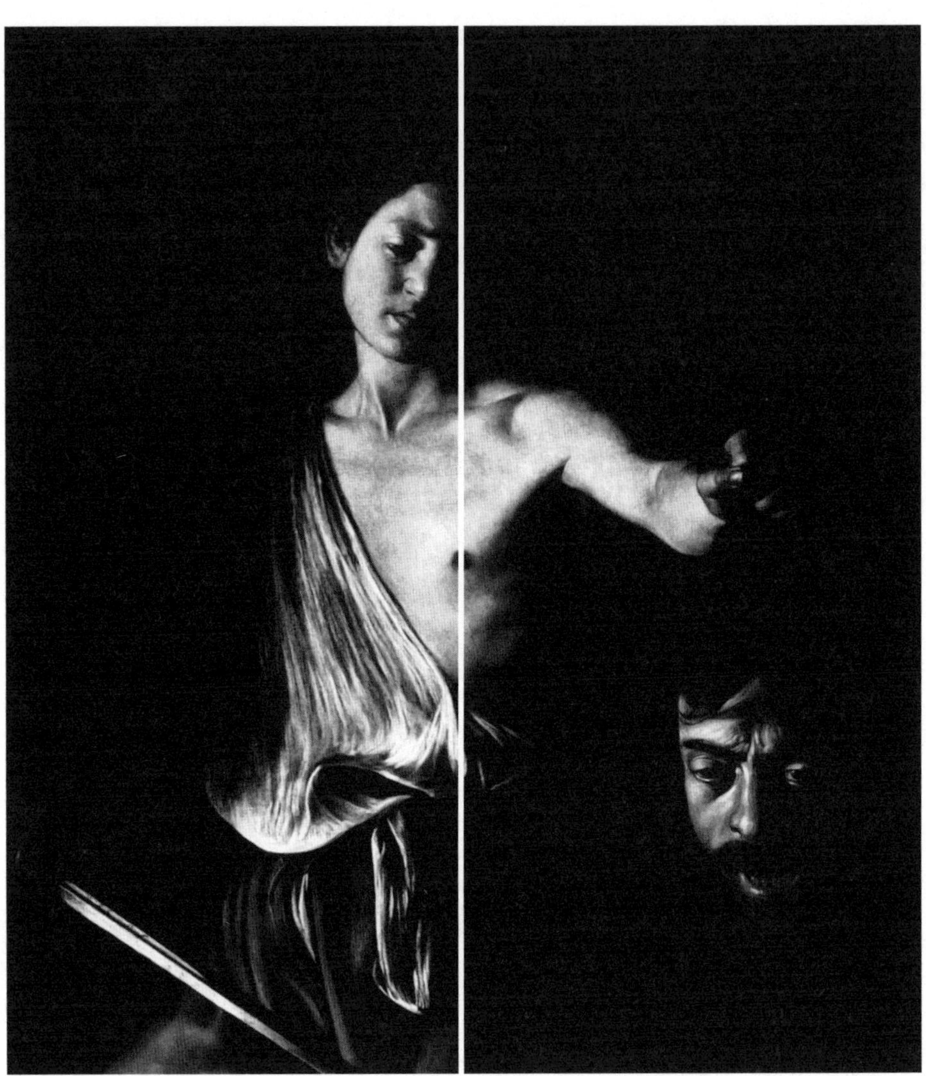

3

Caravaggio: Eros

The Story of Youth

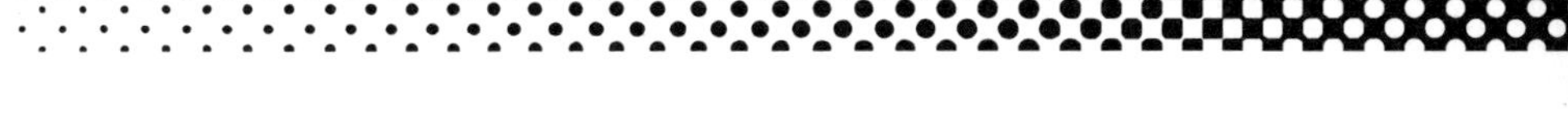

A Monumental Vertical Axis

VERTICALITY To start with, I will concentrate on the figure of David. He dominates the picture. The beauty of youth shines forth, in all its power, vitality and sensuality. He is an Eros. The boy evokes memories of Graeco-Roman antiquity. For that very reason David is a popular figure in the Italian Renaissance: he represents the revival of antiquity. The robust, muscular David in this painting is a proud, upright presence. Caravaggio gives him the dignity of a future king.

The geometrical narrative style is based on a careful vertical composition (fig. II.3.1). The pictorial space is primarily a vertical plane. Vertical lines can be discerned everywhere if you just disregard the representation. The lines running from top to bottom, and vice versa, form the principal compositional elements: the line ending at the left hand, the line from the shoulder to the hip, the line from the other hand ending at the trickling blood. The vertical line is reinforced by the position of the hand in the centre of the picture. You cannot possibly disregard David.

II.3.1 Michelangelo Merisi da Caravaggio, *David with the Head of Goliath* (vertical axis), 1609

ACHILLES Verticality is an index alluding to strength and power. I have arrived in a world of the upright, unyielding. He is the central column that cannot topple. Even more than in Pedriali's photo where you see the body side-on, this David approaches me, the spectator, head-on. The vertical axis is the line along which an arrangement into high and low is organised: the story of a victory. The boy's position versus his opponent confirms his power.

Verticality and power are connected, with verticality determining thinking at various levels. If we follow the vertical axis, the older man is at a lower level than David, for example. In that perspective, the higher-positioned boy is the master. The lower-positioned older man, although stronger and more dangerous as a portrayal, is, with his positioning, the underling. He is not a threat, but a suppressed danger. He is the lesser and, as such, is situated in the darkness—and with good reason. Goliath, in biblical terms, is the dragon at the feet of the archangel Michael.

The direction of the movement can accentuate the vertical logic. The upward movement of the young man's hand works as a metonymic gesture. The hand proudly shows the opponent's severed head. The boy is holding the hair of the man whose powerless head is subservient to the boy's grasp. The hand gesture confirms the mastery of the bare-chested, young athlete.

All this gives the world of verticality something inviolable and the appearance of being shameless and invulnerable. That strength is further underlined by the fact that the muscular torso faces forward. The boy reveals it, uncovered, to the spectator. It is not a gesture of seduction, but of sportive strength. Similar strength is visible in his face, thus reflecting the late-renaissance world of the vigorous young hero resisting death.

THE ADOLESCENT AS A HERO Hans van Driel describes in *De Semiosis: De semiotiek van C.S. Peirce in verband gebracht met het verschijnsel film* (Semiosis: C.S. Peirce's Semiotics Applied to Film, 1993) Charles Sanders Peirce's semiotics as a process of meaning creation between object—what is represented—and subject. I let Caravaggio speak in a process of meaning creation. The story of youth that first emerges is one of the proudly upstanding hero. The concept of "hero" stands for victory, strength and courage. An impression, however rudimentary it may be, starts to unfold. The upstanding vigorous young man comes into the picture as what Deleuze calls "a semiotic machine" (1996, 83). David presents himself as a young Eros, a steadfast protagonist. The older man is the antagonist. Death, which ultimately turns every victory into a Pyrrhic victory, is as yet invisible.

The Targeted Horizontal Axis

HORIZONTALITY Caravaggio's vertical axis intersects the horizontal axis near to David's nipple (fig. 11.3.2). The horizontal axis looks to be made up of three fragments. Every time they tell something different. Together they reveal a dramatic action. Every scene of that action consists of a number of shots that appear simultaneously: pictorial elements that appear and disappear. The difference with the (static) image is that, with film, twenty-four frames are played within the space of one second, thus producing the experience of an authentic timestream. The comic strip does not do that but, rather, works by using space. The three fragments along the horizontal line, from left to right:

1. A large, dark area with a barely visible left hand and

25 The movement in Caravaggio's painting has a hidden spatial arrangement based on logical dramatic action as a series of events in time. *David with the Head of Goliath* (1609) can, therefore be analysed as a fragment from a comic strip.

the hilt of a black-and-white sword. At the bottom, a portion of David's brown breeches is still visible.

2. The entire figure of the boy. I see the head, sinewy neck, chest partially covered with the draped cloth. Lower down: the breeches with open front, and part of the sword that hangs below the crotch.
3. The boy's right arm. In the foreground there is a large, black area (and in it, the older man's head, dripping with red blood).

Together the three focal planes form the scene: a unity of time, place and action. The question is: what does this serial portrayal tell me?[25]

A horizontal composition is a linguistic form reinforcing the goal-orientated character of the action (and so also indirectly the way of the powerful, upright figure). Tension is created between good (young) and evil (old). In Caravaggio's

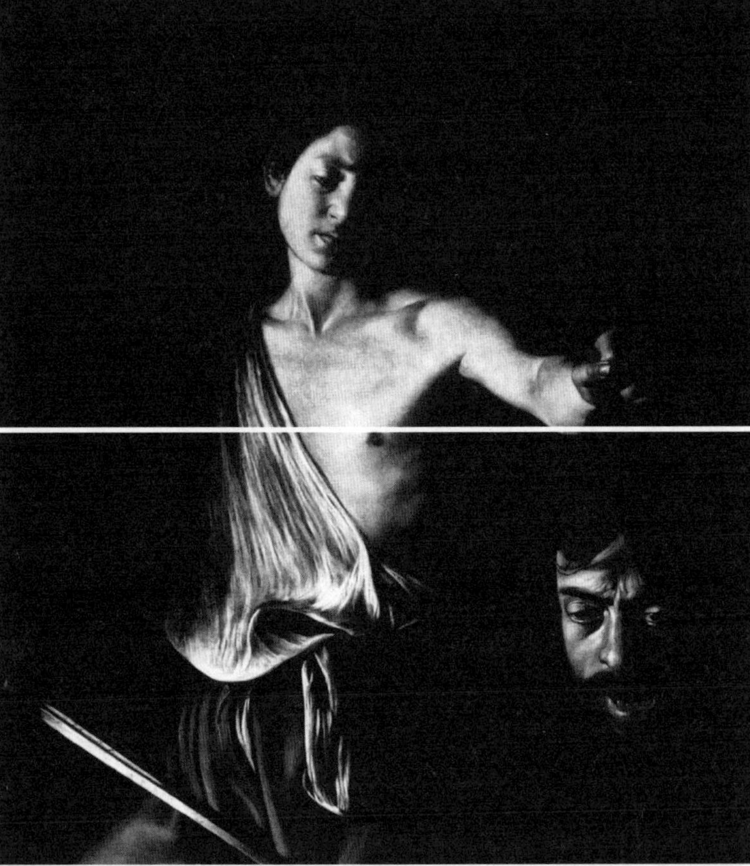

II.3.2 Michelangelo Merisi da Caravaggio, *David with the Head of Goliath* (horizontal axis), 1609

painting the hero, David, has a clear goal: deliverance from the older, wicked man.

This horizontal composition is a recurring phenomenon in film scenarios. According to Dennis Potter, the writer of film screenplays, obstacles are often like "the return of the repressed" (1994, 66): the same obstacle keeps coming back, each time in a different form. The fact that goal-achievement is constantly being postponed produces tension. The protagonist can only realise his goal by overcoming the obstacle.

Using this formula, Caravaggio begins in the left fragment with the formulation of the goal. The young man appears in the darkness with a sword. What will it be used for? Tension mounts. It is difficult to see the hilt of the sword. It evokes the ominous premonition that things might be revealed that the naked eye cannot bear to see. The sword is drawn. Why? By whom? What has happened? For what reason?

The second fragment is a moment when achievement of the goal is postponed. The young hero appears in the spotlight. Light falls on him from above, like a column. It serves to delay. What will he do? Will he tackle the older man? The weapon is at the ready. Then there is the deferred goal. I want to get to know the young man better. He does not seem like a criminal prowling the streets, but a warrior fighting a just cause. I see a charming, attractive, sensual young man. His inclined head and gaze do not indicate aggression but affectionate compassion.

The third fragment: realisation of the goal. We are back with the sword. The older man, the embodiment of evil, appears. His head is bleeding. The young man has accomplished his task by the looks of the sword's blade. The monster has been slain. Tension has come full circle; the young man leaves the picture.

THE ADOLESCENT AS A WARRIOR The adolescent reveals himself as a warrior. Caravaggio's David tells of a combination of strength and gentleness, a virtue that Aristotle describes in *Ethica Nicomachea* as courage: a characteristic somewhere between fear and recklessness. The protagonist faces dangers fearlessly and intrepidly, while "the man who exceeds in confidence is rash, and he who exceeds in fear and falls short in confidence is a coward" (Aristotle 1984, 1784). The warrior shows he is afraid, especially in the middle section, but at the same time he is brave enough to dwell on his fear. The young warrior is innately disciplined. He stands, upright, in this perspective space, focused, knowing what he must do. He is not concerned with minor considerations—he is unmoved by what is happening around him. He does what he has planned to do and finds peace within himself. In fact, this first encounter with the heroic David, this first attempt to decipher the picture, scarcely gives me, the spectator, the feeling I am dealing with a tragic young man.

60

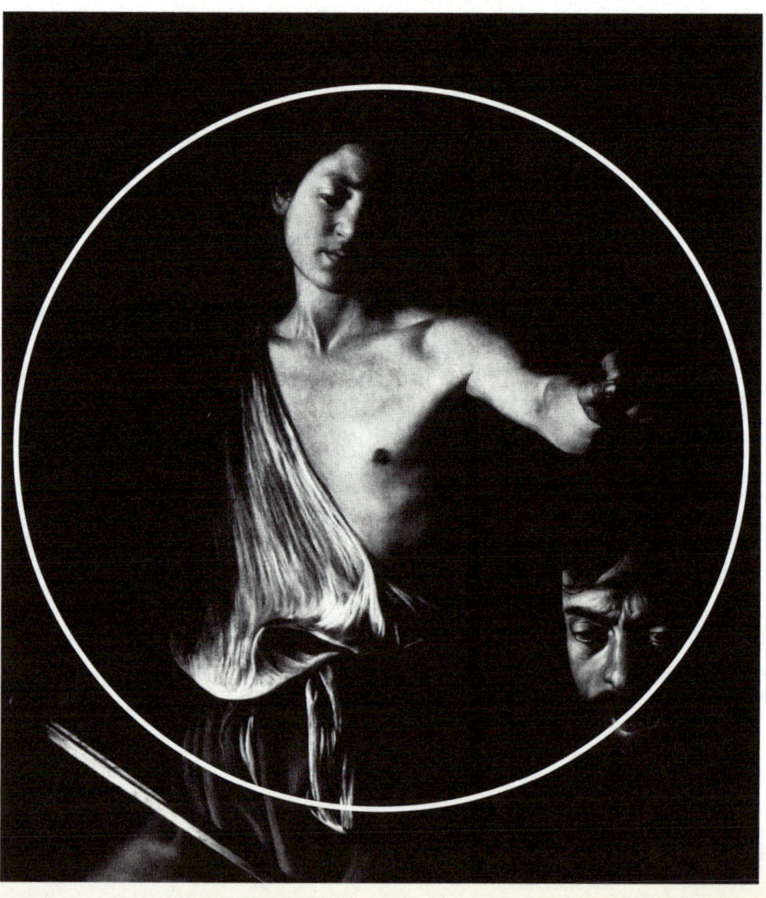

II.3.3 Michelangelo Merisi da Caravaggio, *David with the Head of Goliath* (circle), 1609

The Circle Composition

CIRCLE What is happening with the warrior? Something starts to detract from the so far flawless young hero. I continue to concentrate on the picture. The circle, the third important compositional element, can be of help at this stage (fig. 11.3.3). A circle runs from the crown of David's head, via his left and right arm to the blade of the sword at the bottom of the picture. This element, like the horizontal line, describes a series of events. The events themselves give a different impression from the circle as a whole. The circle shows four dramatic moments which, like in a play, speak all at once:

1. The top: David's face is inclined to the right. He looks past his right arm to Goliath's head.
2. The left side: David's not visible arm and hand which grasp the sword.
3. The bottom: the spot where the sword rests and the pleated fabric at David's crotch, which Goliath can also see out of the corner of his eye.
4. The right side: Goliath's severed head, with David's spotlighted figure behind.

This circle not only shows a series of events. The compositional technique also creates a hierarchy in the picture. The images within the circle are most important. Anything outside the circle belongs in the periphery. Sometimes the periphery is deliberately transformed into the centre of the depiction; that switch forms an exception to the hierarchy.

FREUD The struggle within the illuminated circle alludes to an Oedipal drama. A different composition comes about, depending on the direction in which I follow it. If I follow the circle to the right, the depiction is more extravert. The circular movement starts with David and then arrives at the face of the other character, the older man. The path to the left is more introvert and starts with the young man himself. It is a path inwards. That is the most interesting route, because it can tell us something about the hero's state of mind.

Going to the left, you start with David's face. That area is dominated by the hero's eyes. In fact David's eyes are one of the most defining elements, together with the round, almost feminine face with its narrow lips and gaze expressing solicitude, gentleness and compassion. Caravaggio paints a vulnerable, tragic hero who has performed a task—not for pleasure, but because he accepts the blame. This is not a powerhouse, not a physical victor. I can imagine if a student confronted with that gaze would think of an exalted being: the sacrificial lamb in Freud's *Totem and Taboo* (1950; originally published 1913) enjoying protection from the entire clan and which can only be slaughtered if the entire clan is willing to take responsibility, the chorus in Greek tragedy or the messiah within the Christian tradition who will bear the sins of a people.

The second fragment shows the sword. The young man hardly recalls the weapon at his left side. Since the older man also commands attention, it is easy to overlook the weapon. Yet as I think back to Pedriali's *Davide e Golia,* I immediately realise how important the sword is. Pedriali's portrayal, with no weapon or blood, means something quite different from Caravaggio's representation that does contain them. The missing signs (sword, blood) mean that in Pedriali the sexual significance prevails over that of death. In the circle, the sword plays an important, ever-recurring role. It is an attribute from which the protagonist averts his gaze, as if he wishes to shut out its existence but cannot forget it.

The third fragment draws attention to the lower area. The sword, the shirt and the breeches emphasise the genital area and form an eye-catching, wild and chaotic section of the picture. It is also a part brimming with homo-erotic references. For instance, Goliath's wide-open mouth and David's accentuated crotch appear, in their juxtaposition, to refer to oral sex. The circle crosses an important vertical line here. One side of the line stands for solicitude and compassion, the other side for passion and aggression.

The fourth and final fragment relates to the old man's head. The boy holds it away from himself, as if it were unsavoury. The old man's mouth hangs open. Is he about to say something but is not allowed to do so? His forehead is wrinkled. The blood underneath emphasises the murder. The older man seems like an object, not a living being or subject.[26]

THE STEADFAST ADOLESCENT So far, the warrior appears to be a steadfast, inviolable figure. Thinking in *chiaroscuro* resembles a game between repose and chaos, in which repose overcomes. Perhaps the adolescent falls victim to inner doubt. Etymologically, doubt is related to "two", yet that duality does not threaten David. Despite doubt, he is focused on his goal. As yet David is not a Hamlet. He knows what he wants. He is not distracted by movements in the periphery. He does not allow himself to be dragged into the field of eroticism. Eros dominates as a force, but does not make a victim of him. The psychological drama—the ritual killing of the father—does not make the adolescent irresolute. The vertical and horizontal lines keep the young man in the centre of the story that is characterised by outward strength and action geared to liberation. Art-Based Learning, in line with Aristotle's idea of poetry, can be seen as a lyrical form of contemplation, and in this case results in an epic narrative/legend.[27]

26 The connection between Oedipal drama and tragedy is explained by Kees Nuijten in *Freud en fictie: Literaire genres vanuit psychoanalytisch perspectief* (1999). There he describes that interest from literary spectators with a leaning towards psychoanalysis as regards dramatic art, focuses primarily on tragedy. Tragedy relates to a tragic hero involved in a struggle with an all-powerful person or authority. Here Nuijten makes a connection between the young, tragic hero and the aggressive impulses and fantasies of a father figure. In that context, he quotes the work of Peter von Matt, who characterises the Oedipal situation as the "psychodramatic substrate" of the tragedy. So, in psychoanalysis, our love of tragedy is mainly seen as the unconscious recognition of the Oedipal theme. Caravaggio's painting can, therefore, be considered as a tragic Oedipal conflict. Ultimately, Nuijten arrives at Freud's "speculative anthropological theory" of the murder by the primal horde of the primal father (*Totem and Taboo*) as the key element in a process of identity development (1950).

27 Aristotle sees the process of mimesis—lyrical narrative—as a form of understanding. In *Poetics*, he names three poetic genres: epic, tragedy and comedy. People enjoy imitations (the seeing thereof) because "seeing a picture" is "at the same time learning" (1984, 2318). Aristotle pays particular attention to tragedy. He defines it as "mimesis of an action". "Tragedy is essentially an imitation not of persons but of action and life" (2320). According to Aristotle, the essence of tragedy is the plot, or the relation between goal and events. It is made up of a beginning, a middle and an end, with the beginning not necessarily following from something else, but is by necessity followed by an ensuing event. So Aristotle defines tragedy as a possible world, and, as a form of philosophy, ranks this poetic reality higher than history. The historian tells the story "that has been". The poet and philosopher tells the story "that might be". He pursues how poetry is more philosophical and of greater importance than history, since it comments on "universals where those of history are singulars" (2323). Moreover, tragedy is a spectacle that can generate pain and fear, and then catharsis, in the spectator. A murder that is committed through ignorance has an extremely powerful effect (2326).

Lighting in the Centre

LIGHTING The light in the centre of the picture reinforces the centripetal interplay of forces (fig. II.3.4). Caravaggio's David, the icon of the early-modern adolescent, becomes an illuminated figure in the centre of the painting. This is the place where David is transformed into the baroque pendant of Pedriali's twentieth-century street urchin. We see one of Caravaggio's street kids, "like nonprofessional actors recruited from the streets for modern Italian film" (Moir 1989, 43). The interplay of the pictorial elements is a pictorial theory, with the concomitant internal logic. The point where the vertical and horizontal lines coincide is the point where darkness recedes and the young man says: "Look, here I am". The geometrical composition would seem only to have served to enable the light in the middle to be even more expressive.

In *History of Beauty* (2004) Umberto Eco discusses how every painting is a weird assembly of visual elements, with

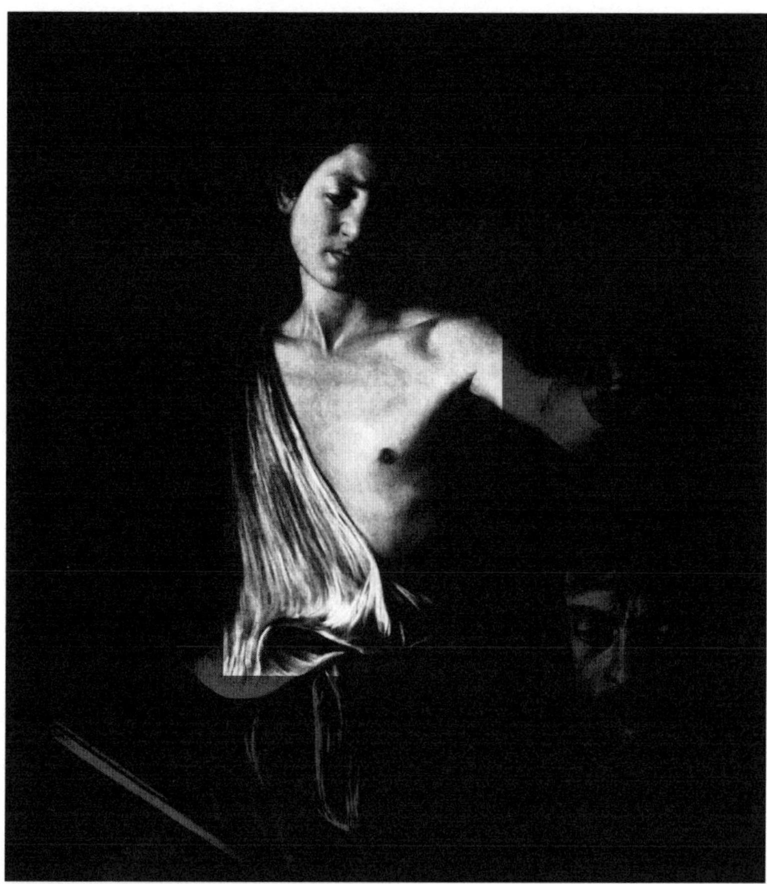

II.3.4 Michelangelo Merisi da Caravaggio, *David with the Head of Goliath* (light areas), 1609

light, representation and composition of lines playing an important part. He refers to a remark by Thomas Aquinas, who suggested that beauty is based on three properties: proportion, integrity and clarity (100).

Caravaggio's young man, as an isolated figure, meets these three criteria. A balanced interplay of lines produces planes. This composition of planes in turn determines the intensity of the light. The adolescent stands in a light world. The bright light (and the way it breaks up into different colours) forms the basic structure that underpins the picture. The planar division in this painting by Caravaggio is in fact determined by the question: "light or dark?"

Light has an important indexical function that is deeply rooted in Western culture. In *Metaphors We Live By*, Lakoff and Johnson show how light and dark, high and low, are meaningful ordering principles. Eco refers to the platonic tradition that associates light with good (2005, 102). David is primarily a light figure. The light planes vary from sharp white to warm, mellow shades of yellow.

The areas in the shadow run from light brown to deep black. The overall light spectrum is not uniform, but consists of a play of supporting colours. The yellows have red accents here and there, particularly at the edge between neck and chest, and in David's face. The dark shades are not uniform either. Here and there, the browns have a hint of moss-green. The whites are backed up with touches of pale blue.
A traveller sees what he wants to see. It is a kind of reading, but also a kind of poetry. As yet, I mainly perceive light in Caravaggio's work.[28]

THE SERENE ADOLESCENT The warrior increasingly turns into a sacred figure. The hero is now a classically serene presence. Caravaggio's David, like the boys in Pasolini's

28 Umberto Eco rejects forced structuralism and introduces semiotics as an "open text" approach. He does not embrace prescriptive formations. He sees semiotics as something that comes about in open fields. These open fields are not limited to art. ABL is a process of ascribing meaning in a third space that can also be seen as an open field. In *History of Beauty* Eco briefly addresses the Baroque, the period in which Caravaggio's work came about. He calls the Baroque a school which is not restricted to art, but also expresses "a dramatisation of life" (2004, 228).

novel *The Street Kids*, is a tearaway warrior with the traits of an angel. The child-like form and clear arrangement add a certain tranquillity and innocence to the picture—which Pasolini's character, Riccetto, also possesses.

A beam of light falls across the youth, virtually a divine blessing. It is a form of presentation that does not give the shadow (and all the demons that lurk there) a chance. Bal refers to the Baroque as a period in which the subject has to abandon his autonomy (1999, 39). However, nothing is lost here. The adolescent has a somewhat stoic attitude. It is as if the God-forsaken world of shadows does not really affect him. He is still the innocent harp-player. Shakespeare's Hamlet, embroiled in a battle with the shadows, reveals himself almost imperceptibly. The tension mounts.[29]

29 I consider Shakespeare's *Hamlet* to be the literary equivalent of Caravaggio's *David with the Head of Goliath*. In *Shakespeare: The Invention of the Human* (1999) Harold Bloom gives Falstaff, Rosalind and Hamlet as three great examples of human nature. In *Genius: A Mosaic of One Hundred Exemplary Creative Minds* (2002) Bloom writes: "Hamlet's study of himself is an absolute, and diminishes what is outside the self as a sea of troubles. Incessantly pondering his own words, as if they both were and were not his own, Hamlet becomes the theologian of his own consciousness, which is so wide that its circumference never can be discovered" (29). Bloom's description of Hamlet's character is a good match for Caravaggio's face of David. The gaze is turned inwards. Like Hamlet, he is overwhelmed by his own thoughts—thoughts that are so far-reaching that they can never be completely fathomed.

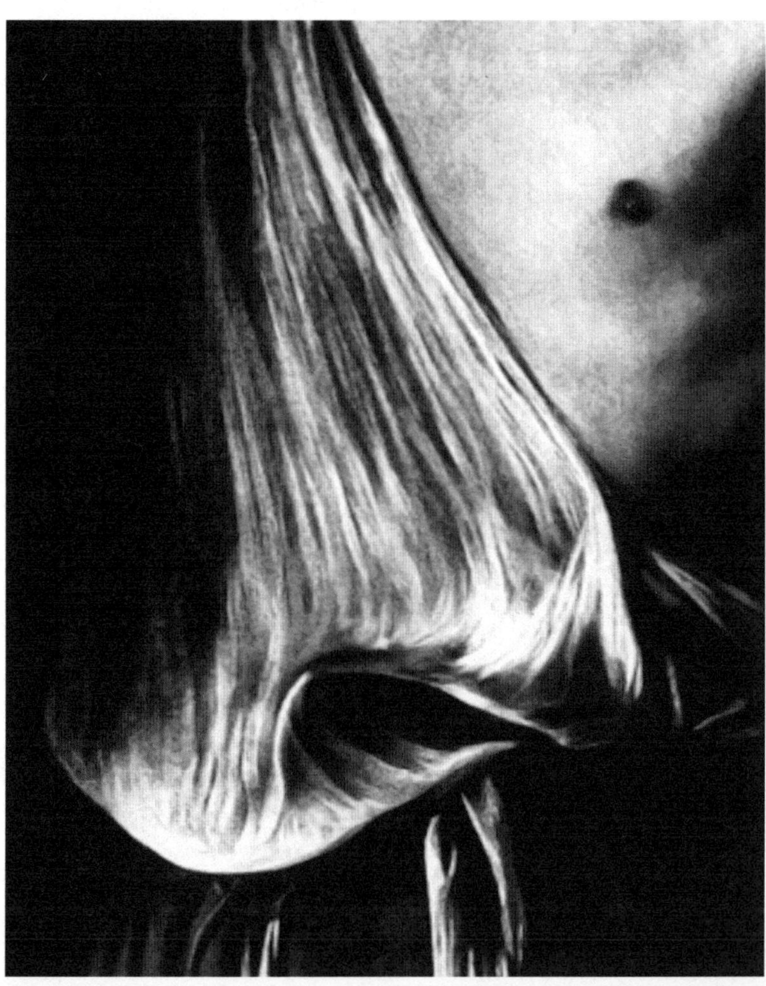

II.3.5 Michelangelo Merisi da Caravaggio, *David with the Head of Goliath* (detail), 1609

At the Centre of the Spotlight

David is standing in the middle of the spotlight, which is aimed mainly from the front. The light underlines the foreground (fig. 11.3.5). The darkness is the background. In all of this, the light intensity is important. Ferdinando Bologna and Vicenzo Abbate describe how Caravaggio uses a painting technique termed *risparmio* (time-saving technique) (2005, 137). It is a technique used with frescoes in which light (transparent) strokes are applied over dark areas.

With this technique Caravaggio realised a tragic-poetic experience. The treatment of the canvas sometimes resembles the paintings from his Sicilian period, like *The Martyrdom of Saint Ursula* (1609/10). The fresco-like areas often have the character of thin lines. Sometimes they are white lines applied on top of black, sometimes thin, yellowish-white surfaces. The light reinforces the experience of distance. The white confronts the spectator. The yellow or brown is more 'withdrawn'. The effect of the light produces subtle differences in distance, but also angular, rounded shapes. The transition to the yellowish-white achieves harmony in the forms. The contrast between black and white is more extreme, more jagged.

The *risparmio* has another special quality. The main strength of the light brushstrokes is not to create shapes, but to create haze. It gives the dramatic representation a somewhat lyrical diction. Is this an answer to extreme naturalism? A subtle reference to a post-naturalist state? Caravaggio is primarily renowned as a dramatic painter. With his specific use of *risparmio* he not only demonstrates his exceptional dramatic strength, but also the more poetic side to his paintings—in one and the same work.[30]

30 Bert Treffers (1991) is one of the writers to stress the importance of *risparmio*. Treffers' Caravaggio is not an angry young man, but an artist working for the ecclesiastical authorities, who saw to it that the theme and rendition coincided with their wishes. Treffers points out the possible theological meaning of the use of light as an artistic principle. Irving Lavin, in his book *Bernini and the Unity of the Visual Arts* (1980), speaks of "the theology of light" that came about in the second half of the sixteenth century. He says: "natural light was incorporated into narrative illustration where it functioned as a supernatural agent" (1980, 155). The "theology of light" also adds special meaning to the image of the adolescent. With this I mean the "theology of light" as a possible element in Caravaggio's thinking in *chiaroscuro*.

The interpretation of the British film director, Derek Jarman, of Caravaggio's work in his film *Caravaggio* (1986) makes it clear that the tragic-poetic experience is produced by the combination of hazy light and sharp *chiaroscuro*. Poetry is the reality of the detail and, with the contrasting illumination from the front, can be fittingly revealed

Jarman makes minimum use of harsh lighting, actually achieving sublimation by way of sharp contrasts. With the bright light he homes in on poetry. The bright light is sustained by slowing down the action. Also, he deploys a décor that is divided into geometric planes, emphasized by a stationary camera. Accordingly, Jarman allows the aesthetic impact poetically to take front stage.

The poetic effect is reinforced as details are repeatedly highlighted. The dry, dusty, weathered South-Italian setting and the relatively pale shades of the housing merely form a geometrical backdrop. They offer restful silence. The true focus is not on the plot, but shifts to the actual occurrence. The contrasting shades are no longer paramount. The spectator arrives in a world where the highlighted detail predominates.

Jarman presents Caravaggio's work by way of powerful, resplendent details. In his representation, Caravaggio's thinking in contrasts is shaped by the way he makes *chiaroscuro* subservient to the luminous poetic detail. And thus the director demonstrates that he is a theorist who—through film—thinks about painting.

Lastly

Thinking not only includes rational logic, but also refined, associative logic, as expressed in dreams. Art-Based Learning is a kind of looking, thinking, dreaming and assigning of meaning, with the art work as the source. In the foregoing pages I have been a spectator and participant, allowing myself to be swept into the 'unthought known', and ending up at Caravaggio's story of *Youth and Death*.

Dream-thought has revealed a connection between Pedriali's *Autoritratto immaginario* and Caravaggio's *David with the Head of Goliath*. With their cinematographic kind of thought, both art works invite us to step into a 'caravaggesque' world. Both also play a postmodern linguistic game in which the adolescent is cast in a specific way. The varying lines of thought in that game can be important for analysing culture surrounding us, even when it does not refer directly to adolescence.[31]

My narration of the adolescent has become a story of a renaissance Eros: a powerful, heroic, divine figure within a balanced composition. What does Caravaggio tell? Is youth really a reality? Even a slight alteration of perspective suffices to overturn the entire image. Eros, the classical, heroic warrior, who had so far been supreme, then disappears into the background. The world of light vanishes. The world of shadows takes over. Straight lines disappear, diagonals emerge. Order disappears, turbulence commences. The beauty of youth will be short-lived.

What more can Caravaggio's *David with the Head of Goliath* tell us? Can youth in the carravagesque view still be plausible as a figure of light? We are at the borderline between Renaissance and Baroque, the area that Foucault keeps on emphasising. In the afterword to *Breekbare vrijheid* (2004), Laurens ten Kate and Henk Manschot describe how time and again Foucault sought to explore that borderland.

The first hairline cracks are becoming visible. One by

31 The term 'dream thought' is used by Jean-François Lyotard. He believes that postmodernism is characterised by "the disbelief in meta-narratives." (Lyotard 2000, 26). Lyotard has been of considerable influence on my idea of Art-Based Learning as a form of thinking in "possible worlds". I emphatically do not see those possible worlds as meta-narratives. After all, they do not constitute a totalitarian claim, but within my approach are a kind of fiction. Lyotard criticises in his essay "The Dream-Work Does Not Think" (1989) a uniformistic idea of thinking. He distinguishes between waking-thought and dream-thought. The latter comprises a process of association and has a transformative rather than a logical character. He cites Freud: "It [the dream-work] does not think, calculate or judge in anyway at all; it restricts itself to giving things a new form" (quoted in 1989, 20). Dream-thought is often a process of transforming by means of transpositioning. That may sometimes be through *Spielerei*, which goes on to generate a process of transgression. The imagination and concomitant metaphors play an important part in this process. Lyotard goes so far as to write: "phantasms, rather than a discourse, should perhaps be classified as dream-thoughts" (1989, 41). The structure of phantasms is more similar to that of a narrative than of an argument. With all this Lyotard reinforces my theory of art as a kind of dream-thought.

one obstacles emerge that can alter my ideas of the phenomenon of "adolescent". So it is important not only to permit the central figure, the adolescent, to speak, but also his surroundings.

The first signs of a world of light that changes into a world of darkness are perceptible. The stationary world becomes a world of motion. The foreground becomes background, the background foreground. The surface makes way for a process of deepening. Life is embraced by death. Young is ousted by old, hope is replaced by despair. Progress becomes regress.

The movement towards the black space—a movement that typifies caravaggesque thought—has begun. The tragic path that ends at the tomb comes into view. Connections with other paintings by Caravaggio, like *Judith Beheading Holofernes* (1598) and *Medusa* (1600) present themselves. Peter Blos describes in *On Adolescence,* "adolescence proper" as a period of love and mourning, which is the result of a "gradual achievement of liberation" (1996, 100). So far, Caravaggio's painting has been about love. The stage which now follows relates to the loss of youth and to mourning.

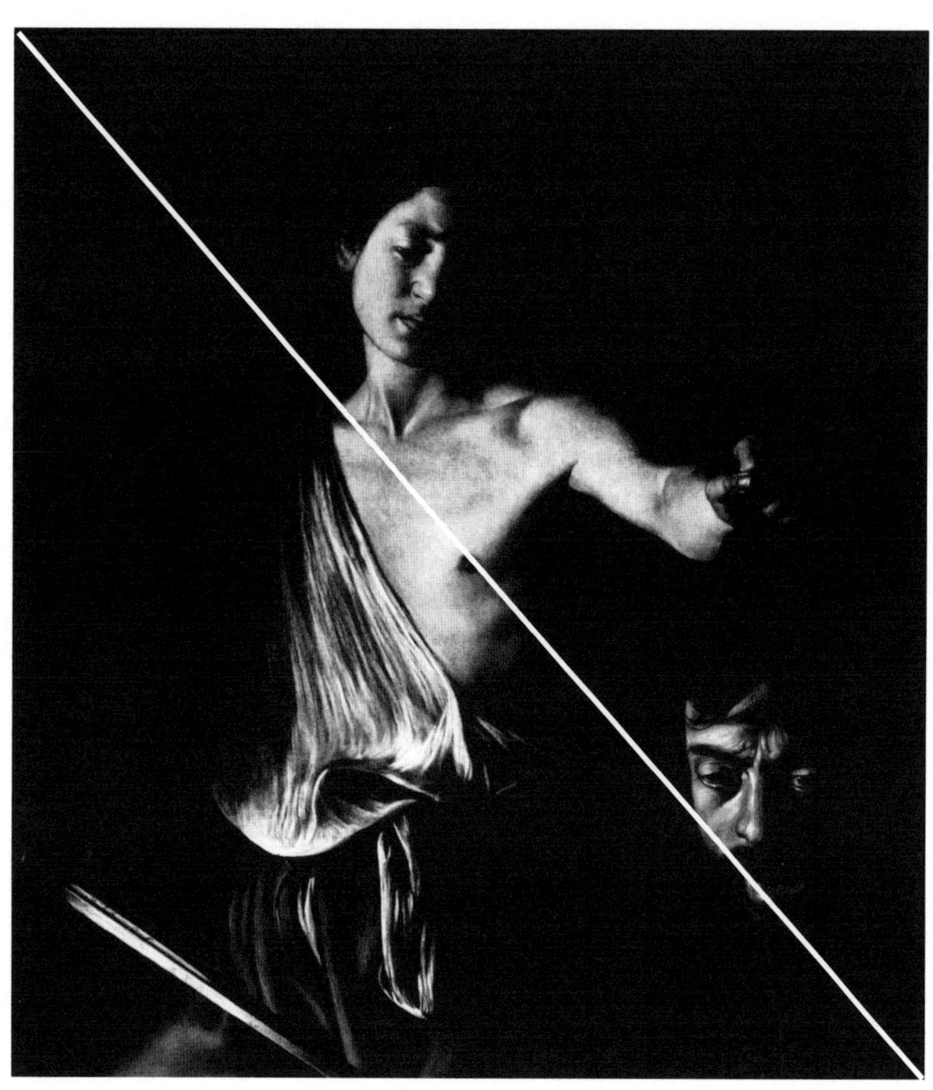

4

Caravaggio: Chronos

The Course of Time

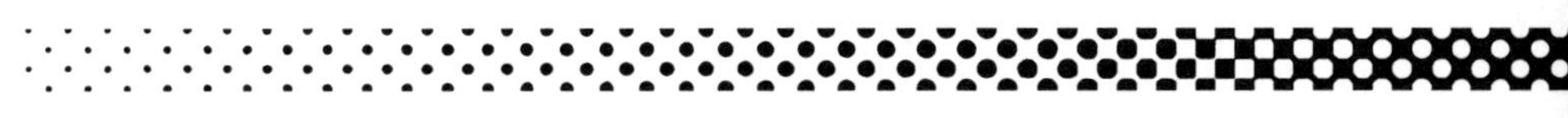

Introduction

A painting may appear like a static object, but—once transformed into a possible world, a dynamic object—it is actually a subject. The inert, material image is set in motion by every new focus. The painting would seem to consist of a series of superimposed, intended or unintended images (sequences) which can be combined in various ways into a living story in the dialogue between the art work and the participant. Bollas refers to a "dialectics of self-experiencing", in which a new ranking of facts brings about a new pattern and a new plot. In *The Poetics of Plot: The Case of English Renaissance Drama,* Thomas Pavel speaks of "moves" that keep on creating new realities (1985, 17). The triptych approach I use gives a new story with every new panel.

So far, a heroic picture of adolescence has emerged, in which my focus has been on the illuminated David (Eros). In the following episode I shall focus on Goliath. The details I explore can be described as Chronos. A dramatic picture

II.4.1 Michelangelo Merisi da Caravaggio, *David with the Head of Goliath* (diagonal), 1609

of adolescence emerges. Now attention is devoted to chaos. A typical baroque world materialises in details and results in movement, as for instance in the clouds in the dome painted by Correggio; every possible fixation is done away with. It is a "correlative; the subject is not given. No stability can be derived from it" (Bal 1999, 39).

Goliath makes his entrance and causes the light to conflict with the underlying shadow. The caravaggesque portrayal of the adolescent—thinking in *chiaroscuro*—gradually turns into the tragic victory of shadow over light. I recall Dennis Potter's *Cold Lazarus* (BBC, 1996)—a contemporary variation on Caravaggio's head with no body. *Cold Lazarus* is a television film about a head of a successful twentieth-century scriptwriter that is artificially kept alive and commercially exploited by media tycoons in the twenty-fourth century. Daniel Feeld's (artificially) living head exhibits similarities with the head of Caravaggio's Goliath, which would seem to have been captured at the time of death.

A Diagonal Viewpont

DIAGONAL I look at the depiction using diagonals (fig. II.4.1). The main diagonal, running from below right to top left of the canvas, generates its drama. This diagonal axis offers an entirely new perspective on youth. The older man (Goliath), the protagonist in the world of shadows, moves to the foreground. The man's severed head with its lined face and open mouth, representing the trophy of a fallen warrior, suddenly becomes the focal point. He shifts from antagonist to protagonist. He was an object (merely an attribute in David's hand), but is now the subject; the carrier of the picture.

David becomes a supporting actor in a dream world. He is pushed into the background—banished from the centre to the periphery. He no longer moves forwards, but backwards. Perhaps the youth is not even a real character, "merely" a construction in the older man's mind: David as a memory of a tormented Chronos.

John Berger examines "the play" as a characteristic of baroque syntax. Alberto Manguel, in *Reading Pictures: What We Think About When We Look at Art* (2000) refers to "the image as theatre", which is characterised by artificial, ever-changing arrangements. This method starts with Michelangelo and continues into contemporary art. The defining aspect of these arrangements is that meanings are constantly being upset. Caravaggio's diagonal line activates "cross-looking": looking at something from an unexpected angle, for instance causing an interruption in the chronology in the picture.[32]

32 The principle of "cross-looking" is discussed in *Hardop kijken: Een inleiding in kunstbeschouwing* (1990), in which Ad de Visser provides an accessible introduction to the way of contemplating art that is so important for the process of Art-Based Learning. A painting by Caravaggio cannot just be captured in a set meaning. The meaning greatly depends on a dynamic interplay with the perspectives, something Damisch sees as typical of the Baroque. If the spectator is focused on the young man, the picture that emerges is different from when the older man is the focal point.

The baroque syntax is a surrealist, non-chronological world which is related in a number of ways to the work of the Italian film-maker Federico Fellini (1920–1993). Fellini quite often takes the present as his point of departure (foreground) for the past (background). His way of filming is narrative-autobiographical. In *8½* (1963) he shows how it can lead to imaginary worlds.

In *8½* Marcello Mastroianni plays Guido Anselmi, the narrator and protagonist of the film and, above all, the director's alter ego. A series of personal memories overlap, sometimes edited in such a way that it is unclear when they actually take place. Childhood, youth, loved ones, the images intersect. *8½* had two closing scenes, one of which was lost during editing.

The scene with which the film finally ends is a splendid

grand finale, with past and present facing each other in a majestic dream. The dream characters descend a staircase in large numbers. An exuberant party develops, in which actuality and memories are reconciled, with the director dancing in the middle. Perhaps, with this second version, Fellini capitulated to his audience, who demanded a happy end.

The missing closing scene of which only fragments are kept in the film archives, is more reminiscent of an impressionist dream: memories disappear into a train like white phantoms. The train is standing in an intermediary space, somewhere between life and death.

In a sense, Caravaggio's world resembles this lost, final scene: surrealistic, ghostly, elusive. The older man looks crosswise (diagonally) to the action. He is both absent and present, both character and narrator. Caravaggio's older man does not reconcile himself with his past, his youth. He lives in inner conflict. We find ourselves in a *monologue intérieur*. The young man in the background corresponds with the possible world of an increasingly elusive memory.[33]

THE ADOLESCENT AS A MEMORY The older man in the foreground turns the adolescent into a fading memory. The older man is the reality. The young man is an illusion, a mental construct of the older man. Steve Blandford describes in *The Film Studies Dictionary* (2001) that recollection (flashback) is an action in the present. In this case, the character in the foreground is the character from the present. The character that appears behind is the character from the past. The adolescent is no more than a mental construct.

Blandford observes that a flashback in films is usually supported by specific "figures of speech", such as dreamy background music. A painting has no soundtrack, but optical tricks can also evoke sound. A dreamy effect is created if you

33 The surrealism in Fellini's work is characterised not only by an unbridled imagination, but also by intensely baroque images. You are struck by his distinctive use of time. In that context, John Russell Taylor comments that "time is appreciated as something within the characters or the maker's head, which may speed by in a swirl and swagger of baroque effect or slow almost to a stop, entirely depending on mood and the emotional structure of the film" (1980, 343). The associative and often archetypal nature of the images of surrealistic film-makers like Fellini can be explained by way of psychoanalysis. Walter Benjamin associates Surrealism with freedom. In "Surrealism: The Last Snapshot of the European Intelligentsia" (1929) he describes what is important in Surrealism, not only as an artistic stylistic feature but also as a philosophy. The concept of freedom of people like Breton, Aragon and Éluard is emblematic. According to Benjamin, their way of life and of working took the following course: "In the world's structure dream loosens individuality like a bad tooth. This loosening of the self by intoxication is, at the same time, precisely the fruitful, living experience that allowed these people to step outside the domain of intoxication" (1999, 208). Art-Based Learning is also akin to Surrealism, particularly on account of the significance of intuition, the unconscious, dream, free association, the drawing of unconventional connections, working with analogies, (urban) cartography, the importance of artistic distortions and manipulations—all based on a radical striving for freedom inspired by psychoanalysis. With respect to the latter, Benjamin writes: "Since Bakunin, Europe has lacked a radical concept of freedom. The Surrealists have one. They are the first to liquidate the sclerotic liberal-moral-humanistic ideal of freedom, because they are convinced that freedom, which on this earth can only be bought with a thousand of the hardest sacrifices, must be enjoyed unrestrictedly in its fullness without any kind of pragmatic calculation, as long as it lasts" (1999, 215).

modify the resolution of the image. By making his painting hazy and shadowy on the left, Caravaggio has produced the "sound" of the in-between.

Andreas Huyssen has addressed the memory as an in-between. In *Twilight Memories: Marking Time in a Culture of Amnesia* (1995) he introduces the concept of "twilight" as an intermediate stage. He writes "Twilight is that moment of the day that foreshadows the night of forgetting, but that seems to slow time itself, an in-between state in which the last light of the day may still play out its ultimate marvels" (3). Movies like *Citizen Kane* (Orson Welles, 1941) emphasise the singsong poetry of the moment as described by Huyssen. The adolescent, visible along the diagonal axis, shows a moment of in-between: the final gleam of daylight, a final attempt to delay, before the curtain falls for youth.[34]

34 Huyssen approaches memory as a kind of representation. For him, representation is, by definition, a time- and site-specific and always topical event: "The temporal status of any act of memory is always the present and not, as some naive epistemology might have it, the past itself, even though all memory in some ineradicable sense is dependent on some past event of experience" (1995, 3). It is interesting to translate phenomena like memory loss and representation into Caravaggio's portrayal of the adolescent. The older man's intellectual world/way of thinking resembles a museum. The adolescent comes from the past, but appears as the representative of the present. The picture might even be a "potentially healthy sign" to combat the pressure of the current situation (ageing) and "to live in extended structures of temporality" out of a "basic human need" (Huyssen 1995, 9).

The Intersecting Diagonal

The painting also contains a diagonal that intersects the first diagonal running from below left to top right. This results in a St. Andrew's or oblique cross (fig. 11.4.2). The centre is in David's chest area. The first diagonal starts in the present and is directed towards the past. The second diagonal also runs from present to past, but begins somewhat later. Incidentally, the diagonals are not the only lines in this complex geometrical composition. Yet I am struck by the fact that most shadow lines can be traced to the cross. Also, the lines overshoot the canvas.

In that respect, Goliath's eyelines point to parallel texts. They are the windows on other possible worlds. The fact that we are stepping outside the frame makes a whole gamut of new combinations possible. The intertextual reality is a kaleidoscope, a dynamic "theatre" that Deleuze terms a rhizomatic ensemble of offshoots and extensions (Deleuze and Guattari 1998, 37). All at once, the space extends into infinity. All that is needed is the (imaginary) construction of a bridge across which I can pursue my journey. Accordingly, images with changing functions appear. When viewed in succession, they create a hermeneutic process, in which one representation copies, the other makes comments and yet another illustrates or verifies.

The diagonal line produces a negative reality. The drama of the possible world, with negative thinking forming the basic structure, affects the diagonals. According to George Steiner, this shadowy side is inherent in life. The tragic approach to life says: "[I]t is best not to be born or, failing that, to die young" (Steiner 1990, 147).

The realm of shadow extends into the world of youth. Steiner's text could have been the caption to Caravaggio's

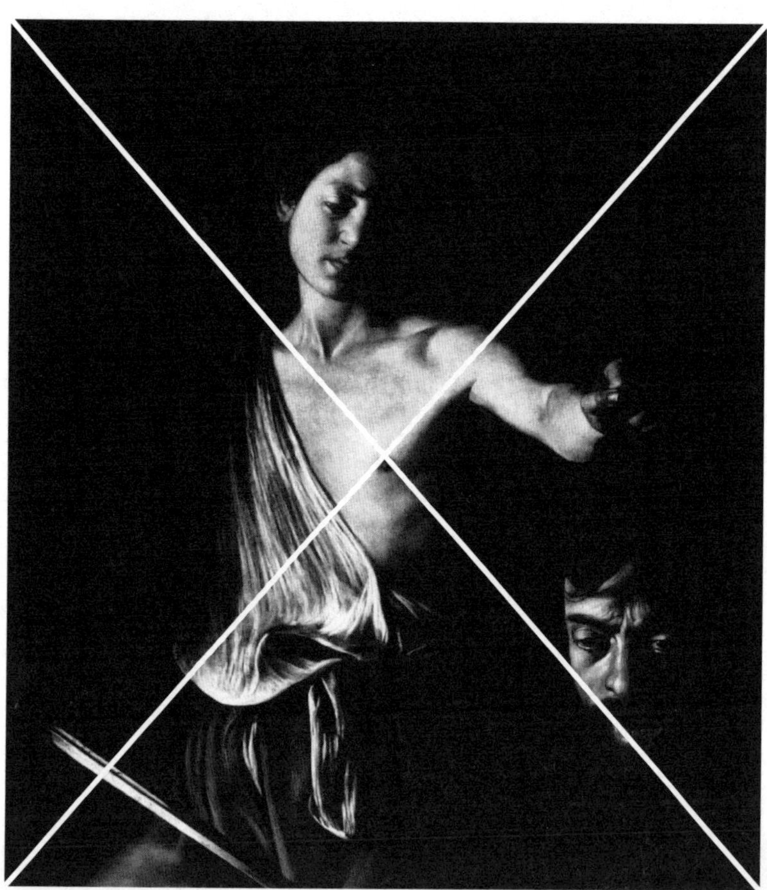

II.4.2 Michelangelo Merisi da Caravaggio, *David with the Head of Goliath* (intersecting diagonals), 1609

painting and goes with the allegory of *Youth and Death*: thc wild head in David's hands—Goliath out of the Book of Samuel from the Old Testament—the wound on the forehead where the stone pierced the head, the severed head, the dripping blood, the inevitable death.

The image would have been much less powerful if Caravaggio had not humanised the older man. Here, the diagonal perspective turns the so far dehumanised object (Goliath) into a humanised subject. The subject (David) becomes the dehumanised object here, although there is still room for negotiation.

When seen from below, with David merely in the distance, a figure suddenly appears that as yet scarcely existed. Goliath has suddenly become a person. He is David's mirror image. He reflects the process of destruction inherent in human existence. The oblique cross as depicted above, over the entire picture, acquires extra significance. The cross through the depiction tells that youth is present, and not.

THE FORGOTTEN ADOLESCENT The negative space, created in shades of black, becomes the protagonist. In the process of transformation, the adolescent resembles someone who comes off worst: a loser of the battle that is part of life. Caravaggio shows how the old man begins to dominate the young hero, the powerful conqueror and positive, purposive youth. Under Chronos' influence, young becomes a negative mental construct. The reference to biblical texts makes you wonder whether humankind is not actually an accessory to his decline.

Goliath is Cain's heir. David, Abel's heir, has vanished. Is the older man to blame for this process of decline? Caravaggio would seem not to exclude this. The older man might be a dual character who has been destroyed by his own sword. Destruction becomes self-destruction. Caravaggio's negative philosophy becomes a fitting system. In the final part of this chapter I shall relate this to the naturalistic mimesis of the adolescent. The divine light, that had preciously still fell as a column of light over Eros, from above to below, vanishes.

The Different Planes

PLANAR DIVISION The geometry of the picture—the diagonals, tones and shapes with a plethora of shadows—emerges as a contextual space, in which three different "characters" appear (fig. II.4.3). They not only move in different places in the space, but also at different distances from me, as a traveller through a possible world:

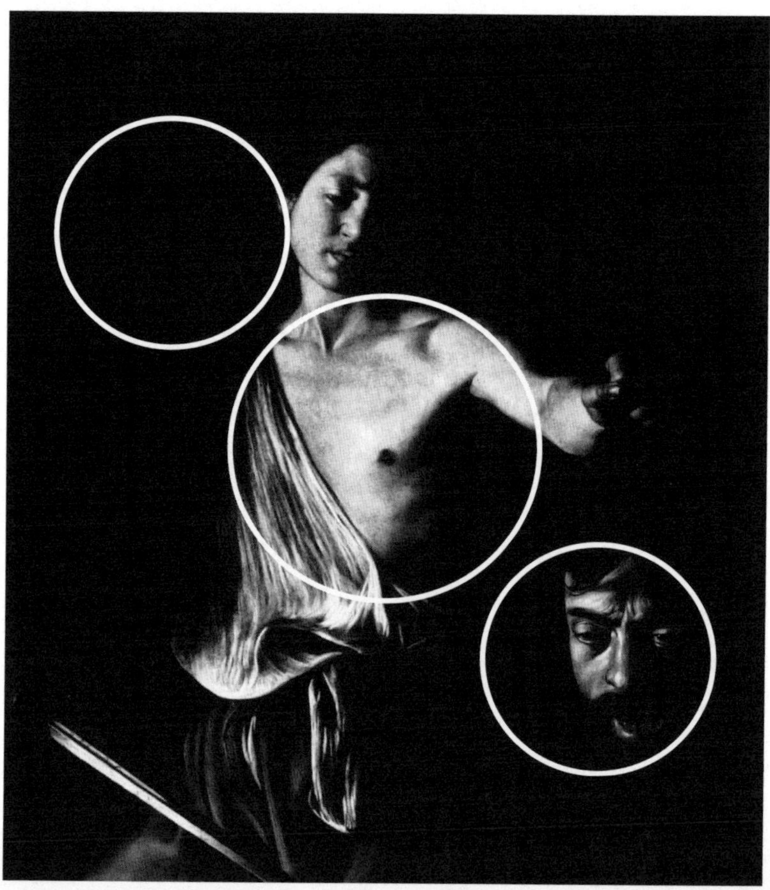

II.4.3 Michelangelo Merisi da Caravaggio, *David with the Head of Goliath* (planar division in circles), 1609

1. Goliath's head in the shadowy foreground
2. David's body as the illuminated centre
3. Unseen death as the black background

The three representations are constantly conversing with one another. Might they possibly look at one another at some stage? If so, one becomes more than a derivative of the other: they become interlocutors. As Freud once said: "Beyond Eros we encounter Thanatos" (quoted in Deleuze 1991, 114). Looked at that way, the old man and the young are playing a game. The focus would seem to shift from one protagonist to the other, though neither disappears—so several protagonists exist simultaneously, side by side. In films, this narrative phenomenon is termed the multiple protagonist effect. The different characters or parties that become visible all have their own story line and, together, form a patchwork of asymmetrical shapes.

Chronos stands for old age, interpreted as sickness and decay. In his analysis of the work of the film director, Michelangelo Antonioni, in *Cinema 2: The Time Image*, Gilles Deleuze states that "Chronos is sickness itself" (1989, 24). Chronos takes the path towards physical and mental decline. Caravaggio develops the projection of old age subtly. The older man's face inclines forward a little. He gazes downwards, he is looking inward. The introspective stance reflects an inner search, a concentration that is typical of someone digging into his memory.

The old man lives in flashbacks. Sometimes he finds something, but more often there is just an accumulation of illusive sensations, similar to the way someone suffering from dementia trawls confusedly through his memory. A pivotal element in the picture with respect to this association is the cruelty of physical aging. The bony, unsymmetrical face of the older man contrasts with the symmetrical, oval face of the youth. The boy's smooth skin is suddenly marked by the wrinkled traces of old age. Caravaggio has caused the controlled, athletic figure of the young man to merge along the diagonal into the powerless savagery of the older body. In a semantic instance, the face displays the ruthless traces of time. The anguished features refer to the pain of this process. The wild hair, the slack mouth and cheeks accentuate the shapeless, disorderly character of aging. The emphasis is found increasingly on the face that, reinforced by the *chiaroscuro,* exhibits the physical symptoms of aging. David is no more than a photo from a distant past. He is a reflection, a childhood memory. He is a briefly glowing moment. Growing old is far-reaching: the black space surrounding the older man.

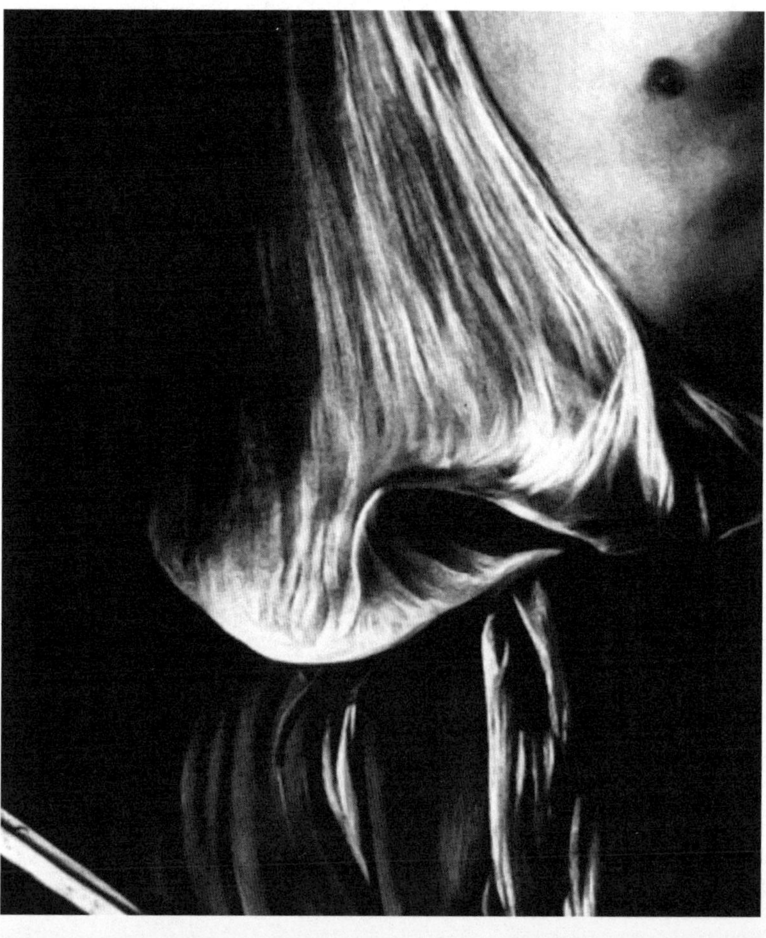

II.4.4 Michelangelo Merisi da Caravaggio, *David with the Head of Goliath* (detail), 1609

THE ADOLESCENT AS A VICTIM The laws of nature have turned the adolescent from a victor into a loser. Youth is a fleeting moment that is past before you fully realise it. George Steiner's concept of "negative ontology" is reflected in Caravaggio's work (1990, 129). "Genetic fixing" is impossible: the incurable process of aging has begun, irrevocably. In this way, Caravaggio anticipates Mathieu Kassovitz' film *La Haine* (1995)—the third panel of the triptych of *Youth and Death*. Kassovitz shows how someone falls off an apartment building. The process of falling, in which you, the spectator, also pass one storey at a time—takes you, story by storey closer to the final "destination". Arrival on the ground, death, is something awaiting us all: inescapable and irreversible.[35]

35 The term "genetic fixing" derives from the science fiction novel *The Stone Gods* (2008) by Jeanette Winterson. The book describes a future society in which aging is no longer natural. Everyone undergoes a medical intervention to "fix" him-/herself "genetically" at a favourite age.

The Rough Texture

TEXTURE The dramatic representation is revealed in an increasing number of details: small, chaotic traces of paint. They are traces of decomposition: microworlds evocative of the structure of a corpse. Particularly in the shadowy area at the bottom of the canvas, Caravaggio worked increasingly in darker details. It is hard to find a point at which youth and old become detached. Where does old age start? Where does youth finish? Is youth merely a passing phenomenon? Is old age an obsessive fixation? What is reality? What is imagination? Shadow and light resemble a chromatic spectrum that can start anywhere. The large planes belong to the harmonic light side we looked at earlier; the shadow side reveals itself in details. Sometimes the details are best seen from a distance. A landscape of fractures. Then I zoom in on the swarming ensemble of traces. The detailed nature of the older man's face (Goliath) is a story in its own right, reinforced by the adjacent space. The young man's clothing (David) has a greyish-white colour, with the structure of a shroud (fig. II.4.4).

The sculptor J.J. Beljon refers in *Ogen open* (1987) to the "ruin effect" of processes of decay. The ruin effect forms the aesthetic of aging. For some it is repulsive and something to be prevented. However, ruin can also possess a weathered attractiveness. Caravaggio does not idealise youth at the expense of old age. Rather, he teaches us to examine the sclerosing process of aging—which he also does with the vitalising process of youth.

Caravaggio's painting depicts, intentionally or unintentionally, scientific, biological ideas on life processes, shaping them here in an artistic way. Also, aging has an inorganic and an organic dimension. Organic aging has a sensual, sometimes even eroticising effect. It can be explained as a spreading process. Organic processes are characterised by jumbled lines and "derailments". The gradual process turns into a process that cannot be slowed down—of fading, decomposition and shrivelling, and is mainly found in nature.

Transient reality even penetrates the painting's surface. Its surface structure, the paint itself, confirms the organic process of decomposition. With Caravaggio, the paint, as a substance, is just as important as the portrayal. The brushstrokes intertwine, like the letters in a sentence. One stroke refines the next. Nothing is fixed. The subsequent action adds fresh meaning to the action that precedes it. Painting as an activity becomes a kind of writing. Brushstrokes become narrative agents, sometimes connecting up, sometimes clashing. Accordingly, the "encounters" round the head—the hair, the blood—acquire increasing significance.

Inorganic aging has different aspects. It is a process of dying. It relates to the mineral world, concerning bones and hair, flaking, tearing, cracking and wearing out. The inorganic processes are reflected in the garments, the organic in the aging of the skin.

APPEARANCE OF ADOLESCENCE The presence of the dark background has gradually become more prominent; the adolescent appears to be nothing more than a painted, cosmetic figment of the imagination. If we look more carefully, we discover that a process of ongoing decomposition is involved. It is the confusing, chaotic, derailing aging game. Freud's naturalistic motto that lack of life existed before life, becomes reality. The beautiful, strong young man actually never existed. In fact, strength and vitality form an unreal, fictitious game that is intended to conceal that human beings are in a process of dying from their very birth. Thus, Caravaggio's work is a symbol for a new biological paradigm. Chemistry replaces theology. Caravaggio's observation punctures every illusion. The depiction says: "Youth is an illusion. Reality is the fascinating horror of aging."

Missing Sound

SOUND Darkness is almost nowhere as clearly visible as in Goliath's wide-open mouth. Ghastly reality is even "audible" here. Caravaggio's obsession with mortality, the moment of the tragic, becomes audibly inaudible: physically material reality and human vulnerability. I see, before the eye of my imaginary stationary camera, an "exchange without exchange" (Derrida 2006, 23). The painting depicts a wordless cry: a howl that turns you to stone.

In terms of composition and materiality, you are inclined to compare it with Francis Bacon's *Study after Velázquez's Portrait of Pope Innocent X*, 1953. Bacon paints an open mouth, from which a cry—yet not a cry—escapes (fig. II.4.5).

The silence of Caravaggio's old man (Goliath) deafeningly conveys the absence of sound: the sound of silence. This silence is so dominant and oppressive that it has the force of a shriek. It is a cry that is so horrifying and so inhumanly piercing that it is no longer audible. It is not a cry of despair evoking sympathy for human suffering. It is a demonic cry, causing suffering rather than being the outcome of suffering. The mouth opens up the path to the dread caverns of the incomprehensible, the bestial, the neutral (*Es*—it). It is the muffled sound of hell.

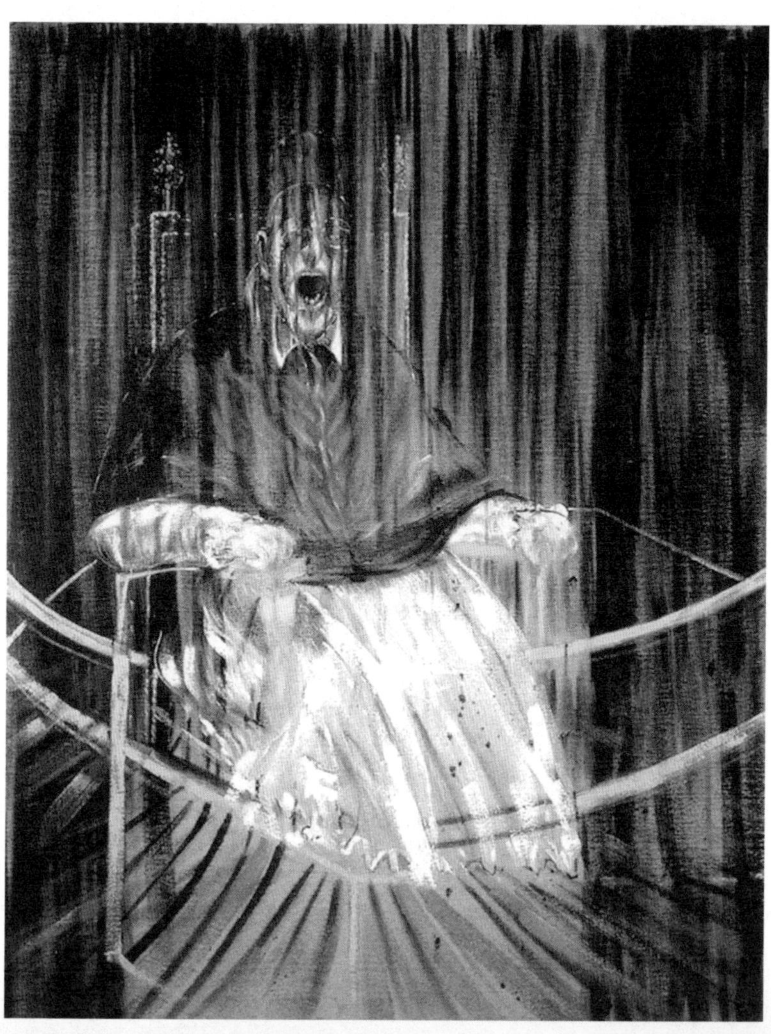

II.4.5 Francis Bacon, *Study after Velázquez's Portrait of Pope Innocent X*, 1953

Silence also has a quality that makes it distinctive. Caravaggio's silence is far harsher than Maurice Blanchot's poetic world of remaining silent in *Literature and the Right to Death* (1995, originally published 1949). In this paradoxical world it holds true that "When we speak we are leaning on a tomb, and the void of that tomb is what makes language true ..." (322). Blanchot sees silence as being of the night, and language as the realm of the day, thus indicating that language is what ignorance leaves behind it as a shadow. Language is the absence of sleep and the abolition of the void, the tomb. Blanchot's language is a poetic voice—quite different from the grim cry with which Caravaggio confronts us: the inaccessible cry, the cry from behind a glass wall. It is a cry evincing inescapable yet unattainable pain. As a spectator, you have the feeling you must look on, powerlessly.[36]

36 According to Ernst van Alphen, when we "read" Francis Bacon's work we are confronted with the dilemma of our own identity. He describes the paralysing pain with which the painting leaves the spectator. Bacon's work primarily confronts us with ourselves. He affects the spectator in his isolation, in his pain, in his nervous system. And that makes a painting like Bacon's *Study after Velázquez's Portrait of Pope Innocent X*, in the series of "screaming popes", interesting for this study. It "challenges death not as a state but as a moment" (Van Alphen 1998a, 95). Our own death approaches us as an experience (113).

THE UNRESISTING ADOLESCENT The caravaggesque darkness turns the once heroic adolescent into a small, inferior cog in the mechanised process of mortality. The shadowy surroundings swell. Darkness seizes power. The adolescent ceases his dramatic fight and becomes part of a machine that is bigger than himself. He is a young adult, who realises that life has its own dynamic, with death as the unavoidable final destination.

In this possible world, youth is an unresisting object and old age is also a cog in the machine. Caravaggio's scream is very different from Edvard Munch's *The Scream* (1893). The Norwegian artist gives despair a human face. However, Caravaggio shows the victory of an inhuman reality. As Deleuze ascertains in *The Logic of Sense* (1990, originally published 1969), the adolescent is not a character but a figure. A character has an autonomous status, a figure is part of a complex game, of a machine that is far larger than he is.

Endless Allusions

PERSPECTIVE Goliath would appear to inhabit unfathomable depths. David recedes farther and farther along the lines of the perspective, becoming a supporting actor (fig. II.4.6). He is looking at me, but then he retreats like a memory that dissolves into the past.

The young man's withdrawal increases until a new point is reached. Memory no longer has any foundation in reality. David has become an illusion. The phenomenon of youth is just a belief. He becomes fiction. Caravaggio creates the adolescent as a phantom.

The *chiaroscuro*—the visual foundation of Caravaggio's thinking—plays an important part in all this. Graphical aspects dominated when I zoomed in on the older man's head. With the young man they were less obvious. Now those aspects disappear completely into the background: form and detail have become irrelevant.

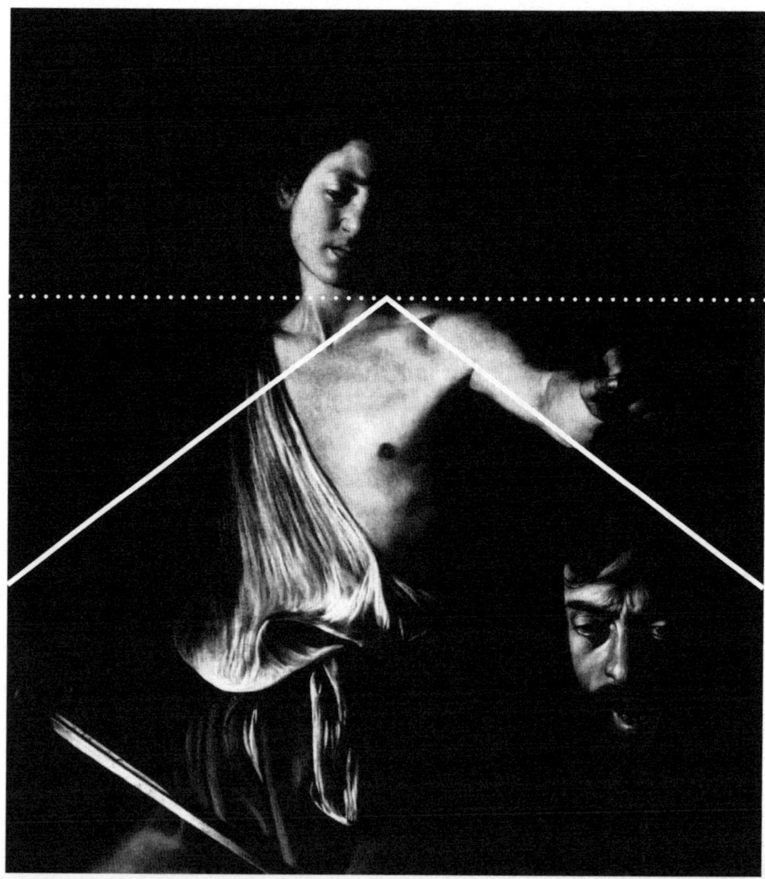

II.4.6 Michelangelo Merisi da Caravaggio, *David with the Head of Goliath* (perspective lines), 1609

Youth is now a glimmer: a dreamy light to which I, the spectator, am drawn. The black of the background produces a contrast, reinforcing the light through which I move even more. Thomas Pavel, in the title of his book, speaks of "the poetics of plot" (1985). However, in this picture it is more a matter of what Gaston Bachelard calls a "poetics of space". The space becomes a light area with a shape that is barely definable.

In *The Poetics of Space* (1994, originally published 1958) Gaston Bachelard writes about "the dialectics of outside and inside" (221). In my analysis of *David with the Head of Goliath*, I follow Bachelard's example, and distinguish between outside and inside space.

Outside space corresponds with the space of the old man. Inside space with that of the young man. Old age dominates the "real space", youth occupies the fictive, inside space. In addition, old age is in the shadows, while youth is in the light. The interior image displays many similarities with a dream image, a game with the subject. The old man's exterior space affects the world of the object.

The Poetics of Space is about architecture. However, the difference between interior and exterior can also be expressed cinematographically. It is an interplay of lighting effects, evoking the illusion of space. Different kinds of light or no light (low key), diffuse light (fill light) and much light (high light) each create a different spatial effect.

Youth, in cinematographic terms, is representation in high light, prompting comparison with science fiction films. David is an idea. He does not exist in the world of the object. The adolescent is an illuminated hologram. He is a virtual manifestation, a phantom. He is form without substance, a mental illusion: he is fiction.[37]

37 Bachelard's *The Poetics of Space* addresses the subject of memory. According to Bachelard, the human psyche creates spaces in which memories are found. When we relive or dream these spaces and then link them together, we can bring about new spaces in a syllogistic process. The poet-scientist can describe the spaces in ironic language, a kind of surrealist dream language that is sometimes difficult to comprehend in its logic. Bachelard's views on the psyche as space correspond significantly with the third step in the process of Art-Based Learning in which it is important to enter a possible world. It is a world where interaction between subject (researcher) and object (art) generates new space. Bachelard opts for a romantic approach that culminates in a poetic, mythical, literary and philosophical form of knowledge production which also characterises ABL. In the essay "Inzoomen, uitzoomen: Notities over kijken en kennen" (2003), Piet Meeuse, writes about the world he perceives through the eye of the camera—in line with Bachelard's work. He suggests that looking can provide us with great satisfaction, provided we allow ourselves to be guided by chance. That amounts to allowing ourselves to be "served by what confronts us" (17). It is the realm of "revelation" in which "everything suddenly seems to come from the other side, presenting itself as something new" (17). In this essay Meeuse describes the process of ABL exactly: you ask yourself a question and wait—poetically—for what assails you. It is a description of an encounter with a speaking object, as also emerges in Bachelard's work.

38 Baruch Spinoza's pantheism ties in with a tragic view of reality that gives way to a poetic view of reality (as in my second triptych). Spinoza was a rationalist and, like Leibniz, an exponent of early modernism. Spinoza's philosophy—in line with that of Parmenides—is based on the idea that there is only one substance: Nature, i.e. God. This substance then appears in infinite forms, which do not, however, have an autonomous eternal existence.

THE ADOLESCENT AS A PHANTOM In this triptych of *Youth and Death*, the adolescent has become a phantom. He has turned from a reality into distorted wish fulfilment—a ghostly figure that, like all phantoms, requires an explanation, according to Bachelard in *The Flame of a Candle* (1988, originally published 1961). This is based on a figure, at this point still in actual reality. The older man's head appears as an indication of a mental space. There, within that mental space, an image appears of youth as a fictitious character.

In fiction, adolescence can be presented with an artistic, psychological or religious slant. Fantasy (art), thought (science) and belief (metaphysics) are, after all, situated in the same field of imagination. In all three cases it is about life in a possible world where everything is possible. One of the possibilities within that space is to "evoke" youth. This possibility is liberating. However, fiction can also have a tragic, inhibiting side. After all, the inevitable process of aging is the end of any form of transcendence. Fiction is linked to the individual as a material component of nature. Spinoza already observed how the individual himself, with his death, is again absorbed in Nature.[38]

Lastly

In *David with the Head of Goliath* I again follow the diagonal course, from below right to top left into the "offscreen reality": the world of the real shadows (fig. II.5.1). The effect of shadow in the painting largely occurs in the bottom right corner. The shadow starts with the older man. His introvert gaze shows the way.

The shadows direct us, calling "this way", back to the past. They now also fall on David's chest—initially I saw him only as an illuminated figure. They then recede further, to fall on his neck and face. The shadow also impacts on the past. Chronos' shadow rewrites the story of youth.

Eventually the shadow reaches past the space of the painting, into offscreen reality. The painting leads me to a black space filled with enigmas. I arrive in the immense world of the text behind the text, and encounter the shocking trail of the dead artist of this scene.

Caravaggio's Goliath is the face of Caravaggio himself. As in the case of Pedriali's *Autoritratto immaginario,* this is a self-portrait. It is a face calling, reverberating "I'm dying!" Here, fiction oversteps its limit and creates a reality.

The seventeenth-century art theorist, Giovanni Bellori, was the first to suggest that Caravaggio painted Goliath as a self-portrait. That is corroborated by the great similarity between this portrait and the figure that is turning away in the background in Caravaggio's *The Calling of St. Matthew* (1600) and a portrait of Caravaggio by Ottavio Leoni (c. 1621).

Yet again Caravaggio has wrong-footed me. This is the effect of the ABL method: you move along with the maker's thinking. I now see youth starting to play a complex game, an unparalleled ego-document and existential drama. The artist appears from behind his easel. He becomes part of the art work. I, the spectator-listener, am involved in a relentless process of self-analysis. The painter deconstructs himself. He 'dismantles' himself: he is no longer the painter, the ingenious creator of the painting. He situates himself in his self-created world. Here we see the first step in the story of the irony of youth that is developed in the final triptych.

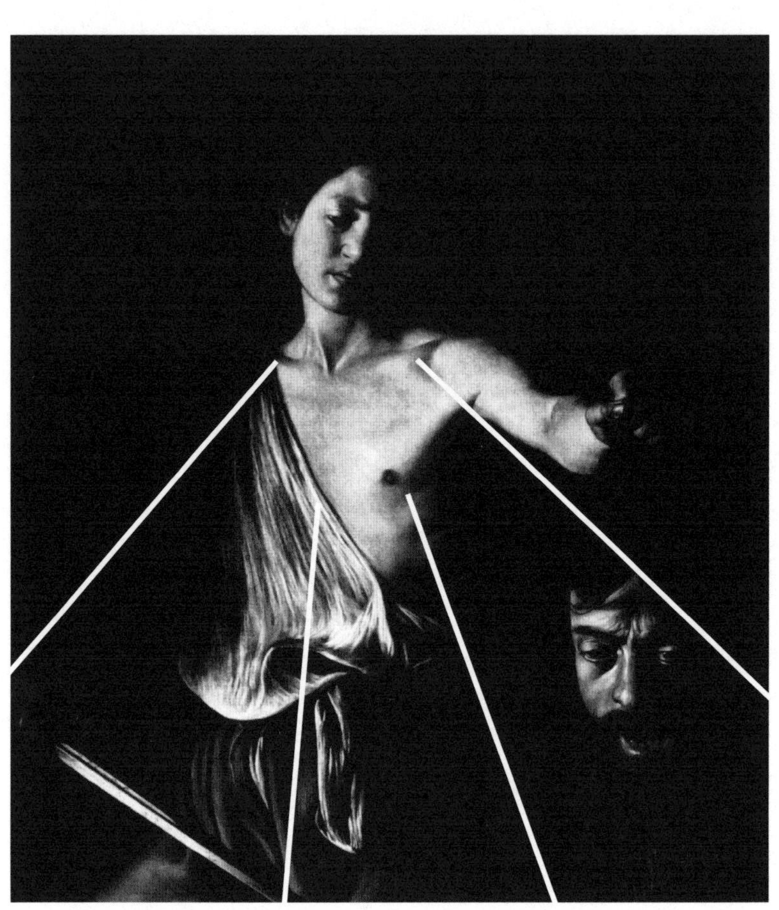

5

Caravaggio: Thanatos

Motionless Space

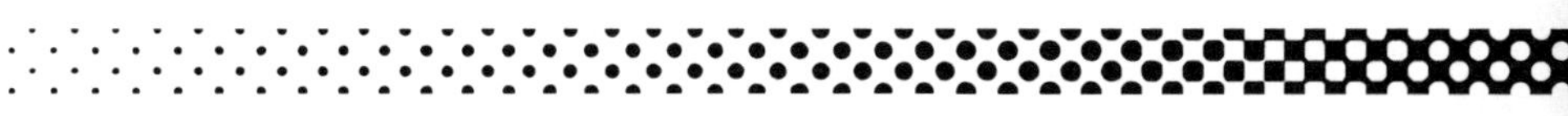

Introduction

The journey through the possible worlds of *David with the Head of Goliath* takes us into the realm of Thanatos. In Greek mythology, Thanatos was a son of Nyx and the twin brother of Hypnos (sleep). We are traversing the area of death. The young man (David), as a speaking object, has told the story of an Eros, a young Graeco-Roman hero. The story of a tormented Chronos (Goliath) has turned the adolescent in Caravaggio's painting into a phantom. Chronos experiences youth as a mere reflection, a distant reality that becomes ever more distant as the years go by. The story of Thanatos, of the visible darkness behind which a hyperreality lurks, is now addressed. It is a mysterious area where chaos prevails.

So far, depictions and forms have gone together. In the young man's world, order dominated—for instance, reflected in his upper body, the structure of which is relatively orderly. In the unsymmetrical world of the young and the older man together, disorder dominates. Here, reflection is found in the

II.5.1 Michelangelo Merisi da Caravaggio, *David with the Head of Goliath* (perspective lines), 1609

young man's lower body: the knot, the bunch, the creeper, the tunnelling, the vortex, the volution, the spiral.

However, the story has not ended yet. In the world of Thanatos, of death that has to come, the enigma and the unfathomable prevail. The noticeable opening in the shirt, the hanging part that is somewhat reminiscent of a wet towel, the open fly—all question the dark cosmos looming behind the young and the older man.

Black space changes the dream-work of youth into an obscure no-man's-land, where Thanatos—neither youth nor old age—reigns. It is the area within the dream. Christopher Bollas writes:

> I am lost in self-experiencing. The distinction between the subject who uses the object to fulfil his desire and the subject who is played upon by the action of the object is no longer possible. The subject is inside the third area of self-experiencing. His prior self-state and the object's simple integrity are both 'destroyed' in the experiential synthesis of mutual effect (2003, 31).

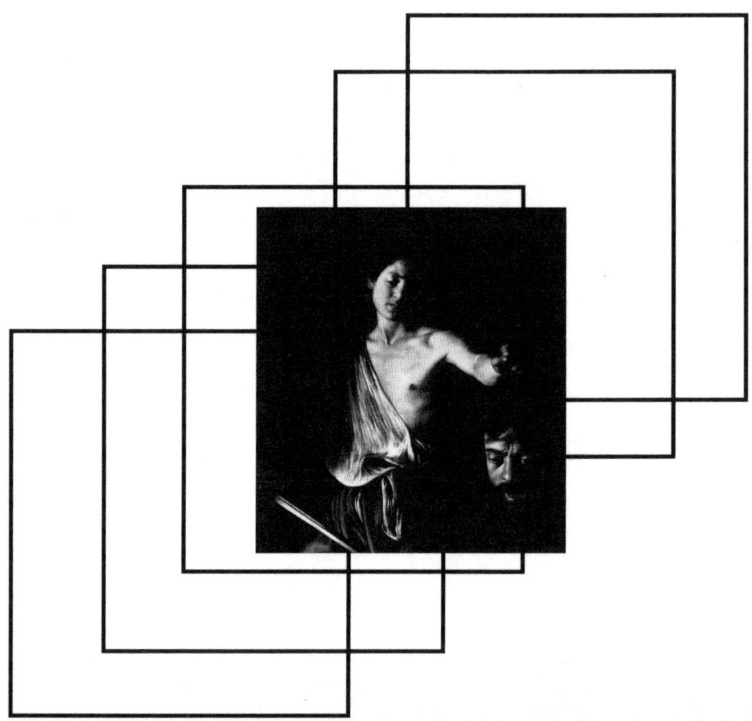

II.5.2 Michelangelo Merisi da Caravaggio, *David with the Head of Goliath* (black space), 1609

The painting takes me ever deeper into the subconscious regions that Freud associates with mortality. It is not easy to enter that world. It requires an extra ability for me, as a subject, to abandon myself to the object of research and thus become subsumed in a series of varying experiences, risking losing myself in contradictions. Time and again, the spectator must allow himself to be carried along by the logic of the illogical. The most obvious reaction is a desire to flee from this place of not knowing, of confusing connections and structures. The desire for guidance and the safety of what is familiar is great. Yet I must allow myself to enter the world of imaginary thought unreservedly, "as if [I were] inside a dream" (Bollas 2003, 21). It is important to postpone my disbelief and continue to give in to the paradoxical appeal of this world.

THE AMBIGUOUS ADOLESCENT The underlying darkness makes every image ambiguous. The painting as a speaking object tells about a possible world in which all certainty vanishes. It is an ambiguity that is characteristic of many baroque pictures. A world is created in which mind and matter mingle.

External Space as a Black Box

BLACK SPACE The ambiguity of the black space is reinforced when I present *David with the Head of Goliath* as an infinite, three-dimensional space (fig. II.5.2). The depth lines challenge you, far more than the diagonals, to continue the virtual journey into the painting. The lines running from the corners to an imaginary horizon behind the boy to the centre of the picture, produce a perspective.

Seen from that point, David is standing in the middle of a black box. He does not look at it. He slides ever farther into it, particularly from the left side. All he still experiences are the different shades of the black space around him—the dominant dark surroundings that many baroque artists always paint first.

It is as if David is gradually disappearing into a universe without end. The perspectivistic composition of the depiction is reinforced by the use of colour. The shadowy greys accost the spectator. The black expands further, while at the same time receding. After black there is Nothing. The black is endless.

Caravaggio's reality is that of a cosmic black hole that draws everything in. In *On the Spiritual in Art* (1946, originally published 1912), Kandinsky contrasts black with white: "Like a nothingness after sunset, black sounds like an eternal silence without future or hope ... Black is something extinguished like a burned pyre ... (68).

II.5.3 Michelangelo Merisi da Caravaggio, *David with the Head of Goliath* (black space), 1609

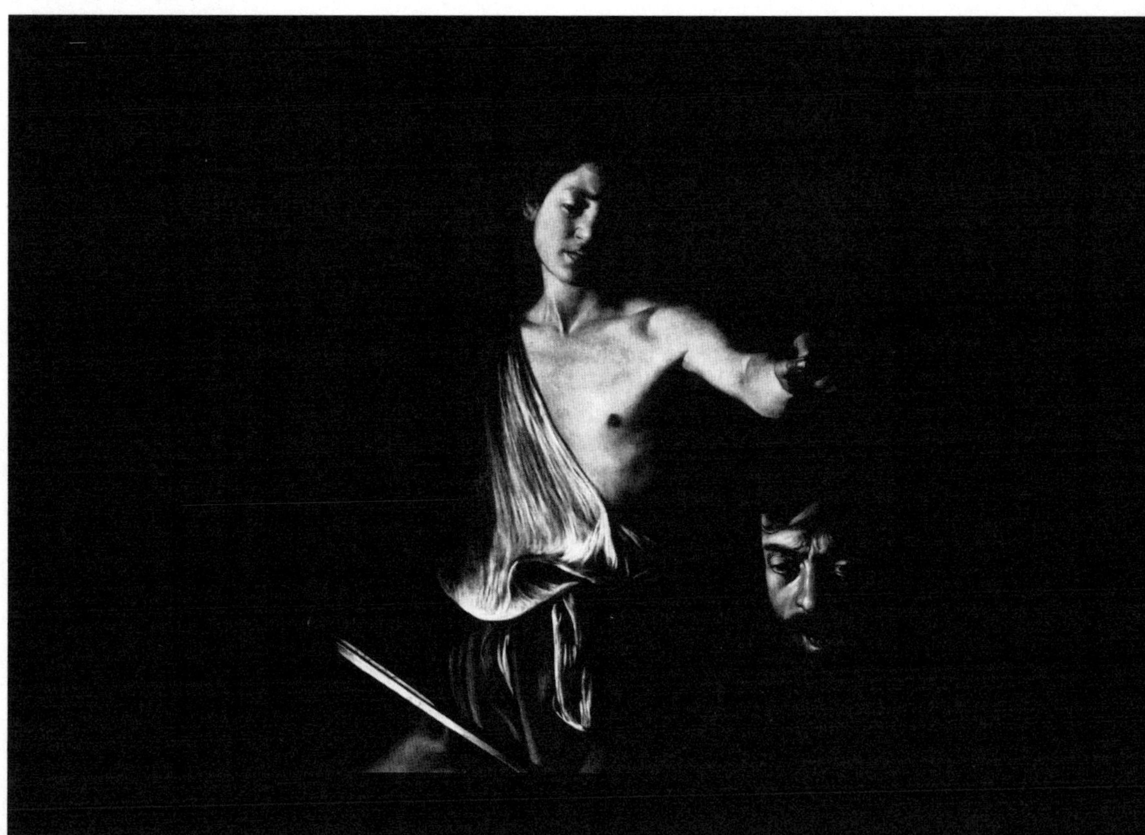

From this new perspective, the black acquires different meanings. I can see it as a cosmic space. David and Goliath are stars in a night sky. Thomas Ruff's *Stars* (1990) and Caravaggio's *David* are on the same wavelength. The black sky of the German photographer is not a void, but an adventurous space waiting to be discovered. It is a world where a new world can come about behind every image. This is an approach that has only been conceivable since the early modern period (in painting, the Baroque). Man begins to chart the physical surroundings, the universe, in all its detail. With Copernicus the geophysical view of the world gradually (starting round 1530) shifted towards a heliocentric view of the world. Man becomes a tiny glimmer of light, a speck of dust in an infinite universe. Caravaggio's David is a speck of dust. He is no longer the centre of the world. He is a space traveller in a vast universe.[39]

39 The vast universe is an important theme for the German artist Thomas Ruff. He makes works in series, since 1981 of the night sky, in particular. The *Stars* series (1990) shows nocturnal space in the way we also see it in Caravaggio (only without the stars).

The Complex Internal Space

Black has the voice of the macrocosm, but also of the microcosm. When we reread the black as a three-dimensional internal space it acquires a psychological dimension. The space around David is an indication of his psychological state (fig. 11.5.3). The space inside David penetrates my own—the traveller's—internal space. Internal space is an infinite universe comprising all manner of possible mental worlds.

It will not come as a surprise that the psychoanalytically-orientated art historian Howard Hibbard in *Caravaggio* (1983) sees a connection between the black space and the unconscious. The painting, for him, illustrates the chaos of conscious. He sketches how, in some of Caravaggio's late works—from 1600 onwards—the large dark areas begin to take precedence.

Hibbard suggests there is a psychological reason. The black space is the representation of an unconscious space, the infinite, black, inner world. He ascribes the way this space is developed to the painter—something that ABL seeks to avoid.[40]

Doležel highlights three normative codes from which we can observe: the rational, the irrational and the insane worlds (1998, 120). These three worlds are found as three virtual projections in Caravaggio's painting. The rational world has the face of David. The irrational world of emotions has the face of Goliath. The world of insanity, of the uncontrolled, has a face in the blackness. It is both space and emptiness. The black plane is an oppressive and frightening space.

It is a world that opens the door to psychiatry. In that black world delusions go their own way, as natural processes. The painting mirrors what is in my mind: the boy and the man are projections. Goliath is the apparition of death, though rigor mortis has not yet set in. In this way, he serves as a final link with the land of the living.

The darkness draws the young hero farther and farther into the hallucinatory depths. He is in danger of falling, out of control, into an unknown ocean of experiences. The young man's battle is a battle against the abyss of death. The unfathomable depths in which he finds himself are an inert, sluggish, mechanical space filled with delusions—delusions that affect him, but which he would seem unable to alter.

THE INSANE ADOLESCENT The black space turns the adolescent into a confused soul. He becomes an insignificant object in a Kafkaesque space. Insanity/Madness lurks. Michel Foucault describes in "Of Other Spaces" (1986,

40 According to Hibbard, the curse of Man is the foremost theme in Caravaggio's work (1983, 267). In *Caravaggio* he addresses the tragic aspects in that work. He says, with respect to the late works: "His paintings have a prevailingly sombre mood that often edges into tragedy: his customary schemes are martyrdoms, burials, or religious experiences that are like death in life" (261). Frequent themes characterising Caravaggio's work, are the vulnerability of Nature, death, dying, inner and outer wounds.

originally published 1967) how the adolescent has left his relatively sacred "crisis heterotopia" that, apart from a few remnants, has disappeared from our society (24). He has turned into a comet, a powerless object in an unprotected, ever-expanding space.

I have already explained insanity as a variant of fantasy: an unwilling suspension of disbelief. Nature—decay—becomes the protagonist. Heterotopia, an 'other' place offering protection for 'otherness', is found in the form a museum or cinema. However, these "heterotopias of deviation" from Foucault's *Madness and Civilization* (1988, originally published 1961) give little consolation. Caravaggio's transparent realism increasingly reveals darkness. It confronts you with an environment that gets you in its clutches, as if it were a machine.

Foucault's work is an example for ABL. In *The Order of Things* (2002, originally published 1966) he walks through Velázquez' painting *Las Meninas* as if passing through a room, allowing the work itself to do the work, as a "speaking object". He starts with: "The painter is standing a little back from the canvas," (2002, 3). Then Foucault goes a step further, not shunning the area of imagination: "He is glancing at his model; perhaps he is considering whether to add some finishing touch, though it is possible that the first stroke has not yet been made" (3) The author descends farther and farther into the "possible worlds". "The arm holding the brush is bent to the left, towards the palette; it is motionless, for an instant ..." (3). With this, Foucault passes judgement, based on a painting's internal logic, on the painting as a photograph that represents a reality. He concludes this first paragraph with the observation that the paintbrush is awaiting the outcome of the painter's gaze, and the painter's gaze is awaiting the painter's gesture. The analysis can also be interpreted as a process in which questions, narrating objects, possible worlds, images and stories interact.

A Compelling Mechanical Structure

The black space absorbs everything (fig. II.5.4). I experience the overpowering force of the space around me. That spatial experience leads me again to recognise Aristotle's description of tragedy. In his interpretation, tragedy is in fact a system in which the plot is pre-eminent, like a powerful machine having everything, every occurrence and every character, in a stranglehold.

The plot is a structure of events which always come first in tragedy. These events interact following a causal logic. In tragedy there is little room for coincidence. Characters have a subordinate position. The tragic aspect evokes fear and sympathy. It resembles an unstoppable train racing farther into the darkness.

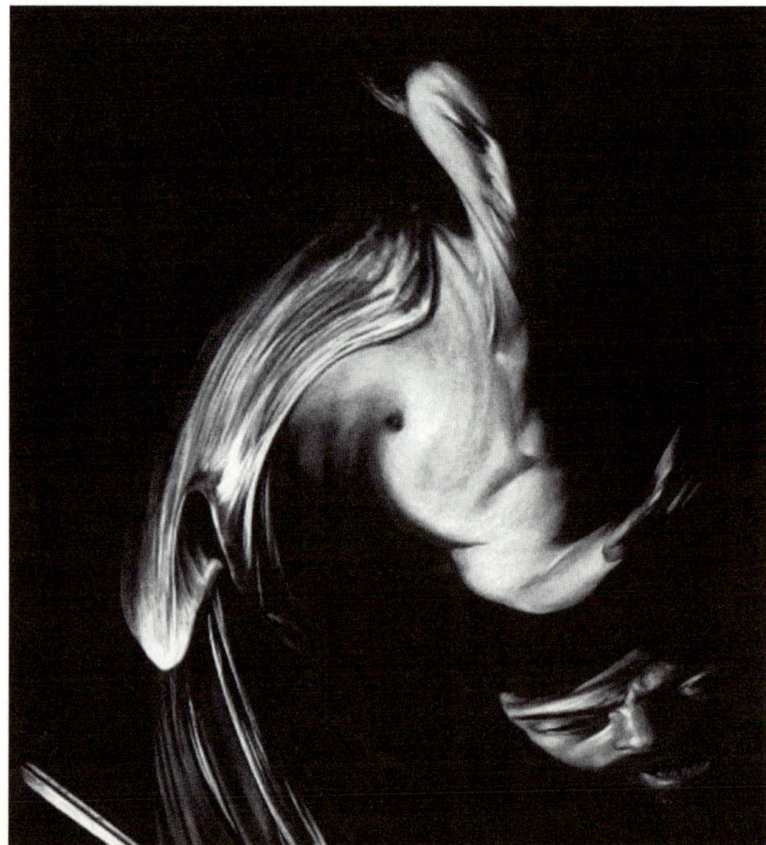

II.5.4 Michelangelo Merisi da Caravaggio, *David with the Head of Goliath* (distorted detail), 1609

The journey into infinity results in an experience that Freud in his lecture on a tale by E.T.A. Hoffmann described as *das Unheimliche* (1983b, 189). This term 'Unheimlich' or 'uncanny' has three characteristics:

1. *Dark space.* In *David with the Head of Goliath* we see a space which (in Freud's terminology) has an 'uncanny' effect. It starts with the black of the dark background as an all-important space. This black reality has a mechanical cause-and-effect structure.
2. *Uncertain status.* This relates to the characters. The portrayed characters are fundamentally uncertain as to their status. Understandably, since none of the characters ultimately steers reality. On the contrary, the sequence of events actually steers the characters.
3. *The doppelganger.* Freud makes the comparison with the terrifying experience of an epileptic fit, in which suddenly an unknown side of the character appears.

In that way David and Goliath become 'doppelgangers': David is the face of culture, while Goliath represents animistic nature, the fearful "return of the dead" (Freud 1983b, 183).

THE DYING ADOLESCENT The caravaggesque way of thinking/mindset grows closer and closer to death. The difference between David, Goliath and darkness becomes ever smaller. *Das Umheimliche* is a feeling of ghastliness. The militancy of the young man, the icon of culture, proves to be a wafer-thin veneer. It is just a matter of time before natural forces surface and the adolescent is irrevocably defeated.

Every attempt to suppress nature's brute force is doomed to fail. Life is an hourglass—to use one of Bachelard's metaphors. Youth is an illusion. The adolescent who takes a good look in the mirror, does not see *Ich* ('I'), but *Es* ('it'). If he builds a fortress, he is merely putting off the evil hour. The adolescent tries to avoid captivity, but meanwhile, in the short time he still has, builds his own prison.

The Heaviness of Substance

The black surroundings, the dead substance, is what ultimately remains (fig. II.5.5). The slowness, the weight, the heaviness—these are important features of matter. The physical world is omnipotent and, in the end, kills everything. Ultimately, substance "kills" every representation. Even the old giant (Goliath) is slain.

The object that has become the subject eventually becomes the object again. Prison, here in the form of nature, makes lifeless 'things' of young and old in the end. The old man's head and David's body have become pieces of matter. The small amount of light in the old man's face is smothered in the omnipresent darkness. The heavy texture of the painting ultimately shapes what the painting is about: matter, lifeless substance that in the end determines everything around us.

II.5.5 Michelangelo Merisi da Caravaggio, *David with the Head of Goliath* (distorted detail), 1609

Ernst van Alphen, in *Armando: Shaping Memory* notes a kinship between Armando's work and that of Caravaggio. Armando's sculpture entitled *Melancholy*, made in 1998, serves as an example (Van Alphen 2000, 96). The work measures about one cubic metre: a modelled 'figure', the characteristic aspects of which are darkness and 'weight'. The blackness is enclosed in itself. The form and texture give the sculpture a compact, seemingly impenetrable appearance. It is a depiction of absolute nothingness. No light can enter this work. It is a radicalisation of Caravaggio's black. It resembles an impression of a black hole: a celestial body from which no light or matter can escape through the strong gravitational field.

Van Alphen analyses how the confrontation with heaviness does not necessarily have to take the spectator into that heaviness. It can affect him. It can remind him of everything it stands for. But the opposite is also possible. Aesthetic pleasure can cause you to move towards the sculpture (41). The fact that the introverted gravity refuses to make contact is the very reason why the spectator moves curiously towards it.[41]

41 Van Alphen describes how the work of Armando (1929–2018) refers to decay and death. The spectator is confronted with wartime experiences which "convince him of the absolute uniqueness" of such experiences. What is impressive about Armando's syntax is, in Van Alphen's view, that it is consistently indexical (2000, 9). The effect of 'indexicality', the referential, results in the spectator of Armando's work being confronted with the "unutterable". Armando's goal is only to "utter or depict what borders on it, touches it" (10). As far as the paintings are concerned, Van Alphen points to the impasto: "we are not only drawn to the depiction, but to the paint that constitutes it" (36). He also compares Armando to Caravaggio's work, pointing in both cases to the tactile element. However: "whereas Caravaggio attracts and invites touch, Armando's paintings repel" (41) The movement present in Caravaggio's dramatic work becomes, in Armando's, impenetrable darkness.

The Materiality of the Canvas

Caravaggio's adolescent, dominated by a naturalist philosophy and artistically represented in *chiaroscuro,* is thus an exponent of the emerging scientific-materialistic thinking at the end of the sixteenth century. The adolescent reveals himself as a mortal individual. The theological portrayals seem like a mere alibi for addressing the theme of nature. At best, religion exists as Spinoza's God: omnipresent and individually invisible. Nature is situated *behind,* or rather perhaps *in* the dark wall (fig. II.5.6).

Caravaggio speaks like an atheist and acknowledges the importance of nature. His attitude is not normative but aesthetic, more material than spiritual. He stands for violence. He is the upright figure and round, innocent face of David. Caravaggio is also the drooping figure, the darkness, the bony face of Goliath. Yet, above all, he is annihilating, impregnable nature. The *condition humaine* is nature, and nature is finite. Man has nothing to say about the most essential matters (life and death). In the end, Man loses.[42]

Catherine Puglisi opts for a biographical approach to Caravaggio's life and work, suggesting a possible development from a physical to a spiritual orientation. My journey through the possible world of Caravaggio's adolescent does not end in a metaphysical, but in a natural world. Caravaggio presents himself as an (early-)modern thinker. He says: "Look, this is the world in which we live". He has no illusions left.

Puglisi, in her extensive study *Caravaggio* (2000), enters the religious world of the Baroque. She describes how, based on the text on David's sword, a comparison is drawn between the fight between David and Goliath, and that between Christ and Satan. It is the power of humility opposed to

42 Catherine Puglisi has the following to say about this painting's tragic story: "In our own post-Freudian era, of all Caravaggio's works the *David with the Head of Goliath* has been regarded as a window into his psyche. Without excluding the homo-erotic implications, recent interpretations have explored the personal meaning of the image more widely by focusing on the visual antithesis offered by the two biblical characters: David projecting youth, virtue, faith and compassion, versus Goliath embodying age, sin, doubt and punishment" (2000, 365). With this Puglisi sketches the antithesis between young and old which is at the centre of in my research. In this approach, youth is seen as something resembling what is good. Old age and decay are described in terms of what is bad.

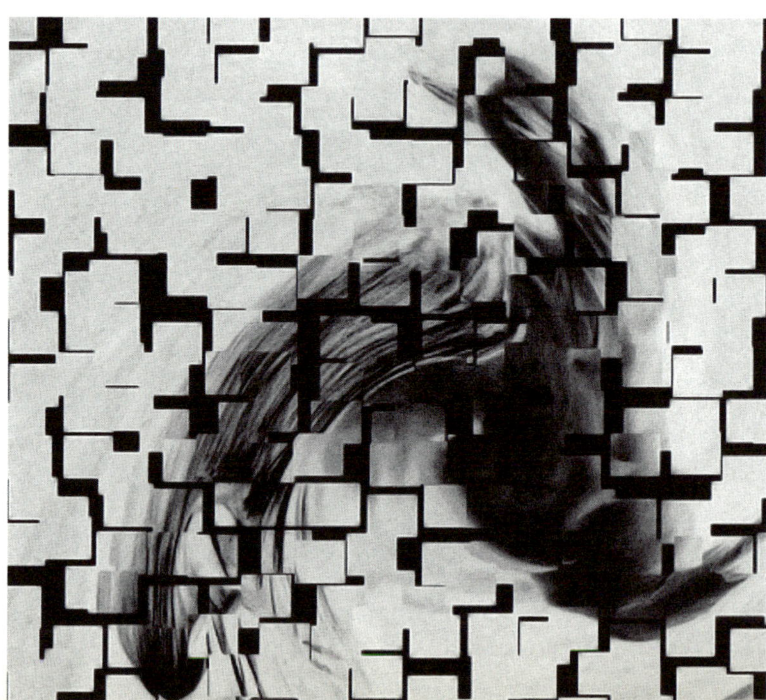

II.5.6 Michelangelo Merisi da Caravaggio, *David with the Head of Goliath* (distorted, negative and fragmented), 1609

pride. David reveals the whole gamut of human types encountered in the Bible. Puglisi cites the shepherd, the warrior, the ruler, the lover, the poet and the sinner (180).

With my analysis I tend to keep company with filmmakers like Derek Jarman. He does not present Caravaggio as a mediaeval man overcome by religion. He allows him to examine and analyse everyday, natural reality (which others conceal). Caravaggio admires nature for its powerful eroticism and relentless decay. In that respect, Caravaggio and Rembrandt have a lot in common. Both think in *chiaroscuro*.

The Dutch master, Rembrandt, and the unmerciful Italian master, Caravaggio, both recognise the diversity of conflicts and contrasts. They paint the play of light and dark, in order to show how darkness—nature—is ever-present.[43]

THE ADOLESCENT AS A NATURAL FORCE Implacable mortality is a natural force to which even youth is subjugated. The young warrior, the conqueror, is a figment of the imagination. He is overcome by dark doubt, physically and emotionally. In order to do good, he cannot always avoid doing wrong. Accordingly, he becomes the older victim. He gets his hands dirty. He becomes a murderer. The adolescent is a plaything in a cruel world.

> *What we have is a simulacrum, a trompe l'oeil, an excess of mimesis.*
> —Louis Marin (1995, 100)

The Simulacrum of Youth

Caravaggio's work is the tragic climax as well as the turning point of classical naturalism. What would Aristotle say when

43 In his work *Caravaggio Studies* (1974, originally published 1955) Walter Friedländer focuses attention on the play of light and dark with both Caravaggio and Rembrandt. He describes Caravaggio's realism as primarily socially committed and, only in the second place, religious. The Dutch caravaggisti were mainly interested in Caravaggio's painting technique. The Rijksmuseum in Amsterdam mounted a major exhibition addressing the relationship between the work of the two painters on the occasion of the 400th anniversary of Rembrandt's birth. In the introduction to the catalogue *Rembrandt/Caravaggio* (2006), Duncan Bull examines the similarities and differences in more detail, mentioning the fact that both painters, deploying pictorial methods (i.e. by thinking in *chiaroscuro*), succeed in emphasising complex human emotions and relationships: "This exceptionally profound psychological insight, this skill to express innermost feelings in paint, is perhaps the point at which, for the modern spectator, Rembrandt and Caravaggio exhibit the greatest kinship" (20). With this, Bull also indicates why Caravaggio's work is so suited for the ABL process, with its focus on human nature (adolescence).

looking at *David with the Head of Goliath*? The *Poetics* qualifies the principles of design, the aesthetic enjoyment of tragedy as the answer to the alarming content. In that way, the ancient Greeks prevent matter from conquering destructive natural forces at the last moment.

Art, the poetic answer to the tragedy of nature, opens up unexpected new paths. And thus Caravaggio's art and depiction of youth triumph over nature. For the maker, the art work is the sublimation of death and, accordingly, a victory over death. It increasingly becomes a blurring representation, a projection out of nothing. Optical phenomena are supplemented with aural experiences.

Michel Chion, in *Audio-Vision: Sound on Screen*, writes that silence is more than a neutral void and always the product of a contrast (1994, 57). Thinking in *chiaroscuro* that

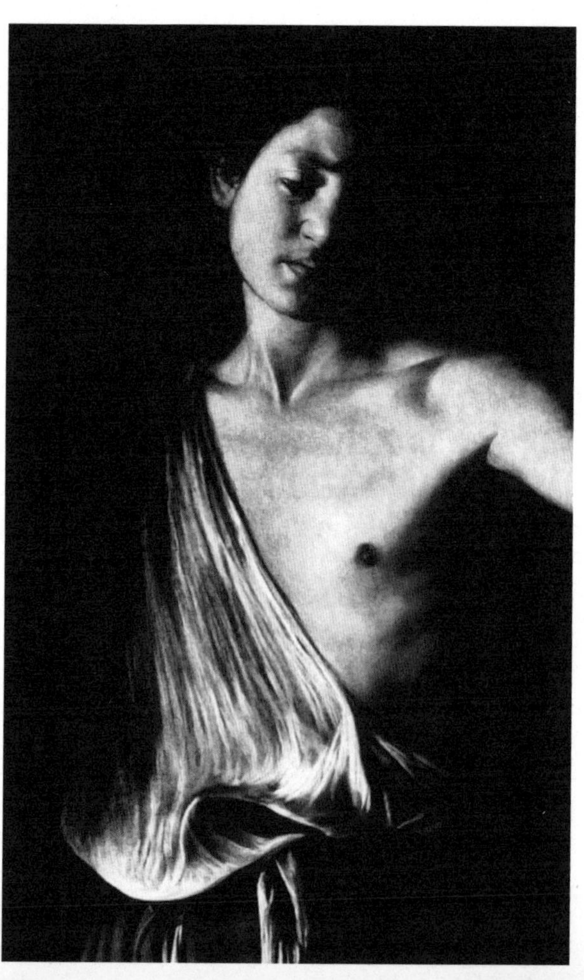

II.5.7 Michelangelo Merisi da Caravaggio, *David with the Head of Goliath* (detail), 1609

characterises Caravaggio's work now becomes thinking in an absence of sound. The contrast between light and dark, between straight lines and diagonals, between area and detail, now resembles musical notation, a score of silence, a composition of ever-clearer darkness. The interface that comes about approaches a new reality.

The adolescent as a figment of the imagination ties in with concept of Jean Baudrillard's: hyperreality as a simulacrum. In *Simulacra and Simulation* (1994, originally published 1981) he suggests that in the postmodern simulacrum, the third space in which we find ourselves, portrayals like that of Caravaggio's adolescent have become fictive figures which refer to themselves alone. In fact, human reality is without validity. The art work is the only reality.

The adolescent in Caravaggio's *David with the Head of Goliath* shows that adolescence is more of a phantom term than a reality. This hyperreality is an artistic reality. The painting is a speech act that opens the way to new fictive realities. Hyperreality is not the elimination of what is tragic, but a way of escaping from it temporarily.

Unlike reality, hyperreality generates new creations. For a long time, the only acoustic experience was the audible soundtrack of silence. But the sound of silence ends: the phantom figure of Goliath starts to speak again. His lips begin to formulate incomprehensible sentences.

David, too, is a hyperreality. Out of the light a new, fanciful reality develops. The young man's mouth was contorted. The red lips clamped together. This silence contrasted sharply with Goliath's muffled scream. The adolescent starts to move again. The strained silence vanishes. The reality of the (as yet) unuttered thought becomes the reality of a carefully uttered thought.

THE FICTIVE ADOLESCENT The adolescent has become fiction. A process of "rereading the previous reading" (Marin 1995, 39) now begins. The tragic adolescent changes into a poetic adolescent. When I reach this stage I have landed in my second narration of youth, in which I will consider a following triptych, comprising the work of William Shakespeare, Virginia Woolf and Thomas Vinterberg. A soft, poetic whisper begins in the distance, with the same implicitness as the melancholic (Pensky 1993). The idea of youth as a trauma, as an expression of the unexpressed, finds an escape route. It is the tender sound of the poet.

Lastly

Art-Based Learning, the dialectics of self-experience, has taken me from experiencing, understanding and ascribing meaning into an associative area. Experiencing and thinking, subject and object, fact and fiction, nature and culture, the focus of my studies and my personal memories are interwoven.

A dialogue with the work of the artistic philosopher Caravaggio has ensued. Focus, illumination, the inner voice and the outer voice have created a picture in which the young man recedes farther and farther into the background, while old age and death have changed from antagonist to protagonist. Decayed nature, with its chemical processes, has ousted the young god.

The caravaggesque world is a way of thinking—a linguistic game—of *Youth and Death* in *chiaroscuro*: a rhetorical game in which youth (light) loses and death (dark) wins. Youth becomes a virtual figure. David is a recollection that is hard to recapture. Youth acquires something reminiscent of an empty, projected presence: a picture without an original. The adolescent is now a "pseudo-form". Youth evaporates, blurs, and is overshadowed by death. Old age, death, as part of an individual's physical nature, is all that remains.

In *Representation* (1997), Stuart Hall asserts that images influence our social behaviour. In that respect, Art-Based Learning concentrates less on the maker's intention, but more on the significance of a work in bringing about a cultural reality. Questions like "What is the significance of pictures like those of Caravaggio for present-day culture?" should no longer be understood in terms of representation. Fiction is not a reflection of reality, but a relative concept. We give the figments of our imagination reality status.

The actual intention of Art-Based Learning is to discover how art produces topical realities, the rationale being that pictures like that of the tragic adolescent in fiction consciously or unconsciously create a specific cultural reality. And this takes us into the field of anthropology. Does a narrative modality exist of *Youth and Death* in culture? Does a *chiaroscuro* exist in thinking? Is it conceivable that certain social phenomena are the consequence of a possible world that goes beyond time and space? Is it conceivable that by degrees, with repetition of this figure, a social identity is created as "ethnographic reality"?[44]

In the following chapter I will allow the caravaggesque world to engage in a dialogue with this contemporary ethnographic reality, via the right-hand panel of this first triptych. What do we see of the world that is also outlined in Freud's biologically-inspired thinking?

Fiction is used as a way of describing contemporary urban narratives about youth, as filmed by the director

44 Hall's thinking is set in a framework of reception theory. The relationship between product and reader centres on this semiotic approach. He describes this with two terms related to the work of Barthes and Foucault: "encoding" and "decoding". The basic assumption is that meaning is generated by language. In *Representation: Cultural Representations and Signifying Practices* he refers to a "representational system" based on "the production and circulation of meaning through language" (1997, 1). Production and circulation of meaning through language is precisely what happens in the four steps in the process of Art-Based Learning. The process of a "telling object" via a "possible world" to a "story/essay" is an outstanding linguistic process.

Mathieu Kassovitz, for instance. Whereas the past was the prime focus in this chapter, I shall now address the past in the present. My knowledge of youth and death derived from studying Caravaggio will be of assistance. In the analysis of *La Haine*—a socially and politically topical film about youth—we will see if it serves a purpose for understanding the anthropological reality in our everyday surroundings.

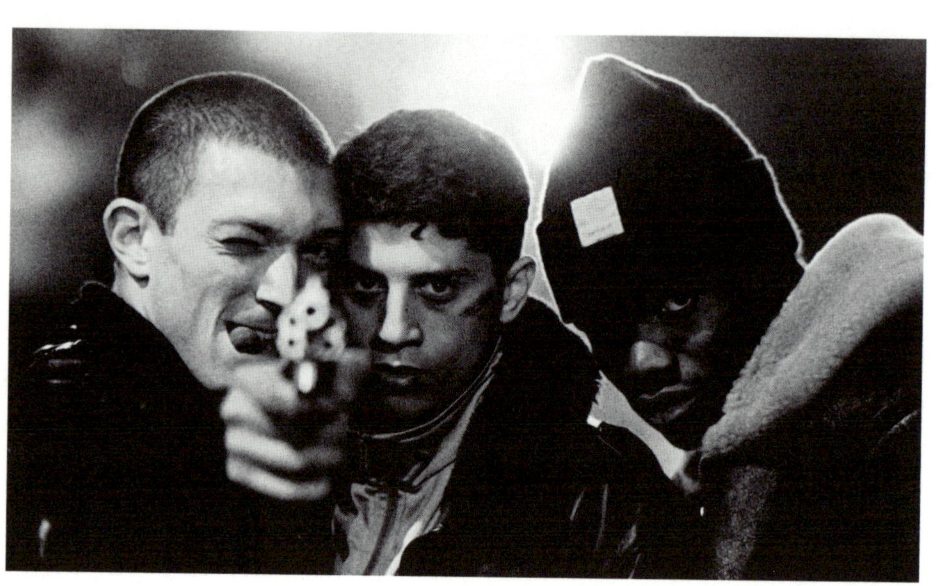

6

Reprise: Kassovitz

The Rhetoric of Death

Introduction

The early-modern caravaggesque rules of play, which also determine our way of thinking in the third panel, have become visible in the two previous panels: the left-hand one with Pedriali's photo and the central panel with the Caravaggio painting. I shall now concentrate on the third—as yet empty—panel, which will be the frame of reference for the last part of this case study (fig. II.6.1). Once I have explored a cultural memory, I shall return to contemporary culture. This dialectic movement turns art into a relevant kind of knowledge.

We are dealing with the past-in-the-present. It is now the reader's turn to speak. What is the significance of acquired artistic knowledge for a contemporary cultural context? What does adolescence mean in a contemporary ethnographic perspective? What does the rhetoric of *Youth and Death*—the story of the hero, his fall and his death—mean in an urban, twenty-first-century setting? Nowadays, we can recognise a return of thinking in *chiaroscuro*.

II.6.1 Mathieu Kassovitz, *La Haine* (film still), 1995

Judith Butler says, repeatedly in different terms: "reality is fabricated"; it is "an effect and function of a decidedly public and social discourse" (2007, 85). Language is not only the representation of a reality, it also creates a reality and, in that way, becomes performative. This performative dimension of language creates a historical-anthropological reality. In this final part, I am not so much analysing an art work, as primarily examining the production of a caravaggesque reality (the story of *Youth and Death*). The focus will be on reality as an art work, with all the concomitant normative, aesthetic, philosophical and political implications. In addition, I see a film like *La Haine* (1995) as the logical consequence of the rhetoric of *Youth and Death*, a rhetoric that is part of our cultural heritage and is being rewritten, time and again. Instead of being the reader of an art work, I now react as the author of a cultural reality. In fact, that cultural inscription must be seen, like the art work under study, as a new art work, a performative linguistic act that not only represents the story, but brings it to life.

THE WRITER AS AN ADOLESCENT The best way to tell this story is to construct it, shot by shot, into what I have described metaphorically as a cinematographic narrative. This kind of narrative can be compared to an essay based on a personal experience. In his thesis *Een drempelwereld: Moderne ervaring en stedelijke openbaarheid*, René Boomkens calls essays "exercises in 'free thinking'" (1998, 42). The essay is like an argument that exists thanks to "a stringing together of events into a meaningful plot" (Abma and Widdershoven 2006, 54). The essay moves from orientation on the past to orientation on the future. As Barthes put it, it turns the reader into a writer. The best essayistic annotations even turn the author into a character—Bollas' "self as object".[45]

45 Boomkens' thesis is a substantive source of inspiration for this study, because in it he provides a picture of present-day urban culture, against which background this story of the twenty-first-century adolescent takes on meaning. He discusses Paris, Amsterdam, New York and Los Angeles. He even calls Amsterdam "the adolescence of modernity". However, the chapter on Los Angeles is the most important because it provides considerable insight into the world of Kassovitz, Vinterberg and Jarmusch. Boomkens' work is also interesting in terms of method, because he makes a stand against a rigid, positivist, scientific approach, and advocates an essayistic approach to cultural science. Art-Based Learning is a cross between a poetic and an essayist view of science. Boomkens argues that: "the essay is written without the prospect of a set goal, but in the conviction that author will reach a meaningful place, a clear conclusion, an attractive perspective, however temporary it may be" (1998, 42). He aligns himself with Nietzsche, Foucault and Benjamin who see thinking as a fictive process.

The Specator as a Close Reader

La Haine is set in Paris of 1995 and is an allegory, a broadly developed metaphor. Kassovitz' metaphor contains a specific way of thinking. In this film still three elements stand out:

1. *The characters*: the three young heroes, Vinz, Saïd and Hubert.
2. *The time*: the gun, the first step towards the drama of the performance (fig. II.6.2).
3. *The space*: the darkness of the Paris metro, the tragedy of the story.

FRACTURE SOCIALE The possible world we enter is a world as it could really be. *La Haine* belongs to the *cinéma du look* or *cinéma verité*: cinema with a documentary-like style that suggests that film is more than fiction.

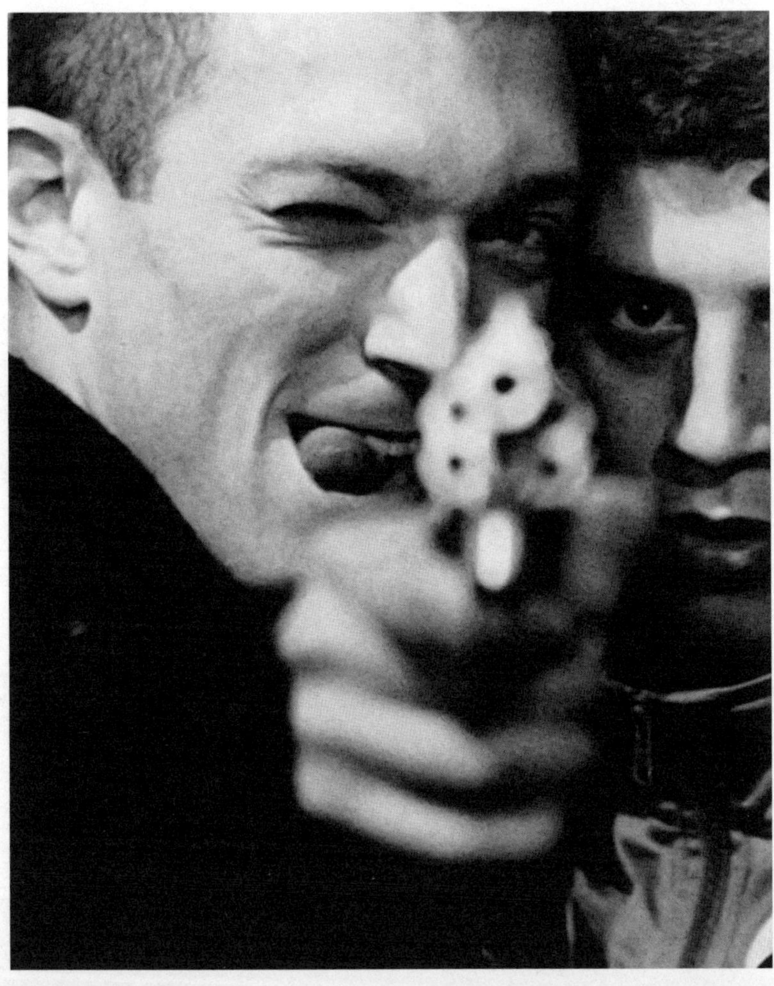

II.6.2 Mathieu Kassovitz, *La Haine* (film still), 1995

It is a film taking place in the same field and sphere as news broadcasts about explosive French banlieues—the emblems of a 'fracture sociale' (Higbee 2006, 67). *La Haine* is a variation on Danny Boyle's *Trainspotting* (England, 1996) and John Singleton's *Boyz in the Hood* (US, 1991). It is a striking film because of its subcultural aspects like music, dance and street art. Moreover, I consider hip-hop and break dance, and graffiti and rap as equivalents of Caravaggio's brushstrokes. They are the lines in the darkness. *La Haine* opens—appropriately—with Bob Marley's *Burnin' & Lootin'*, a number he wrote in reaction to brutal police action in Kingston, Jamaica, in the nineteen-seventies.

THE URBAN ADOLESCENT Kassovitz' camera shows us that adolescence in art can best be interpreted as an experience. It is the linguistic game of *Youth and Death*, set in a contemporary, western metropolis. Thinking in *chiaroscuro* returns, in the spatial design: a transformed caravaggesque world of the present.

II.6.3 Mathieu Kassovitz, *La Haine* (film still with horizontal line), 1995

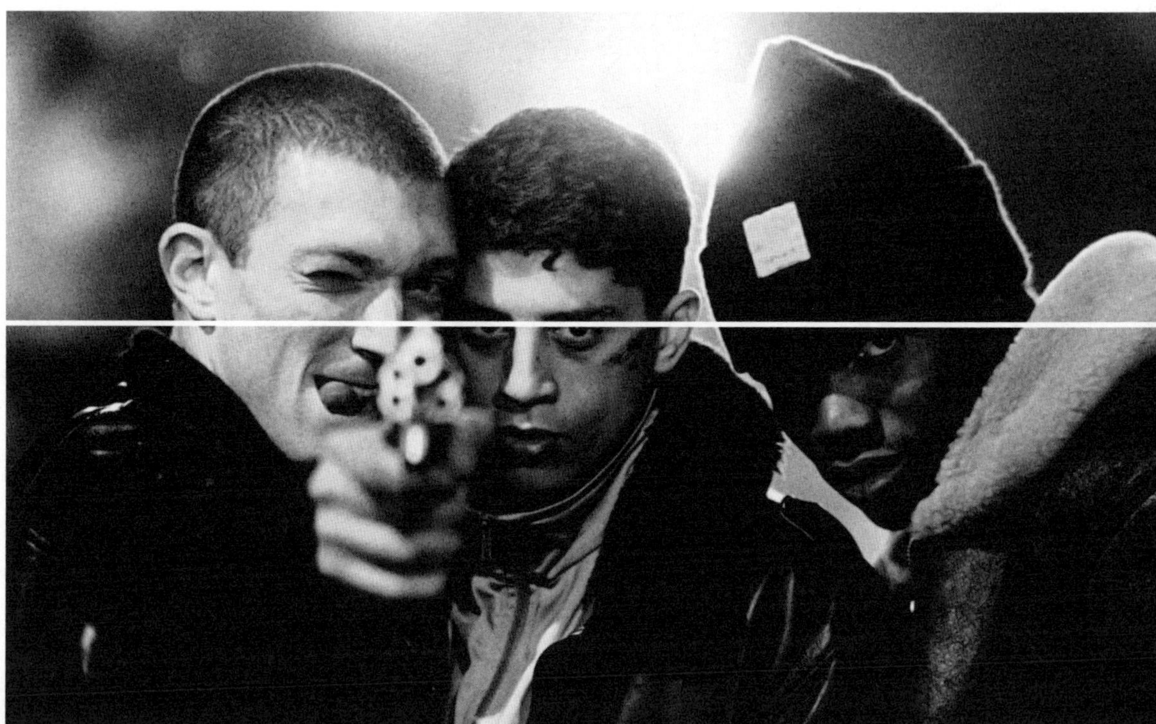

The Importance of the Plot

The three young heroes—Vinz, Saïd and Hubert—take an almost mythological journey by TGV (high-speed train) to "the end of the night"; they are shown side by side (fig. II.6.3). They are part of the French hip-hop scene. In the still, the boys stand in a horizontal line, one another's equals. All three live in the suburbs of Paris, which from the start are characterised by what Higbee calls a "site of struggle", a "space of marginality" (2006, 62–67).

The three protagonists—Vinz (Jewish), Saïd (Arabic) and Hubert (African)—are without prospects for the future. Violence, poverty and ethnic differences are commonplace. The only remedy for boredom is to smoke dope or plague the authorities. Kassovitz creates an atmosphere in which it is almost impossible for young people to be young. In the ghettoes it is all about survival. Threats come from gangs and corrupt, violent police alike. This is the dismal reality of metropolises like Paris. Young people are born old.

The attention paid to the characters, the close-ups in this film still, betray the influence of the director, John Cassavetes. The narrator, with the frequent use of close-ups, focuses on the details and expressive faces of the characters. In his monograph *Mathieu Kassovitz*, Will Higbee defines the three protagonists as specific cases of "youth aesthetics" (2006, 35). Tragedy and aesthetics coincide. The focus on details is directly related to the *cinéma du look* of Luc Besson, the director of films like *Subway* (1985), *Nikita* (1990) and *Léon* (1994). These films portray young people as both heroes and tormented victims. The element of recognition that is generated no doubt contributed to the film's tremendous success.

The ensuing politico-social debate takes place at a micro-level. With his three heroes, Kassovitz mirrors a French society that cannot fail to move supporters and opponents. The film is almost exclusively about survival. Death is breathing down the necks of the heroes in a chaotic world, in which there is but one law: kill or be killed. Death is an everyday reality for the youth of the Parisian banlieues, and subsequently permeates their culture. Law and order are mere illusions. The State is Goliath, a corrupt power in the service of the underworld, which ultimately controls everything. The city is a lethal no-go area in which Goliath walks abroad: a setting in which youth stands excels as a hero, but perishes in the end. David, youth, is constantly embroiled in this dramatic battle and will, ultimately, lose.[46]

46 Cassavetes' cinema is fundamentally subject-orientated. With improvisations playing such an important part, the work makes a very natural impression. In that respect Cassavetes said: "the emotion was improvised. the lines were written." He wanted the camera to follow the actor rather than hampering him. The camera often takes a long time to capture the character's inner life. Cassavetes' interaction with space differs from that of the French Nouvelle Vague and the German "School of Fear". In the Nouvelle Vague, with filmmakers like Godard, space has a non-totalisable, incomplete, open and even musical character. The School of Fear, in which he includes directors like Rainer Werner Fassbinder and Daniel Schmidt, focuses primarily on a deserted exterior, and has a minimum of connections. Kassovitz' approach conjures up an urban environment. However, the filming method is such that the actor is the key focus. The exterior is imposing, overwhelming, desolate. Yet it is never depicted in such a way that the spectator loses his connection with the actor.

THE ADOLESCENT AS A GLADIATOR The adolescent appears in the middle of this chaotic world of violence as a contemporary gladiator. And Vinz is a variation on Caravaggio's David (Lorenz 2002, 106). Vinz, Saïd and Hubert—the gladiators—know from the start they are entering the arena that has signed their death warrant. The 'unthought known' we saw with Pedriali's photos slowly

II.6.4 Mathieu Kassovitz, *La Haine* (film still with diagonal line), 1995

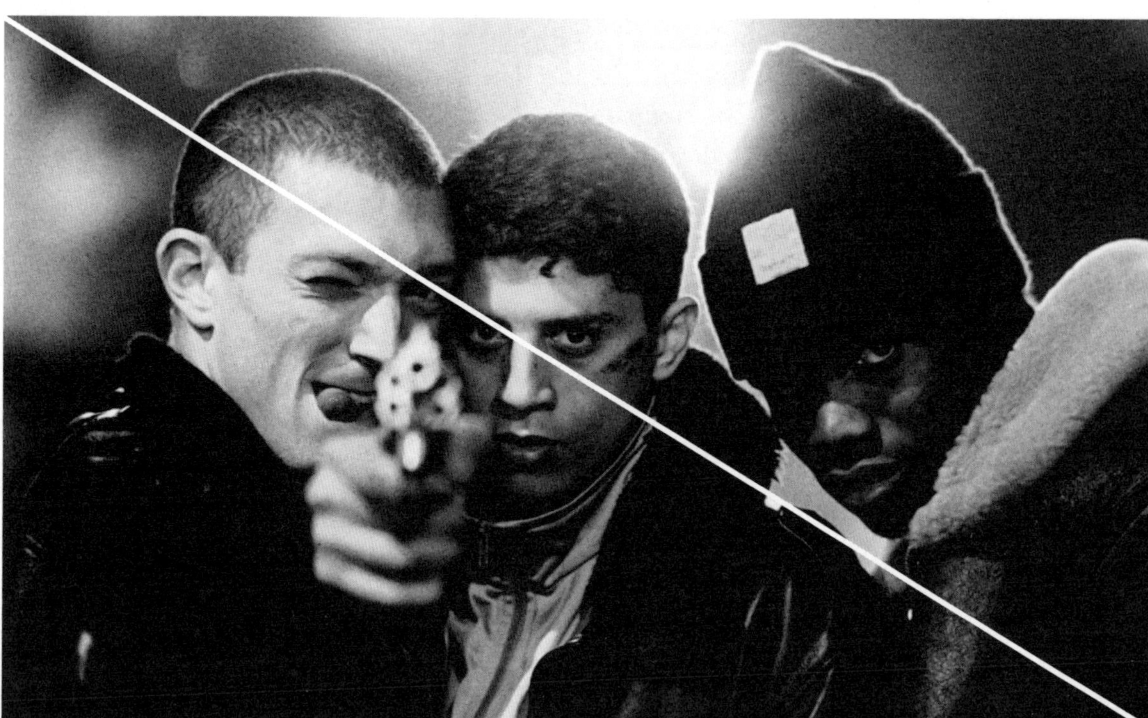

changes after the confrontation with Caravaggio's work into a 'known' when we see this film.

The Protagonist at the Centre

The protagonist, Vinz (Vincent Cassel), the boy on the left in the illustration, is the David of *La Haine*. He is pointing his pistol straight at the spectator (fig. 11.6.4). Like most of the characters, his status is uncertain and, ultimately, he comes off worst in a criminal universe. From the very start in the film, it is uncertain whether he will survive as the show-off in the group. He is controlled by fate, like a cog in an unstoppable machine. His resistance as a tragic hero is in vain. Saïd, in the centre, watches along with the gunman, but does not touch the gun. "I'll shoot"—but he doesn't. He does not lead, but follows the boy with the gun who, biting his tongue, is ready to shoot.

Hubert, on the right, does not look at the pistol, but at me. He is the witness. He does not commit himself in expressing approval, or not, of what is going on. He is powerless. In the image you sense the adage: "No matter how hard you fight, nothing can help, the space has already been established, the outcome preordained."

Julia Kristeva describes in *Powers of Horror: An Essay on Abjection* (1982) the theme of 'abject heroes'. The negative character of the abject hero illustrates the fatal reality. He is unpleasant, dissonant, abject and, in the process, contemptible. All three characters have an abject element. They do no shrink from burglary or violence.

As in Caravaggio's *David with the Head of Goliath*, we follow the line from top left to below right. Top left, Vinz and

Saïd strut their stuff as the offenders. Hubert appears, below right, as the victim. However, the impression he makes is the opposite to Goliath. To start with, he receives most sympathy from the narrator. Hubert occupies a special position. He represents more of a Hamlet-like figure. He is vulnerable and has a "Hamlet-complex", while (in psychoanalytical terms) his Oedipal wish-fantasies—necessary for healthy maturation—are not realised. He is a boy whose thoughts hamper his deeds. What he has repressed gets the upper hand. Hubert does not have a father.[47]

47 Oedipal confrontation is a term in Freudian psychoanalysis which is already found in *The Interpretation of Dreams*. It is rooted in "our first sexual impulses towards our mothers" and "our first impulses of hatred and violence toward our fathers" (1997, 157). Hamlet cannot take vengeance on the man who did away with his father and "shows him in realisation the repressed desires of his own childhood" (1997, 159).

THE ADOLESCENT AS AN ANTI-HERO With his three gladiators, Kassovitz portrays three anti-heroes, wandering powerlessly in a fatal caravaggesque universe. Vinz falls victim to chaos. Saïd is the active spectator. The melancholic Hubert is even so lacking in resistance to what is abject that at the end of the film he lands in an explosive 'Mexican standoff' with a corrupt policeman. This touching scene coincides with something that has been present throughout the film: the permanent threat of self-destruction. In the voice-over you hear Hubert's voice in the background: "Do you

II.6.5 Mathieu Kassovitz, *La Haine* (edited film still), 1995

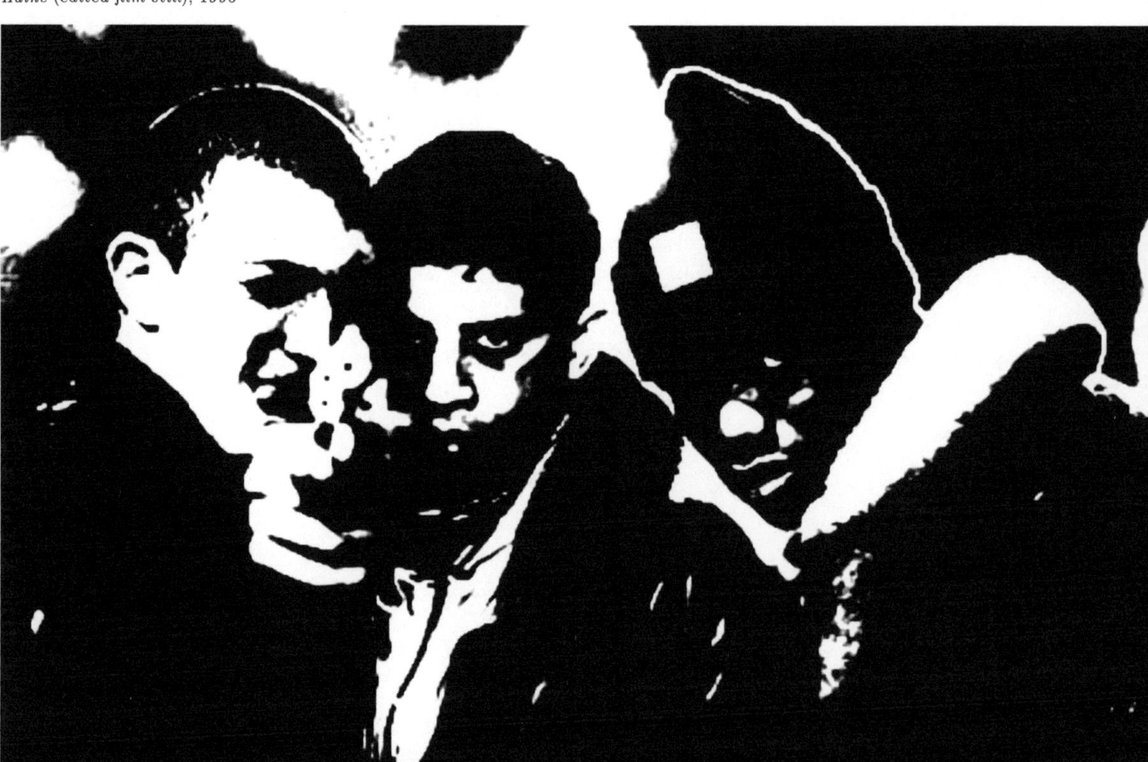

know the story of the man who fell from the apartment building? At each floor he says *jusqu'ici tout va bien* [So far, so good] Yet it doesn't matter how you fall, but how you land." It would seem that the TGV has reached its final destination; Hubert, the innocent one, falls. Abjection draws everyone with it into its maelstrom. It is the dramatic "night's end".

The Effect of Light

Caravaggio's *chiaroscuro*—the dark background with the illuminated characters—is revived. Now, however, the dots of light together form a chaotic rhythm, more so than in Caravaggio (fig. II.6.5). It is the kind of chaotic rhythm found, for instance, in breakdance and rap. The negative surroundings become even more prominent. The characters have already lost. The baroque reality of Foucault's other spaces (1986) takes shape; the individual feels lost. The muddled, twilit world of matter prevails. The final metaphysical foundation has gone. Time and space merge. Darkness, death: the irrevocable end is ever-present.

HIP-HOP Hip-hop is a musical style that uses the language of the street: it started in New York in the 1980s and spread from there to Europe. It is an art form characterised by revolt against a world steeped in 'lostness'; it is a language of chaos and darkness. As such, hip-hop extends to thinking in *chiaroscuro*. Life in a metropolis is an ongoing confrontation between life and death. Kassovitz' anti-heroes flee and offer resistance. Such resistance is reflected in subcultural stylistic features as a response to the repressive bourgeois culture. The struggle for survival is expressed in rap, as the exchange of cultivated abuse. That struggle for survival is also echoed in 'battles' (fights in dance), freestyle, (sports) clothing and graffiti as forms of linguistic expression.

THE DANCING ADOLESCENT The adolescent dances. Hip-hop endeavours to overcome what is tragic and form a response to the *memento mori*. Beauty (poetry) but also laughter (irony) will be examined in more detail later in this study, as answers to oblivion.

The Choice of a Perspective

The composition and perspective of the picture underline the dramatic development (fig. II.6.6). Vinz, in the foreground, has screwed up one eye. Tension causes him to bite his tongue. It is clear from the outset: the shot will be fired. Everyone is a participant. It is not a question of whether, but how and when. Vinz is a powerless individual whose status is uncertain. He is a ticking time bomb that can explode at any moment. Every step forward is in fact a step closer to the grave. The plot of *La Haine* has a rigid—almost mechanical—composition. The sequence of scenes, the lighting, the

II.6.6 Mathieu Kassovitz, *La Haine* (film still with perspective lines), 1995

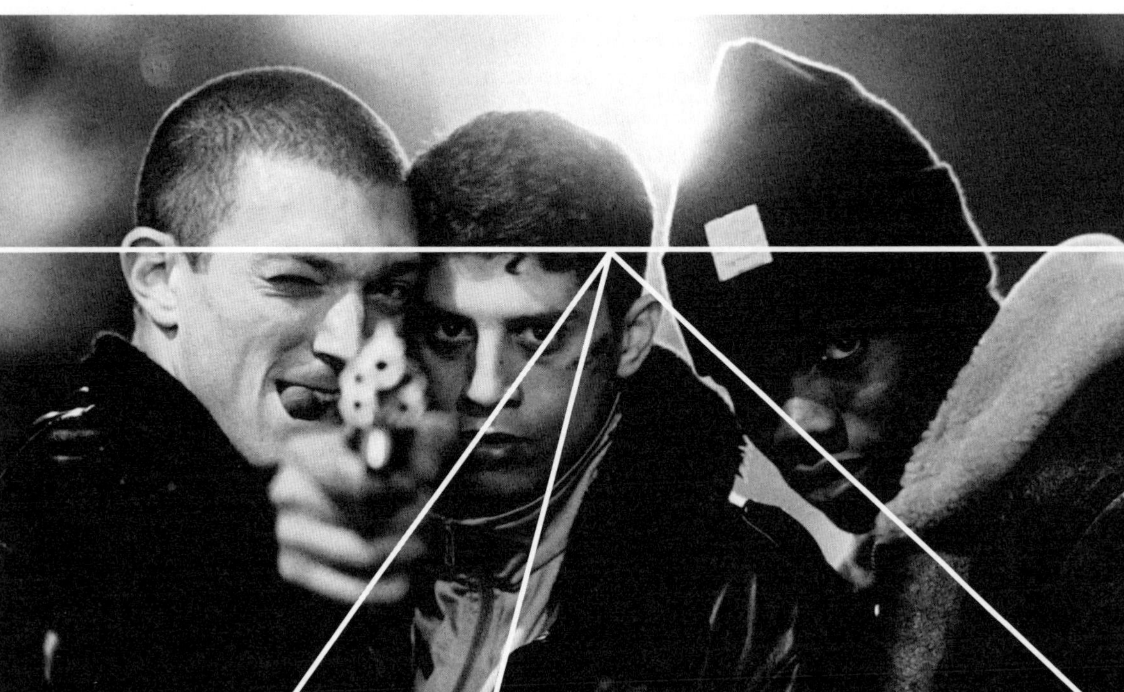

spatial composition from high to low, and the visibleness of the invisibleness all point towards what this photo already foreshadows: the merciless passing of time.

Jean-Luc Godard once remarked sarcastically that a gun and a woman are enough for a good film. *La Haine* does not have a woman, but the gun plays a prominent role. Actually, the plot line of the film is even supported by the gun—in fact it is the protagonist. It marks the time. The point at which the gun appears is the motoric moment that already harbours the tragic developments.

Godard uses film elements like long takes and deep focus (elements in the fore- and background are portrayed with the same focus) to evoke the mood of a desolate landscape. In the part of *La Haine* set in the centre of Paris, it may seem as if life is still vibrant, but the film in fact portrays a modern *ars moriendi*. The Paris suburbs form an inorganic, dehumanised urban environment. At that stage, the centre is already involved in an unstoppable process of decay.[48]

THE URBAN ADOLESCENT The adolescent becomes a pariah in the city. Susan Buck-Morss, in *The Dialectics of Seeing* (1989), speaks of processes of degradation which were very much in evidence in the Baroque and which eventually indicate death. The baroque aesthetic is characterised by decay, ruin, catastrophe and transformation into dust. The shanty towns round cities like Rio de Janeiro, reflect those processes of decomposition. The environment that Kassovitz painted goes a step further. The film offers a variation on the inorganic reality of Godard's *Pierrot le fou* (1965). The world has changed now, in the clinical mortuary of Godard and Kubrick.

48 Godard set the tone for the Nouvelle Vague, an independent movement that rebelled against the dominant Hollywood films that were inclined to lull the audience to sleep. Godard wanted to emphasise the autonomy of film as a medium, using such techniques as the hand-held camera, actors speaking into the camera, illogical jumps in editing, and non-synchronised sounds. He did not seek to represent reality, but to construct it.

Reading Outside the Frame

If we look at this film still as a painting forming part of a hidden film, the time outside the 'frame' of the still is characterised by a series of successive, rapid images (fig. II.6.7). In the cinematographic reality in which the still becomes visible, these merging images turn every image of the tableau in time into a component that can only be captured in the imagination. The context of the still, the periphery, on the one hand shows the world of cold, glaring light, and on the other hand, daybreak following a journey through the night. The journey comprises three episodes. The action covers the space of 24 hours. The journey on the TGV serves as an intermezzo between the episodes.

1. *The start* The *cité*—the boys clearly (still) feel at home and believe they are in charge of the undertaking. They have appropriated their surroundings. They make the impression of being unaware that they live in a cold, clinical, stone environment. It is light in the blue-collar neighbourhood, the territory of youth. The emptiness is their space. They have barbecues on the roof. DJ Cut Killer's music resounds between the apartment buildings, through an open window. It all makes a surreal impression.

Hip-hop alternates with Édith Piaf's chansons. Seen from a helicopter, the apartment buildings spin and sway. A stray cow wanders over the asphalt. Hubert smokes a spliff in a room hung with photos of the boxer, Muhammad Ali. Vinz imitates Robert De Niro (*Taxi Driver*) in front of his mirror. It is all somewhat reminiscent of *ars moriendi*, the

II.6.7 Mathieu Kassovitz, *La Haine* (film stills), 1995

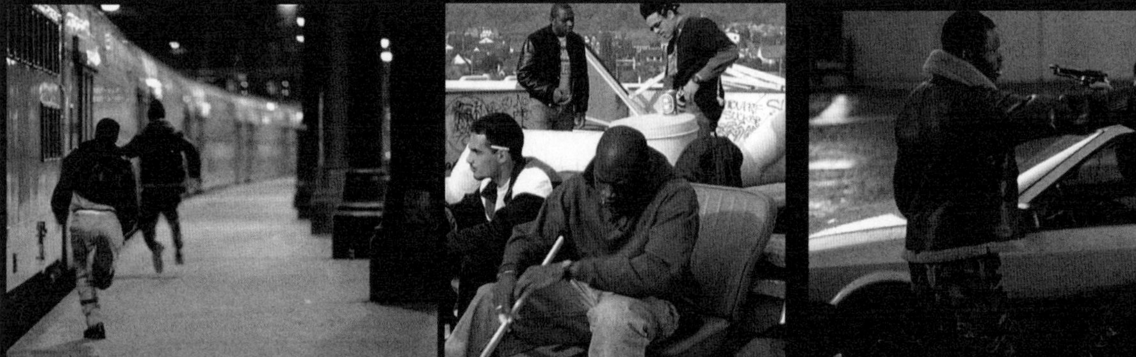

characters are caricatures circling the theme of death, but as yet they do not fade. Saïd is the hedonist graffiti artist, calling "seize the day!" (*carpe diem*). Hubert is the melancholic, reacting with "all is vanity" (*vanitas*). Vinz is a hypersensitive avenger, who reacts aggressively (*nemesis*). Saïd and Vinz are the protagonists in the first part of the film. The rhetoric of death gradually takes shape in Saïd's uninhibited, overcompensating vivacity. He deploys texts like "le monde, c'est (v)nous" (the world is you/us) to express his naïve optimism.

2. *The middle* The TGV. This part starts around 6.22 p.m., at nightfall. Confrontation with the surroundings begins. The friends have arrived in the centre of Paris and embark on their journey through the night. Here, Vinz has a leading role. In Cassel's interpretation Vinz is a brawler. However, his belligerence proves to be all talk. His bravado hides his fear of death—as the scene with the skinheads confirms. Hubert dares Vinz, after a brief fight, to kill a skinhead. Then something surfaces that had so far been submerged: Vinz turns out not to be an avenger, but a little, vulnerable boy. Vengeance assumes the ability to kill—which Vinz does not possess. According to the mediaeval *ars moriendi*, unbelief, despair, impatience, pride and greed stand in the way of dying. Vinz brags, curses and constantly plays first fiddle, but in the end, he is more attached to life than his swaggering would suggest.

3. *The end* The station, after midnight. The surroundings predominate. The friends have again crossed the "Styx", on their way back to the banlieues, the run-down suburbs. The African, Hubert, increasingly becomes the central

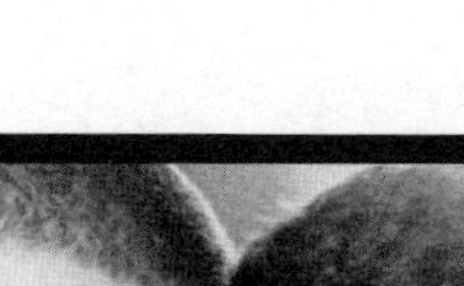

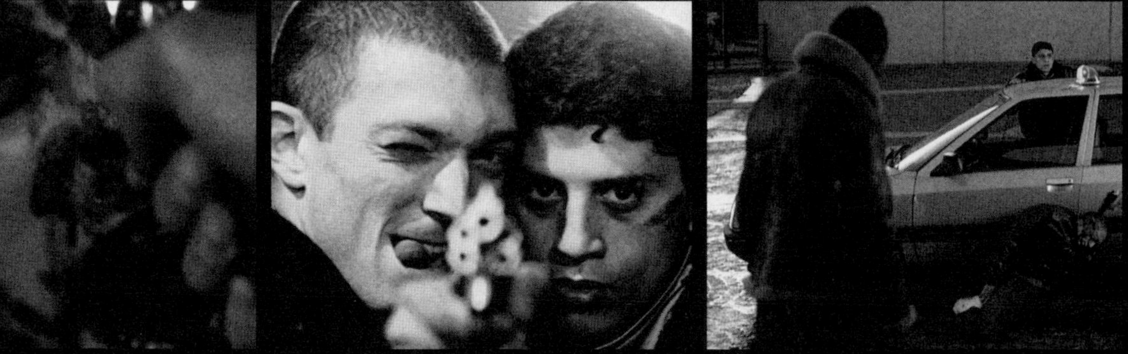

49 *La Haine* is a modern variant of the mediaeval *ars moriendi*—the art of dying—which confronts the spectator with death. In addition, dying is seen as an art. *La Haine* confronts the viewer with death in a big European metropolis. In the film, present-day incarnations of mediaeval devils, priests and fools keep on appearing.

character. Saïd represents dancing on the volcano, Vinz inner struggle. Hubert is the tragic hero. Without anyone noticing, he has already distanced himself from the world. He is the relative outsider who nurses within him the 'vanitas' theme. Sixteenth-century vanitas paintings warn that all is perishable. Youth is a mask, a veneer, a fictitious state beneath which the only true figure is found: death. Hubert, who is stoned, lives in a different world. All lines converge in him. He is the symbol of the hopelessness of youth.[49]

THE ADOLESCENT AS A TRAVELLER The film rushes like a high-speed train towards the disastrous ending. The adolescent is now a traveller, watching through the window of a racing TGV as life whizzes past. The three characters in the TGV belong to a group in society with which politicians do not want to dirty their hands. Youth belongs in a no-go area where, according to Kassovitz, corrupt policemen have seized power. The distance between the classes is poignantly clear in a scene in a gallery. The trio happens to visit a reception where they are obviously out of place. The uncomfortable encounter of the underworld with 'upper' world creates a feeling of alienation. It is reflected in the attitude of several pseudo-progressive, art-loving intellectuals vis-à-vis the ill-mannered young people. The gulf between the elite and the youth with no prospects would seem to be unbridgeable.

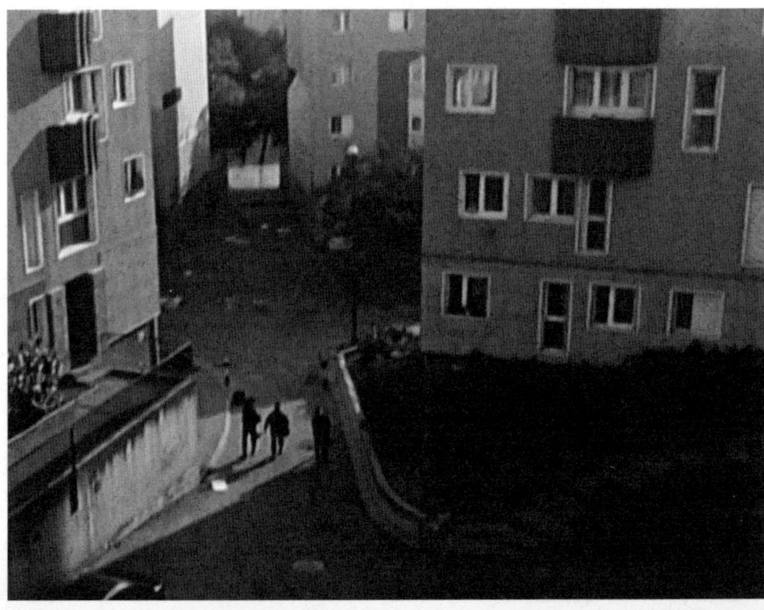

II.6.8 Mathieu Kassovitz, *La Haine* (film still), 1995

The space between the frame of this still which is possible to envisage using the imagination, speaks as a black-grey, tragic space (fig. 11.6.8). Characters and time are permanently subservient to the effect of the negative space. The spatial setting—a fragment, extracted from the time sequence, like a painting—becomes the film's protagonist.

It slowly becomes increasingly clear that any development in time is, just like the characters' sense of freedom, ultimately a mere illusion. In this tragedy, time as a (hopeful) development is just a dream. The only real time is the time experienced, the duration in absolute darkness, with no development. The underworld, the experiential world that colours everything, is a static prison with no possible means of escape. Any idea of something else is in fact a fairy-tale. Music, drugs, dance: they are the opium that briefly makes you forget you are incarcerated. From the very start, the possible world is one with no hope of liberation. It is a world with a ruin-effect: a permanent, immutable dead space where, during your life, your awareness grows.[50]

50 The philosopher Henri Bergson distinguishes between two kinds of time. The time he relates to life is what he calls 'duration'. You can understand duration if you have a special kind of thinking in which the immediate, inner experience plays a part, a living force which Bergson distinguishes from intellect, which focuses in general on a more limited form of understanding related to mathematical time. I consider duration (of time) as experienced time. It is not an objective élan vital, but a tragic experience of time. Duration does not affect a metaphysical core of life. It actually relates to the experience of onrushing death.

DANTE'S INFERNO Kassovitz has developed his version of the Inferno as a dead city. The overwhelming portrayal of the banlieues, the outskirts of the city, primarily plays an important role in the first part of the film. Here, the underworld manifests itself in its most ruthless guise. The boys seem to feel at home there. Yet the spectator, left momentarily with a feeling of uncertainty, knows better. The freedom they feel is an illusion. The characters pale to insignificance, but are barely aware of any loss. The apartment buildings in the Paris banlieues are ever present and the individual, the subject, is no longer the focal point. The dead surroundings choke out any normal feeling. The surroundings have been reduced to stone and are, therefore, the dead protagonist. Much of what you see is related to unoccupied properties.

The narrator keeps repeating, with his images: "There is no life left here. The space these boys occupied is dead." Death is not what adversely affects life, but the absence of life is. Poverty, abandoned buildings and desolation create a vastly run-down environment. There, the characters look for shelter, but in fact they no longer count. They are obscure, marginalised figures. The buildings are monsters from which the living are banished. Decay seems to take an increasingly prominent place, while youth vanishes into the background—into the darkness.

THE IRREDEEMABLE ADOLESCENT The caravaggesque world is the world of the damned. The three boys

II.6.9 Mathieu Kassovitz, *La Haine* (film still), 1995

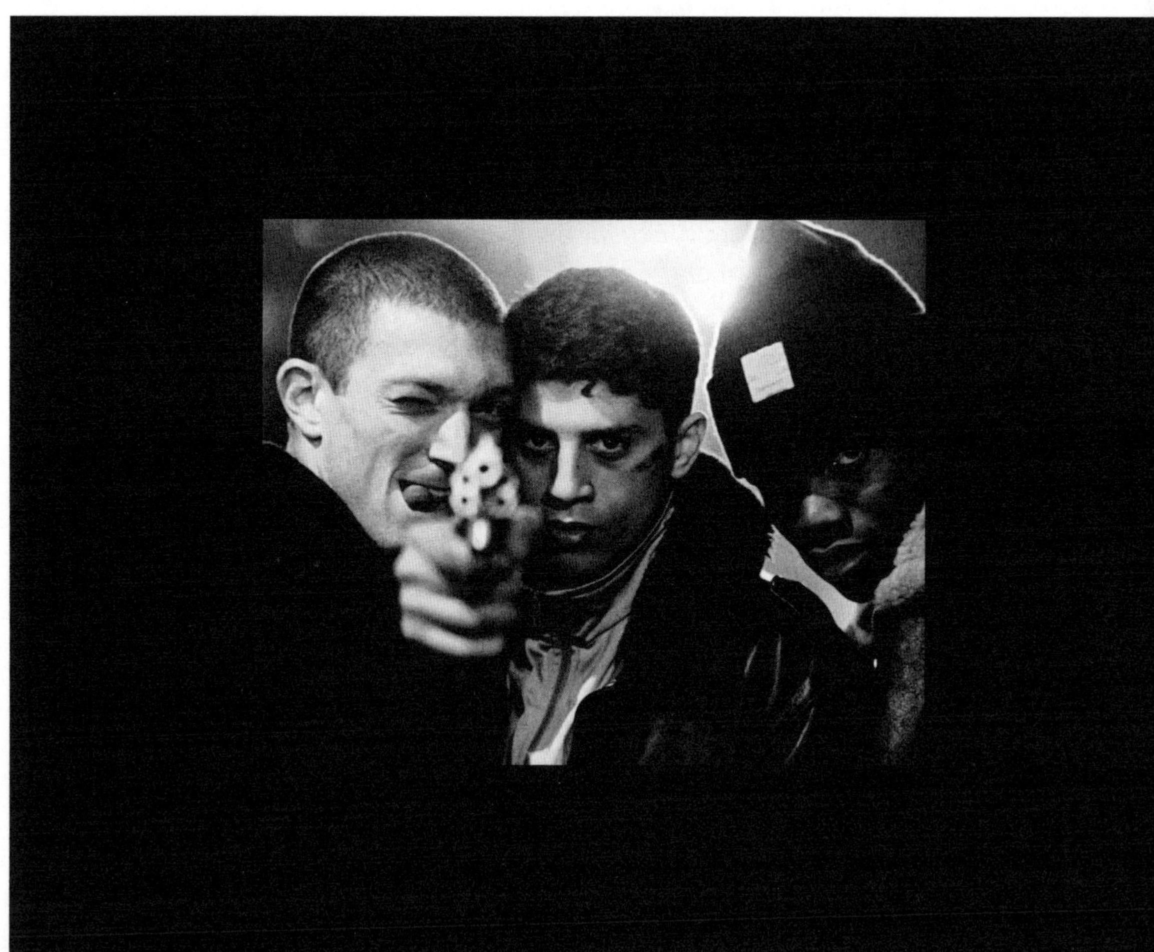

in *La Haine* saunter through the surroundings, stealing, mutinous and rowdy. They are anti-heroes: lost souls in circumstances beyond their control. They are not handsome, smart, strong and noble like Caravaggio's David. A human tragedy is taking place; they are completely lost in their despondent deprivation. Adolescence is the time to realise it. Youth, belief in the future is, at most, a fragile dream, an illusion. Higbee points out that in the year *La Haine* was first shown it was one of the top three best-attended films in France, and very popular with young people. Was it a wake-up call, because many recognised themselves in an alienating, bleak, late-modern world?

Standstill through Repetition

Space is the most defining contextual theme in the illustration (fig. 11.6.9). The world beyond the frame of the still is the stationary, dark world of absolute tragedy. The movement of the various images may pass us by and draw us with it into a trap, but the overall picture has already been outlined in the recurring black-and-white backgrounds. In the end, the absolute tragedy is not defined by the downward movement, but by the absolute absence of movement. It is in fact that radical standstill that assigns meaning to these surroundings.

LOCUS TERRIBILIS Caravaggio's cosmonaut, David, wanders through the unpredictable labyrinth of the city. The director's shallow focus blurs the background and the resulting contrast accentuates the expressions on the characters' faces.

Lakoff and Johnson (1980) write that metaphors often have a specific meaningful structure, like high/low or in front/behind. The world that now moves from background to foreground is a nocturnal world. It has the appearance of wealth and happiness, but is in fact a *locus terribilis*, an arena where there is always suffering. A characteristic feature of the *locus terribilis* is that everyone entering it knows he will lose.

There is no hope. It is a place of decay that erodes, image by image, a place devoid of light and air. The setting of *La Haine* is one of remorseless death. Unlike in Caravaggio's painting, death in this film is not only created using trails of blood, phantoms, demons, decay and immorality. Death is inherent in human decay, but also in the empty brick buildings, surrounded by cold, depersonalised police officers. As a *locus terribilis*, *La Haine* resembles Pasolini's neorealistic space, a post-apocalyptical landscape.

Hades has become the protagonist: the metaphor of the stationary, dreary space where young people have to grow up. Thanatos, who still held sway in the analysis of Caravaggio, is replaced by Hades. The impersonal surroundings—the décor, the lighting, the sound, the camera viewpoints, the extras—determine the story. Hades becomes visible in the dead matter, the inorganic.

THE CONTEMPORARY ADOLESCENT The prominent presence of darkness turns the adolescent as depicted here into an icon of contemporary Man. The dead city is a labyrinthine environment from which there is no escape. Ariadne's thread has been cut. Man becomes a wanderer, irretrievably lost in the universe. Youth, as with Caravaggio, is a simulacrum: anyone not belonging to the elite, has no youth. Even friendship amounts to nothing. At best, it is a painful contrast with tragedy. Music, dance, fashion and language seem like an interesting counterculture, but are of little consolation from the narrator's perspective.

Lastly

In this first exercise in Art-Based Learning, the path of observation, association and creation, I have sought to show how you can learn by entering into a dialogue with art works. This introduction to ABL reveals that art works are speaking objects that can take us into possible worlds and bring about a personal meaning.

Speaking objects, as a source of knowledge, are very valuable for students and teachers, because they provide an opportunity to acquire greater insight into important, contemporary cultural issues. The secret lies in allowing the art work to speak, in detail. In that context, Bollas' hermeneutic and associative method is of importance in giving the speaking object space. So far, I have turned to three visual sources: Pedriali's photograph *Autoritratto immaginario* (1989), Caravaggio's painting *David with the Head of Goliath* (1610) and Kassovitz' film *La Haine* (1995). In this, the allegory of *Youth and Death*, a concept from the visual arts and literature, has been the binding agent.

Bal's approach to art as the "telling object" has been a major source of inspiration. It pointed the way to the possible worlds I mentioned earlier. My central premise has always been to consider art as a product of thinking, a logical fantasy. I have arrived in worlds that need not, but can be true.

And so, for now, "the assignment of personal meaning" is the answer to the question "what is adolescence in contemporary culture?" This is the rationale for further analysis of the work of (early) modern artists—from Caravaggio to Kassovitz—but also of various postmodern philosophers like Deleuze and Baudrillard. New speaking objects traversed the depiction of the art work—and sometimes the periphery only.

A new reality came about that I went on to describe as "thinking in *chiaroscuro*".

Bal describes the attribution of meaning as a process of story-telling. Perhaps that is the most important outcome of this study. Acquired knowledge could acquire significance. "What is this?" Bollas repeatedly asks himself. In *The Evocative Object World* (2009) he notes how important it is to allow the quest for knowledge to restart, again and again, with curiosity and astonishment, and from there to develop "psychic genera"—an accumulation of impressions in a psychic setting that can ultimately result in a new perspective of the past, the present and the future of the Self (29).

Is that the final image of Western cultural history? Has life become a tragedy? Does the black of this first triptych have the last word? The answer is "no!" In the adjoining cultural space a second theme appears for a triptych entitled *The Beauty of Youth*. Works by William Shakespeare, Virginia Woolf and Thomas Vinterberg are the new speaking objects. We shall see how the movement of time tries to conquer static space there.[51]

51 Cultural history is a creative process of attributing meaning. In *What is Cultural History?* (2004) Peter Burke cites Mikhail Bakhtin, alongside Foucault, Elias and Bourdieu, as one of the most original culture theorists of the twentieth century, even though Bakhtin was only discovered by culture historians after the publication of *Rabelais and His World* (1984, originally published. 1965). His basic concepts are terms like "carnivalization", "marketplace speech", "uncrowning", "polyglossia" and "heter[o]glossia"—all designations for a world that is not uniform, but withdraws from centralist control. So Bakhtin's approach provides a very useful framework of terminology for this study as regards the reception of youth and youth culture as a complex network of interconnected linguistic games (possible worlds). Bakhtin's methodological term "quoted speech" is also very useful for ABL. In her introduction to the translation of *Rabelais and His World* , Krystyna Pomorska describes this term as: "[W]e are actually dealing with someone else's words more often than our own. ... In each case someone else's speech makes it possible to generate our own and thus becomes an indispensable factor in the creative power of language" (1984, ix). "Quotation" is an important element when analysing the world of today. In this context, Bal's concept "preposterous history" (1999) merits particular attention. "Quotation" is also important when, by way of a dialogue, a new reality is created which is the basic structure of the process of story-telling as found in ABL.

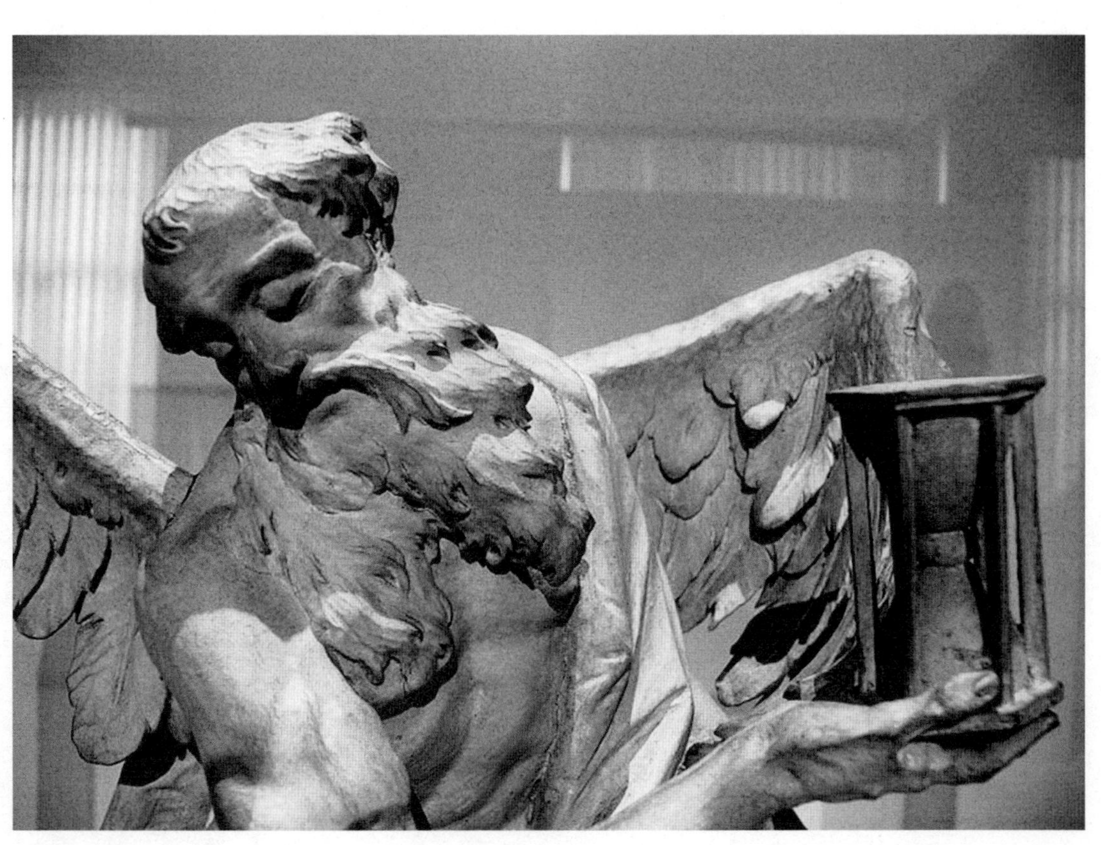

II.7.1 Ignaz Günther, *Chronos*, c. 1765–75

III

The Beauty of Youth

Concerning Literature

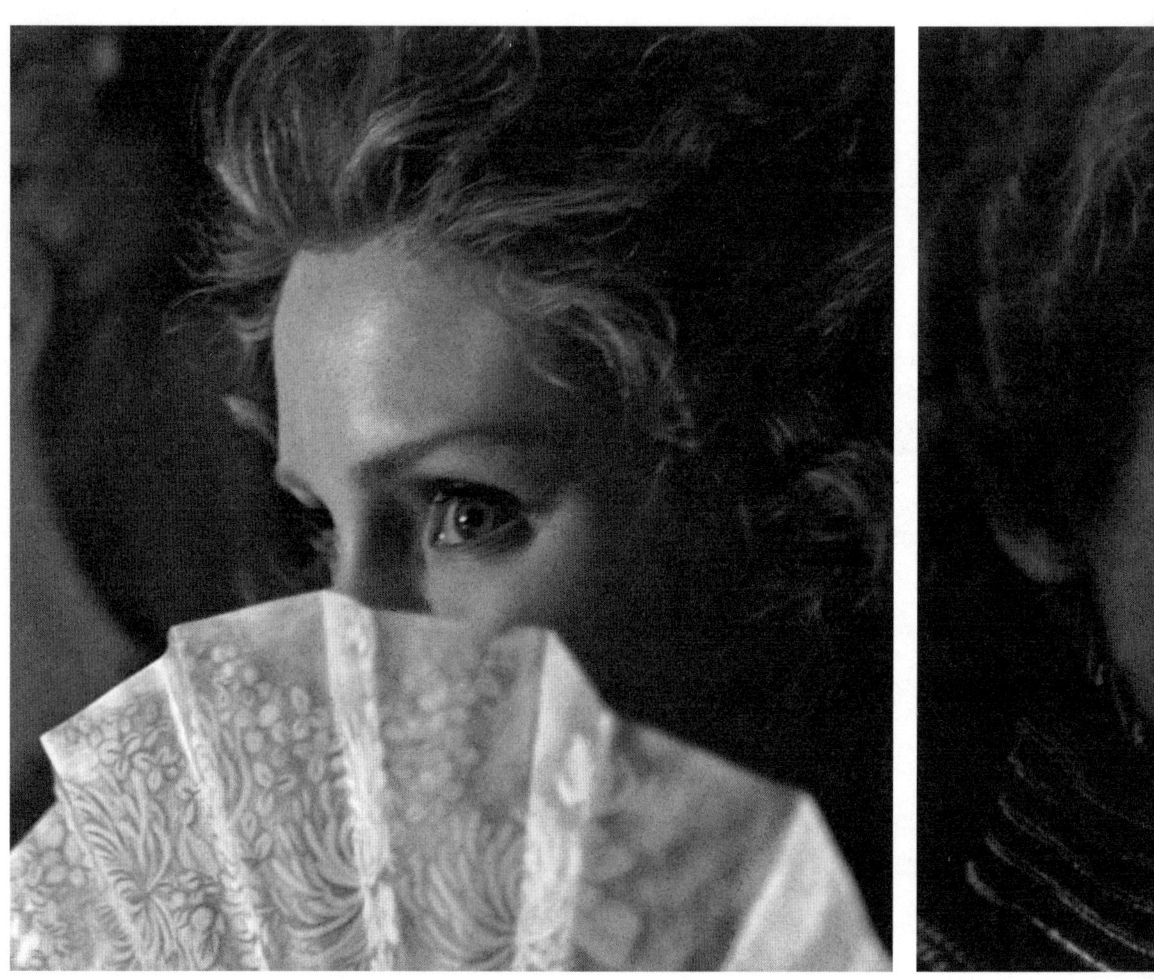

III.1.1 Triptych Shakespeare—Woolf—Vinterberg

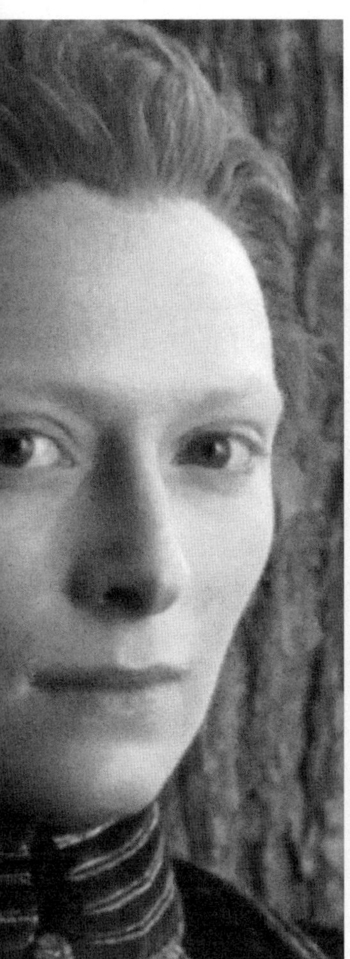

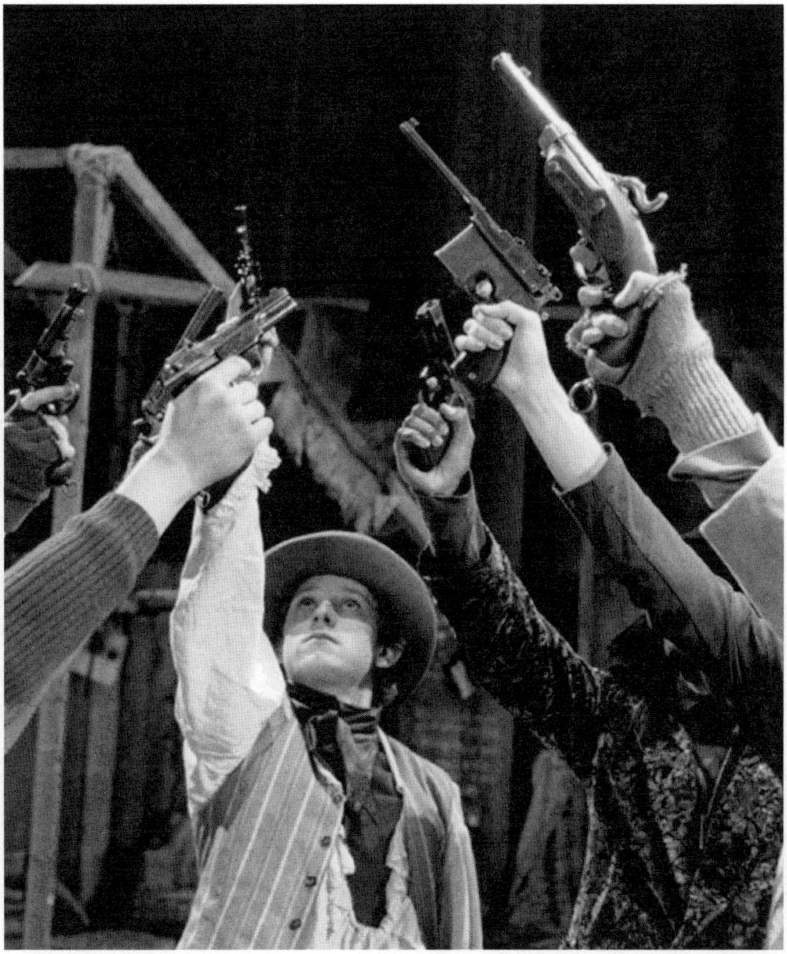

Thinking as a stream of consciousness

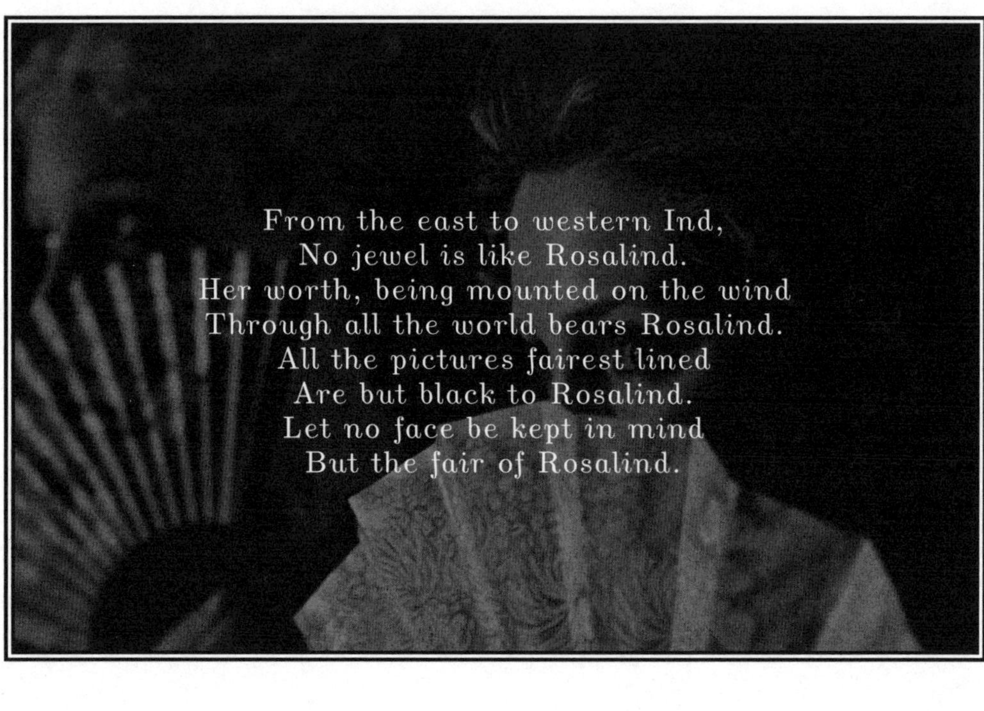
From the east to western Ind,
No jewel is like Rosalind.
Her worth, being mounted on the wind
Through all the world bears Rosalind.
All the pictures fairest lined
Are but black to Rosalind.
Let no face be kept in mind
But the fair of Rosalind.

1

Exposition: Shakespeare

Do you know what turns darkness into light? Poetry!
—Lemmy Caution in *Alphaville* (Jean-Luc Godard, 1965)

Introduction

What does the term 'adolescence' mean now? In this new triptych I again start, in the first side panel, with the present, and then go back in time. This triptych is entitled 'The Beauty of Youth'. It relates to a new possible world. It is a Shakespearean world culminating in Woolfian modern aesthetics. It is the kind of world that is reflected in Shakespeare's play *As You Like It* (1599), Virginia Woolf's novella *Orlando* (1928) and Thomas Vinterberg's film *Dear Wendy* (2005).

The content of our research object changes, and so does the medium. The depictions that are now explored are fragments from two literary texts and a film. A new journey begins through a world of text that ends in an area I shall call "the rhetoric of life". Words replace paint and colours.

III.1.2 Kenneth Branagh, *William Shakespeare's As You Like It* (film still), 2006

Letters provide the modern aesthetic with a possibility to tell more about the interior than the exterior, more about the imagination than reality, more about mind than matter, and more about life than death. In a recording for the BBC in 1937, Virginia Woolf said:

> Words, English words, are full of echoes, memories, associations, they are out and about on people's lips, in their houses, in the streets, in the fields, for so many centuries, and that is one of the chief difficulties of writing today. They are stored with other meanings, with other memories and they have contracted so many famous marriages in the past. (1993, 137–43)

Literary texts can be speaking objects. The encounter with text is not only a visual, but also an auditive experience. Words sound and make sentences, which in turn make pages. The text moves in an intertextual space. Focaliser and focalised object get carte blanche.

David Hume's essay *Of the Standard of Taste* (1757)—further explained by Patricia De Martelaere in "Hume over smaak" (Hume on taste) (2001)—describes the acquisition of knowledge as a process in which knowledge and experience transform through the imagination. Ultimately, that produces an opinion of one's own. This is similar to what the ABL method does.[52]

The three panels of this triptych are filled with words, words derived from carefully selected sources. Yet the fact remains: selection is to some extent an unconscious process. It is guided by the Bollas principle of 'unknown thought', as encountered earlier. The spectator selects an object which he senses might contain further information. An arrangement like a triptych makes it possible for the three sources to 'converse' with one another:

52 Hume's approach to knowledge as a secondary quality is helpful for understanding the process of ABL. De Martelaere argues that Hume's view of what is aesthetic does not differ fundamentally from his view of science. In fact, according to Hume, they are comparable ways of thinking. He distinguishes between an object world and a subject world. The object world has a primary quality. Knowledge, be it scientific or aesthetic, belongs in the subject world. That knowledge is a secondary quality. Beauty, on the side of the object world, has a number of characteristics in the realm of "a construction of parts that give a pleasure or satisfaction to the soul" (De Martelaere 2001, 175). The subject side, where the learning of art also belongs, is not an objective process, since there is no monitoring body—it is a process of probabilities and possibilities which, based on reflection and correction, can acquire a gradual value. The quality of knowledge that generates a process like ABL depends on the extent to which, based on a question, the student is able to select securely (intelligence), to speak openly (detachment), to represent sophisticatedly (subtlety) and judge with common sense (De Martelaere, 2001, 171). It goes without saying that higher education can supply the necessary skills.

1. *The left-hand panel*: Words from *As You Like It* against the background of a portrait of Bryce Dallas Howard in Kenneth Branagh's mainstream film based on the play. She plays Rosalind in Shakespeare's late-renaissance comedy. Youth and the odd whims of fate are exposed by linking up fragments of text. The adolescent appears as a "poet of the detail" (Bal 1997, 121).[53]
2. *The centre panel*: Words from *Orlando* against the background of Tilda Swinton. She played the leading role in the film based on Virginia Woolf's fictitious biography *Orlando*. The novella *Orlando* is a prime example of thinking as a stream of consciousness. Woolf also writes in a stream of words. For instance, the first paragraph of *Orlando*, goes as follows: "He—for there could be no doubt of his sex, though the fashion of the time did something to disguise it—was in the act of slicing at the head of a Moor which swung from the rafters."[54]
3. *The right-hand panel*: Words from the lyrics of a song by The Zombies with a still from Thomas Vinterberg's *Dear Wendy* (2005) forming the background. Here, the concept of the beauty of youth is combined with a contemporary urban environment. Image becomes décor.[55]

This journey is reminiscent of science fiction: I imagine we're some thousand years later. In that case, the pictures will tell something about the cultural history of our present day. I see a culture with youth as its icon and art as its prime source. Literary art now gives us the next step in our journey.

In *S/Z*, Roland Barthes demonstrates a kind of ABL. He 'converses' with a literary text by Balzac. A reading- and

53 *As You Like It* marks the beginning of Shakespeare's mature work that culminates in plays like *Hamlet* (c. 1600–1). The text I used with English annotations is from *The Norton Shakespeare* (2008). I also discuss the most recent screen version: that of Kenneth Branagh dating from 2006.

54 The stream of consciousness is even more manifest in books from the same period, such as *To the Lighthouse* (1927) and *The Waves* (1931).

55 The leading role of Dick Dandelion is played by Jamie Bell, who became famous for his role in the film *Billy Elliot* (2000). This film by Stephen Daldry shows, like *Dear Wendy*, how growing up is a process of both pain and beauty.

learning-attitude emerges as a kind of close reading. Peter Brooks says, with respect to *S/Z*: "What may be most significant about *S/Z* is its break away from the somewhat rigid notion of structure to the more fluid and dynamic notion of structuration" (1992, 19). Barthes has an ear for words. For him, texts are complex, auditive experiences that the reader can never overcome (1974, 30). This semiotic approach to *S/Z* is also found one of Barthes' last works, *A Lover's Discourse: Fragments* (1990).[56]

56 Barthes' *S/Z* is an analysis of *Sarrasine*, a short story by Honoré de Balzac. He divides the work into 561 *lexias*. Barthes' method is geared to turning the reader into a writer. In *S/Z* various significant perspectives are addressed: (1) hermeneutic (theme-related), abbreviated as HER; (2) proairetic (action-related, abbreviated as ACT; (3) symbolic (contrast-related), abbreviated as SYM; (4) semic (characteristic-related), abbreviated as SEM; (5) cultural (reference-related), abbreviated as REF. Barthes' work is particularly relevant in the final stage of ABL.

As You Like It

From...

EXPOSÉ *As You Like It* begins at Court, where we meet Orlando, a reckless, rebellious adolescent. Orlando's father, a righteous man, has died and Orlando's arrogant brother, Oliver, is taking care of him. It ends in conflict. Oliver does not honour the conditions of his inheritance. He even tries to murder his brother, but Orlando defies death at the last minute and flees the palace.

The second act takes place in the Forest of Arden. It resembles the Garden of Eden, a place of love. Rosalind and Orlando know each other from the Court. She is the daughter of the old, exiled duke, a good friend of Orlando's late father. Rosalind secretly follows Orlando into the forest. She appears, dressed as a boy, in the hope of discovering Orlando's feelings for her—a complicated plot, familiar from *Twelfth Night, or What You Will* (c. 1600–1).

Maidens, writers, jesters, farmers and shepherds come on stage. Rosalind, initially a lesser character, develops into the protagonist of the play. She and Orlando change places, and he retreats into the background. He becomes a figment of the imagination. Rosalind's becomes the main voice in the play around whom all the other characters gather.

In part three, the worlds of the Court and the Forest of Arden fuse into a carnivalesque procession. It ends with the removal of masks, the end of differences. Rosalind and Orlando marry. Rivals and lovers are reunited and the two worlds become one.

Friedrich Schiller's *On the Aesthetic Education of Man in a Series of Letters* (1967, originally published 1795) is a fitting place to start to reveal the development from girl to young woman. Schiller combines his positive, romantic view of human development with the theme of beauty.

In his letters, Schiller, differentiates between three aspects in Man: matter, form and play. Matter relates to material nature in its perfect manifestation. Form refers to the elaborate soul in its perfect manifestation. Beauty is somewhere in between. It is the domain of play. It is the (as yet) incomplete space between matter and form.

Play drive is an intermediate state. It is the area of the living form and of freedom—a nascent state in which perfection is strived for. In his fifteenth letter, Schiller says that beauty can be seen as the "fulfilment of human existence" (2009, 55). Plato's cave, the world of archetypes, echoes as a background theme.[57]

Schiller's theory clarifies why beauty is always described as an intangible third space. C.S. Lewis, the author of *An Experiment in Criticism* (originally published 1961), explains the experience of beauty as something for which an open mind is needed: "the first demand any work of art makes upon us is surrender. Look. Listen. Receive. Get yourself out of the way" (1992, 19).

57 Romantic thinking about youth might provide an answer to tragic thinking about youth. Aristotle's tragic concept forms the logical system of *Youth and Death*. The romantic-aesthetic concept of the beauty of youth starts with Plato and continues, via Schiller, to Kristeva.

THE BEAUTY OF 'OTHERNESS' Adolescence in *As You Like It* is a story about the beauty of otherness. The adolescent tears himself away from the laws of nature and constructs his own identity. Shakespeare's work expresses what Bollas terms the revolt against the "fascist state of mind" (2003, 193). It is the story of the free-and-easy adolescent, of beauty and of life. In the twenty-first-century Shakespeare's adolescent appears on the TV screen in the sitting room. The text, the images and the flood of sensations provide an answer to the tragic adolescent from the previous section.

The Black of the Letters

Orlando is the poet who composed "From the east to the western Ind." In the BBC's 1979 film version of As You Like It, we see Helen Mirren in the role of Rosalind, running down a hill, laughing as she reads how Orlando has described her as the prettiest girl in the world, to whom nothing and no-one can compare, all others pale in comparison.

...the east
to the western
Ind...
No jewel is like
Rosalind

The character Orlando carves rhymes in tree trunks and hangs verses on the branches. He is proud, hot-tempered, easily misled, and sentimental. He is fixated on the past, his father Roland de Bois, his lost inheritance and the injustice done to him by his brother Oliver.

Shakespeare's Orlando is a gullible young fool. He recites poetry that, according to Touchstone (the jester), can hardly be taken seriously. When Touchstone hears Rosalind reading Orlando's poem he warns: "this is the very false gallop of verses. Why do you infect yourself with them?" (3.2.102–3). Nevertheless, Orlando continues to speak to his subjects as if he were king ("that would I, were I of all kingdoms king," 5.4.10).

Orlando is led by platitudes. When his beloved Rosalind stands in front of him, disguised as Ganymede, wearing a jerkin, he does not recognise her. He addresses her as a young man, "fair youth" (3.2.348). Even when Rosalind goes a step further and, as Ganymede, 'plays' Rosalind, Orlando has no inkling who is really there with him. He is blinded by clichés.

Rosalind is his "jewel", a precious possession. He reduces her to an object of his imagination: an object he desires and on which he depends. Sentences like: "I beseech you, punish me not with your hard thoughts" (1.2.152–53) indicate the extent to which he is the victim of his desire. Riches lead mainly to the fear of losing those riches, as in *King Lear* (1605) and *Macbeth* (1606).

"All the world's a stage" (2.7.138), Jaques says. Orlando plays a part in which the people around him barely take him seriously. He has nothing new to say. He occasionally assumes another role, temporarily, and we see a little more, for instance when he practises proposing to Rosalind in her guise as a man: "I take thee Rosalind, for wife" (4.1.116). However, such moments are few and far between. On the whole, Orlando is very predictable.

If the spectator wishes to discover Rosalind, he/she must listen to the spaces between the words. The reading of Shakespeare is a visual and an auditive experience. The literary work contains a whole gamut of unexpressed thoughts. When you listen, every sentence and every word proffers new riches: a new variety, an overwhelming, unique and unexpected aesthetic variation, a possible world.

Erich Segal notes in *The Death of Comedy* (2001) that one of the lines along which culture is organised is the world of comedy. It is a place where unexpressed thoughts can become visible in the white space. Comedy is a world that

58 The romantic genre and the comic genre are sometimes very similar. Segal argues that *cosmos* is a combination of *chaos* and *eros*. And says with respect to Shakespeare: "In Shakespeare love is renewal, regeneration and rebirth" (2001, 296).

often appears in the pluriform space between the words.

In the white space, music by the baroque composer Purcell is heard. It does not occur in a dramatic or antithetic way, as with thinking in *chiaroscuro*. Adjoining worlds do not repel each other, but seek each other out. The sentences respond to one another, like instruments in an orchestra. Every dramatic action follows on from or contrasts with the main theme of love as a creative force. The forest forming the backdrop is a good metaphor for that creating life force.

Segal's view of love coincides with the triumph of tragedy. He remarks that the lightness of love has a regenerative character. Love gives rise to rebirth; love conquers death. Love can be a sign of restored harmony resulting in epiphany. In the tragic construction of reality, the rhetoric of death is also present. In this comic-romantic construction I see the rhetoric of life.[58]

...Through all the world bears Rosalind...

THE ADOLESCENT AS A CLICHÉ The adolescent speaks empty, meaningless words; they do not represent intensely-felt values, thus giving each word an element of exaggeration. They become hyperbole. They make too much of what is not present and so drown an underlying emptiness. The meaning of the text is dimmed. Beauty is reduced to kitsch. Love is reduced to sentimentality.

The White between the Words

THE PROTAGONIST Rosalind becomes audible in the white between "through all the world bears Rosalind". The white is the space where the text relations are formed. Rosalind does not speak in hyperbole. She does not read someone else's text. Rosalind writes her own play and, for it, disguises herself as Ganymede. Love is not doggerel for her. Her language is unique, down-to-earth, humorous and at the same time, poetic. A good example is how Rosalind-in-love does not wallow in emotion, but comments matter-of-factly: "there is a man haunts the forest that abuses our young plants with carving Rosalind on their barks" (3.2.326–27). Thus revealing that, although she is love, she possesses a sobering humour and does not take doggerel in the least seriously.

"Love," she says, "is merely a madness, and I tell you, deserves as well a dark house and a whip as madmen do; and the reason why they are not so punished and cured is that the lunacy is so ordinary that the whippers are in love too" (3.2.359–62). In other words, rather than wallowing in emotion, Rosalind remains clear and quick-witted. She does not repeat, but has her own point of view. She reacts by taking an alternative view—sometimes as a feminist *avant la lettre* with her "woman's wit" (4.1.138), sometimes in a homoerotic role-play with Orlando, who is blinded by convention.

Rosalind pokes fun at Orlando and puts him in his place: "if you break one jot of your promise or come one minute behind your hour, I will think you the most pathetical break-promise, and the most hollow lover, and the most unworthy of her you call Rosalind that may be chosen out of the gross band of the unfaithful" (4.1.162–66).

Ted Hughes describes *As You Like It* as the beginning of Shakespeare's mature work. He sees Arden as an alchemistic, mythical place, where not only Rosalind and Orlando come together, but also the two brothers (one dark and one light), who are involved in a ritual drama.

Rosalind in the palace is a metaphor of childhood. Rosalind in the forest symbolises adolescence, and Rosalind back at the palace reflects adulthood. This adult role forms a new spiritual relation with the ego and the universe. In all of this, according to Hughes, Rosalind is the representation of a psychological function; the female soul of the character Orlando that elevates itself to mystical heights: "She is the feminine aspect of Orlando's mythic self" (1993, 113). Hughes emphasises the psychological dimension in contrast with the physical dimension that was addressed in the caravaggesque world.

I can understand that *As You Like It* is explained in terms of the maturation process. However, I am in doubt as to whether maturation automatically implies a process of spiritual growth. Hughes assumes that maturation and spirituality are comparable. Shakespeare actually avoids such moralism. His thinking is not linear, but based on ever-changing perspectives in which the assigning of value is closely connected with perspective.

...the fair of Rosalind

THE CRITICAL ADOLESCENT The adolescent becomes critical. He lives in a complex world filled with strange occurrences and ambiguous characters. He is in an open space and does not dare to deviate from the normal path. He rebels against the laws of nature. The death of the old challenges him to create something new. What disappears is the rebellion against nature by replacement. In all respects, it is the opposite of Caravaggio's darkness where Thanatos rules and youth is ultimately drawn in.

The Genesis of Free Verse

Rosalind plays a game with fact and fiction. She resembles free verse with no arrangement in stanzas. She "writes" and "rewrites" herself, depending on the goal she has in mind.

One version proceeds from another, as if they were offshoots of a root system.

At Court Rosalind must comply with the strict "direction" of Duke Frederick and Orlando's older brother, Oliver, but it is different in the Forest of Arden. There, as a woman, she can play the many parts Jaques refers to (2.7.141). The heavenly Forest of Eden is the setting for the uninhibited process of 'growing and blossoming'. The place resembles a dream world where everything is possible. The 'polyphony' of the characters can be activated. There is a new story round every corner. It is a vibrant world with its own laws. Every tree, every path opens the way to something new, to an unknown new space.

Ganymede gives Rosalind all the scope she needs. She acquires a different sex. She shakes off all her fears by wandering as a man with "a gallant curtal-axe upon my thigh" (1.3.111). The transformation also means she sheds all possible sexual obstacles. For instance, Ganymede flirts openly with Orlando; in "his" texts we can detect a distinct homo-erotic undertone. Love and eroticism can no longer be captured in a monogamous, primarily heterosexual structure. Similarly, as Ganymede, Rosalind is courted by Phebe, whom she rejects on the one hand, while tying Phebe to her with evasive remarks like "I will marry you if ever I marry woman" (5.2.104–5). Ganymede represents the liberated adolescent. That happy state will continue as long as youth lasts, because, in Rosalind's words, "maids are May when they are maids, but the sky changes when they are wives" (4.1.125–27). In other words, after marriage, freedom is finished.

In the end, Rosalind is the one, as the leading lady, to speak the epilogue, thus repositioning the whole play. She states that it is her task to conjure (Epilogue 9): she wants to bewitch the audience. During the play, Rosalind changes from a woman into a man, and from a man into a woman again. Here in the epilogue, she insinuates that she has never been a woman. The phrase "If I were a woman ..." (Epilogue 14–15) alludes to the historical fact that in Shakespeare's day female parts were played by boys. So all the gender roles are jumbled up, causing you, the reader, to completely lose your way.

In *Introducing Shakespeare* (1991), George B. Harrison notes that the use of prose or blank verse invariably had a set significance in Elizabethan works. Characters adopting a more elevated standpoint, use blank verse (Harrison 1991, 177). Rosalind uses both. A baroque interplay is created between ordinary prose and more elevated blank verse. In the epilogue, her tone is self-assured ("If I were a woman"), while she also refers to the commonplace reality of "beards" and "sweet breaths". Shakespeare's paradoxical game means that Rosalind eludes unequivocal definition.[59]

When all is said and done, Rosalind stands for an ultimate freedom. There are no more barriers. Rosalind, who even makes gender a matter of editing, is the complete opposite of cliché-ridden Orlando.[60]

In *Shakespeare: The Invention of the Human* (1999), Harold Bloom describes the writing reader. He sketches the figure of Rosalind not only as the loving heroine or mystical presence, but more especially as a sincere young woman who, more than the other characters, speaks plainly and honestly. She is an adolescent who arouses in her listeners "our most humane faculties" (204).

Bloom proceeds, saying how vibrant and beautiful Rosalind is, in body, soul and spirit. In his view, she deserves a better lover than Orlando, and better conversation than with Touchstone and Jaques who, with their dissolute verses

59 Art-Based Learning is characterised by a poetic stream of thoughts. It starts with the speaking object. The reader is also sensitive to the text and permits it to be "articulated". Articulation is hearing more than what the text says. In Shakespeare's case, it is listening to what Harrison refers to as the "game [...] with words" (1999, 168), the "movements of his mind", and (in the case of *Richard II*), "a poetical stream of consciousness" (176).

60 In "Feminist Editing and the Body of the Text" (2000) Laurie E. Maguire examines the curious last passage of *As You Like It* in which Rosalind refers to herself as 'he'. In the past, it has sometimes been considered a mistake by the editor of Shakespeare's text, but it may refer to the fact that Rosalind is a character who "steers" her gender herself.

actually beat about the bush (1999, 205). In Bloom's opinion, the glory of Rosalind and of her play is "her confidence, and ours, that all things will go well" (207).

In this character, the opposite of Caravaggio's David speaks. Rosalind is a cheerful "representative of life's possible freedoms" (Bloom 1999, 211).

Rosalind's world is not only one of beauty and natural love, it also contains a liberalism that the other characters lack. Walter Pater, whom Bloom regularly quotes, describes in *The Renaissance: Studies in Art and Poetry* (originally published 1910), this uninhibited mentality as authenticity. He believes authenticity to be the source, the aesthetic experience: "the power of being deeply moved by the presence of beautiful objects" (2010, 2). It is the composition of a possible world that clarifies the internal logic of a character like Rosalind: sincere, pretty and superior.

In *Where Shall Wisdom Be Found?* (2004) Bloom continues that Rosalind, when honestly expressing her thoughts, is not speaking according to the lofty conventions of wisdom, but *is* wise. Hamlet represents the heart of darkness, Rosalind unspoilt nature.[61]

THE CREATIVE ADOLESCENT The adolescent has become creative. That ties in with Eveline Crone's findings in *The Adolescent Brain: Changes in Learning, Decision-making and Social Relations* that adolescents "[are] often far more creative, idealistic and inventive than adults" (2016, 149). She has a biological explanation for this that is connected to the development of the brain.

Shakespeare, with Rosalind, adds the image of the creative adolescent to the existing series of images. Rosalind is the story of the beauty of the adolescent in his/her constant

61 For Bloom, art is more than emotional expression or skilled technique: it is a form of thinking. In *Genius: A Mosaic of One Hundred Exemplary Creative Minds* he writes that Shakespeare was one of the greatest psychologists ever to have lived (2002, 26). In plays like *Hamlet* he interprets human beings as self-analysing beings. In fact: it was Shakespeare "[who] discovered [or] invented [...] the self-recognition of self-overhearing." Moreover, he calls listening to the speaking self "the royal road to change" (27).

'otherness'. It is the adolescent who plays parts: an inventive character who is capable of leaving behind fossilised cultural structures, thanks to his poetic abilities.

For Bloom, Rosalind is even such an important character that he has renamed *As You Like It* into *As Rosalind Like It*. The character transcends, anticipates and knows, in her uninhibited shrewdness, the language of the other characters (Bloom 1999, 204). She is Elizabeth Swann (Keira Knightly) in *Pirates of the Caribbean*. She is Alice in Tim Burton's *Alice in Wonderland*.

C.S. Lewis would say: here speaks authentic free verse, the "regenerative stream" of renewed life.

Lastly

A palimpsest now results: the new poetic text is superimposed on the foregoing tragic text. The old text continues to exist, but disappears, like memories that sink into the subconscious. Until, at some point, it is revived. The new text points to a new underlying metaphor. The reader becomes a time traveller. He traverses an infinite universe characterised by polysemy: a world in which fact and fiction may mingle.[62]

The parallel space that now comes about is characterised by a positive ontology. It is a light world that has a direct connection with stories about youth. Rosalind, one of the icons of youth, represents that light possible world.

Rosalind's world rebels against decay in nature. Shakespeare shows how the adolescent, in her sincerity and otherness, shies away from the laws of nature. It is his play about love, written two years before his play about death: *Hamlet*. Rosalind escapes from Plato's cave. She climbs up to

62 The way fact and fiction can intermingle is explained by John Rajchman, among others. In his introduction to the translation of Gilles Deleuze's *Pure Immanence* (2001), he describes Deleuze's empiricism that assumes that no "sensus communis" exists. According the Rajchman, the art work is a good source because it does have some connection. Similarly, ABL addresses art works. Rajchman translates "speaking object" in deleuzian terms as a "logic of sensations". According to the author, Deleuze is taking a step towards a "logic of multiplicity" which is comparable to the idea of parallel possible worlds. Finally, he ends in a world of "constructivist logic of unfinished series" —the domain of story-telling. Rajchman argues that Deleuze's logical empiricism is a knowledge process, inspired by Hume, Nietzsche and Bergson, of unfolding complexity. Instead of simplicity, an "immanent plane" comes about during the process which, unlike consciousness, is a work in progress: a realistic, undifferentiated and so rather vague experience of singularities. Rajchman, like Bollas, does not see thinking as a process giving increasing certainty, but rather a process that tempers and complicates without offering certainty.

the world of ideas. Young Rosalind tells the story of someone who says what she thinks and thinks what she says. Her beauty rests on the character's inner freedom to enter any domain she may wish. It is the positive world of light and life. At the end of the play, this approach to life even entitles Rosalind to speak the epilogue, while she divests herself of all pretence and also reveals the actor playing Rosalind. A development towards freedom of this type is also found in Woolf's character, Orlando.

It is now time to build a bridge to the middle panel of this triptych: the work of Virginia Woolf. Richard Halpern argues in *Shakespeare Among the Moderns* (1997) that Shakespeare is for the masses and Woolf for the minority. To my mind, such assertions are both absurd and incorrect. I hope, in the dialogue with the middle panel, to show by way of the Art-Based Learning method, how both can be relevant sources of knowledge.[63]

63 The importance of art as a source of knowledge is upheld by Hubert Damisch and Ernst van Alphen. Van Alphen's essay "Het intellectuele museum" (1998b), calls for a different way of contemplating art and different positioning of the museum: not as an archive of works or a place for emotional perceptions and experiences, but a place for intellectual work. Van Alphen believes that the museum educator should no longer seek to explain art in relation to other art. Like the conceptual artist, he should use art to say something about the world about him. The museum would be an intellectual meeting place where art would be deployed to discuss the world outside the museum.

He—for there could be no doubt of his sex, though the fashion of the time did something to disguise it—was in the act of slicing at the head of a Moor which swung from the rafters. It was the colour of an old football, and more or less the shape of one, save for the sunken cheeks and a strand or two of coarse, dry hair, like the hair of a cocoanut. Orlando's father, or perhaps his grandfather, had struck it from the shoulders of a vast Pagan, who had started up under the moon in the barbarian fields of Africa; and now it swung, gently, perpetually, in the breeze which never ceased blowing through the attic rooms of the gigantic house of the lord who had slain him.

2

Continuing Impact: Virginia Woolf

Let me imagine, since facts are so hard to come by, what would have happened had Shakespeare had a wonderfully gifted sister, called Judith let us say.
—Virginia Woolf (2000, 48)

Introduction

The speaking object addressed in the middle panel is a fragment from *Orlando,* a fictitious biography by Virginia Woolf (fig. III.2.1). On 22 March 1928 Virginia Woolf wrote in her diary: "Yes it's done—*Orlando*—begun on 8th October, as a joke; and now rather too long for my liking. It may fall between stools, be too long for a joke, and too frivolous for a serious book" (1953, 122).[64]

Virginia Woolf's fictitious biography is about a young poet, who barely gets any older in the course of four centuries: a boy who turns into a girl and travels a road of personal development. In this story, the adolescent as a poet becomes increasingly prominent.

64 Woolf's *A Writer's Diary* (1953) is a selection taken from the 26 parts with diary entries that Woolf wrote between 1915 and 1941 (until four days before her death). It was compiled by Leonard Woolf. In the diary, the writer looks at every book she undertook. The diary fragments concerning *Orlando* (1928) are limited. That may be because Leonard Woolf wrote in the preface that he considered *The Waves*, *To the Lighthouse* and *Between the Acts* to be major literary works. He describes the rest, so including *Orlando*, as readable, but of less literary quality.

III.2.1 Sally Potter, *Orlando* (film still), 1992

ORLANDO The book begins with the story of the budding young poet. Orlando lives at the court of Queen Elizabeth at the end of the sixteenth century. He is one of Elizabeth's favourite servants. The aging queen (Quentin Crisp in the film of the same name) perceives in Orlando (Tilda Swinton) the strength of youth which keeps her alive during an unremitting process of isolation and physical decline. Orlando feels he is surrounded by opulence and enjoys the court's protection.

One winter's day, a Russian envoy appears. One of the members of his noble retinue is the ravishing Sasha. Orlando first thinks she is a man. He immediately falls in love. However, the love does not last long. Sasha prefers pleasure to a long relationship. She steals away in the night and her ship disappears over the horizon. This is Orlando's first experience of a disintegrating paradise.

As he tries to overcome his heartbreak, Orlando falls asleep for seven days and then goes on to seek comfort in writing. He wants to be a poet. The castle Elizabeth gave him as thanks for his services is transformed into a writer's library. He chooses Greene—a name derived from a contemporary of Shakespeare's—as his teacher. However, Greene turns out to be a fraud who wants only wealth and fame. In a publication *Visit to a Nobleman* he totally derides Orlando.

In the second half of the story, the theme of otherness is addressed. Orlando has lost faith in everything that is dear to him and decides to take up the offer to become an ambassador. He becomes the representative of the English throne in Constantinople. However, the situation in the Ottoman empire is unstable and, after a period of relative peace, civil war breaks out.

Orlando is lying in his room and falls into a deep sleep (for the second time), once more for seven days. He awakes, completely changed. Orlando is now a (young) adult woman. Conditions change in the country. Orlando changes. He, who is now she, decides to go away, into the desert. In the desert's unspoilt nature she finds herself. Yet the world of the desert people is not hers. She feels like an outsider and decides to return to England as a woman.

The eighteenth and nineteenth centuries pass by in rapid succession. Orlando, because she is now a woman, has lost everything. Lawsuits follow. She meets new and learned friends, though they barely take her seriously as a woman. She can only be herself during night-time visits to shady bars.

In the last part, Woolf describes the mature writer of free verse. The nineteenth and twentieth centuries form the backdrop: Victorian and Edwardian England. Orlando meets the man of her dreams: Shelmerdine, an adventurer, globe-trotter and, like her, both man and woman. They marry and have a child. It is 1928, the time when Woolf's book is published—and Orlando also published her first major work. She is thirty and looks as young as she did at the start of the story, even though she has lived for four hundred years.

Peter Blos writes in *On Adolescence* that *Orlando* is a story about becoming a woman (1966, 148). He ushers in what I will examine when looking in more detail at the world of the sleeping, dreaming and fantasising adolescent. "Becoming a poet": youth transforms from warrior to poet, with disconnected fragments forming a new picture, like in the editing of a film.[65]

65 In *On Adolescence: A Psychoanalytic Interpretation*, Peter Blos explicitly devotes attention to *Orlando*: "the theme of bisexuality in the girl is most intriguingly told by Virginia Woolf in *Orlando*, in which the main character is transfigured from man to woman" (1966, 83). Blos not only describes Orlando as an example of gender-bending, but also as an illustration of a process of self-realization and the "various roles the maturing self learns to live with" (148).

He... it...
Orlando

3

Woolf: Hypnos

The Sleeping Identity of Youth

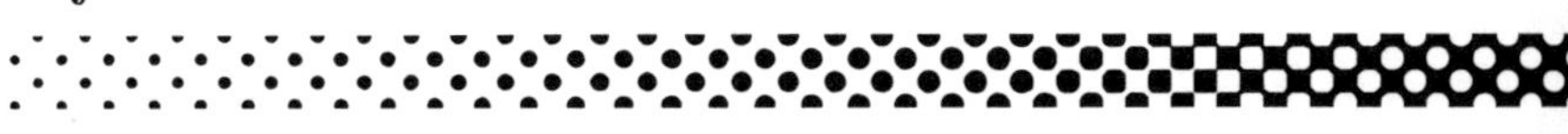

The Stream of Time

TIME SERIES I start this part of the triptych with the opening of *Orlando*. The fragment enables me to see how a small detail like this can serve as an index for the entire work. It gives access to a further level in the phenomenon of adolescence, the focus being on aesthetics as the answer to the tragedy of existence. Again, the primary question relates to the story of the adolescent.

When you open the book you encounter a language that works as a dreamlike sequence in time. William James' term "stream of consciousness" is often associated with Woolf's work and is in evidence from the first sentence. Like Laurence Sterne's *The Life and Opinions of Tristram Shandy* (1759), the text is highly serial in character, with a casual, improvising touch. It is a compositional approach that in psychoanalysis is sometimes generalised, wrongly in my opinion, as feminine, and so contrasted with static, masculine compositions.

According to some Woolf experts, the language flow relates to Henri Bergson's *élan vital*, the vital force of words. However, Ann Banfield emphatically refutes a relationship between the work of Bergson and Woolf. She actually stresses that we should look more towards England than to France when establishing the internal logic of the text. Seen in that context, Woolf's thinking can be traced primarily to the epistemology of Moore, Fry and Russell, and has its foundations in modern English thought, starting with the Scottish philosopher David Hume. Banfield writes: "The universe of Virginia Woolf's novels is a monadology whose plurality of possible worlds includes private points of space and time unobserved, unoccupied by any subject" (2000, 1). The apparent improvisations do not form an uninterrupted line, but an atomistic spectrum that is characterised by:

1. *Thinking in continuity*: Woolf's adolescent is distinguished by an endless series of primary and secondary associations that manifest themselves as a subjective stream of consciousness, as waves of light and sound. It is an atomistic world, but also a world of a regular time and accent division—a world of continuity within an invisibly expanding universe.
2. *Thinking in contiguity*: Woolf's adolescent is distinguished by a way of thinking in contiguous areas. The text has a metonymic quality; freedom of the psyche and not the restriction of the body is at the fore. Contiguity creates a universe of "particularia".
3. *Thinking in polysemy*: Woolf's adolescent is distinguished by a varied, rich and colourful inner reality where freedom for otherness and a multitude of meanings become increasingly prominent. The varying

compositions turn polysemy into a dynamic complex. Words interweave into a picture.

A continuous line from Shakespeare to Sterne and Woolf becomes audible. In "Shakespeare's Sister" (*A Room of One's Own*, 2000; originally published 1929) Woolf sketches a picture of the Shakespearean adolescent who speaks the language of the psyche. Caravaggio described and commented on the adolescent in his physicality. There, the biological process played a key part, and painting proved to be an excellent medium for it. Shakespeare and Woolf comment on adolescence in *As You Like It* and *Orlando* respectively, as a psychological phenomenon. Literature is a highly suitable medium in that context.

The theme around which everything centres with Virginia Woolf is youth as an identity process. Three subthemes are addressed: identity, alterity and fictionality. It relates to the genesis of the individual as a process of awakening; sleep (Hypnos), dream (Morpheus) and fantasy (Phantasmos) are the three most important stages.[66]

THE DEVELOPING ADOLESCENT The Woolfian poetic adolescent is defined by the emphasis on growth and development, as also found in the composition of the story. This poetic adolescent opposes the tragic immobility of Caravaggio's. The adolescent in *chiaroscuro,* dark thinking and the domain of death disappear into the background. The "rhetoric of life" begins. Light thinking appears: a stream of consciousness that in terms of form and content is marked by movement, life, an upwards striving towards perfection.

The world of the adolescent that is now under review has the organic character of improvisation. It relates to a kind of beauty that J.S. Bruner describes in *Actual Minds, Possible*

66 In the same year that she wrote *Orlando*, Virginia Woolf was working on a lecture to be held at Girton College, Cambridge: *A Room of One's Own*. There, she introduces Judith, the imaginary sister of Shakespeare who lives on in a character, as Orlando. Shakespeare's 'sister' dies young. She never wrote a word. However, Woolf is of the opinion that "this poet who never wrote a word and was buried at the cross-roads still lives. She lives in you and me, and in many other women, who are not here tonight, for they are washing up the dishes and putting the children to bed. But she lives; for great poets do not die; they are continuing presences; they need only the opportunity, as I think, it is now coming within your power to give her" (2000, 111–12). The underlying theme of this lecture is woman in art. Woolf draws a comparison between Shakespeare, Sterne, Coleridge, Keats and Proust. All five authors are characterised by pronounced androgyny. "Shakespeare was androgynous; and so were Keats and Sterne and Cowper and Lamp and Coleridge. Shelley perhaps was sexless. Milton and Ben Jonson had a dash too much of the male in them. So had Wordsworth and Tolstoy. In our time Proust was wholly androgynous, if not perhaps a little too much of a woman" (2000, 102). Androgyny for Woolf is a characteristic of ideal creativity.

Worlds (1986) as more like associative thinking (A-thinking) than a logical and rational form of thinking. (R-thinking). The underlying pattern has the features of positive ontology.[67]

67 Art-Based Learning is more consistent with Jerome Bruner's associative way of thinking than with the rational form. In *Making Stories: Law, Literature, Life* (2002) Bruner tells how literature "offers alternative worlds that put the actual one in a new light" and how "[i]t explores human plights through the prism of imagination" in a more subversive than pedagogically-founded way (10–11). According to Bruner, literature has a number of advantages with regard to the visual arts, because it can paint "human plans gone off the track". Literature can think, using genre theory in reasonably predictable forms, "to restore or to cope with the situation" (31).

Words as Sentences

FIXATION Orlando, as heard speaking here in the first paragraph and expressing himself in the first two chapters, is not a split personality, but a seemingly homogenous character, suited to a simple plot that takes you into a closed, balanced world. The world of Chronos vanishes. The world of Thanatos evaporates. We now enter the world of Hypnos, in Greek mythology the son of Nyx and brother of Thanatos. The first word from the selected fragment of text, "He", is a "word sentence", an envelope. The fragmented hero has become a sleepwalking object. He reveals a mere fraction of the melancholic, meditating subject and nothing of a consciously acting subject. He is a character who speaks, even though his motives remain a secret. The classical beauty: perfect in his physical proportions, but without any recognisable inner self.

He–

The narrator of this story fulfils the picture Michel Chion sketches of the 'acousmetre' in *The Voice in Cinema* (1999). This character stands behind an imaginary curtain and comments on the action of a largely invisible person. The narrator describes Orlando, accompanied, somewhat ironically, by commentary. The narrator has already spent time in the world of absolute beauty, to which Orlando has no access as yet.

The "he" is the third person. The "I", the adolescent, is the first person and, so far, has not awakened. The use of "he" gives the impression of an observation. It makes the main character elusive, just like Mrs. Dalloway in the eponymous novel (1925). "He" is a phenomenon, the word of the acousmetre. It might be a poet, but seen from an external perspective.

The only "me" in the story is the narrator: a character that coincides in the imagination with Virginia Woolf. The biographical interpretation corresponds with the fact that the story of Orlando is a humorous and loving reference to the life of Virginia Woolf's friend Vita Sackville-West, to whom the book is dedicated. That is why Nigel Nicholson, Sackville-West's son, called *Orlando* "the longest love letter ever". Woolf's acousmetre can also coincide with the alter ego of Orlando, although it is not an autobiography, but a (fictitious) biography of Orlando.

The correlation between the narrator and Virginia Woolf was portrayed well in the stage version of *Orlando* by the Oostpool theatre in Arnhem based on an adaptation by Joeri Vos. The relationship between the narrator and Orlando is reflected in the layout of the stage—in a division into two halves. Left (for the audience) we saw half the characters from the novel. The right-hand side was the narrator's domain. They continually passed the baton back and forth.[68]

Roman Jakobson, in "Two Aspects of Language" (2004) points out that an argument, a process of attributing meaning can pursue two lines: one of similarity and one of contiguity. Hypnos' world, the sleeping world addressed here, coincides most with that of similarity. The world is still what it is: the king is the king, the teacher is the teacher, the beloved is the beloved. That is what dominates Orlando's way of thinking in chapters one and two of the first part.

This world of similarity is still static. *Orlando as a Boy*, the depiction on the cover of the original Hogarth Press

68 Joeri Vos' script for Orlando was published under the title *Orlando: Een werkboek*. Concerning the text, Joris van der Meer says: "Joeri Vos' adaptation is not only a fluent reconstruction of an impressive story. Vos mirrors Woolf's self-reflective research of the genre of biography in a text that not only seeks to capture the essence of biography, also challenges the how and why of this actual adaptation. Through, and together with, the actors—the subtitle is not without reason—*werkboek* (workbook) —he questions terms like dialogue and acting style, and the need for theatre. By adding texts of his own, Vos also makes his own voice heard. All this means that this version of Orlando is a combination of adaptation and play script. A script that might not be in keeping with the classical tradition, but actually makes an object of it, thus, inspired by Virginia Woolf herself, also seeking to do justice to the greater significance of *Orlando*" (Vos 2009, 3).

edition of *Orlando* published in 1928, is consistent with that: a boy, in elegant garb, has been forced to stand beside a table in a pose that is not appropriate to his age. It is a static, vertical pose. Here, the world of similarity has a hierarchical character and the appearance of calm. A homogenous world of solemn simplicity is presented.

The possible world in which we now find ourselves is that of a closed monad. The curtains are drawn. The closed monad is very different from Bertrand Russell's open monad (which ties in better with the third part of *Orlando*). Russell describes the world of the monad as one with open windows and doors that are always connected to areas adjoining them in time and space. That is not yet the case here.

Robert Wilson who, together with Philip Glass, pioneered the opera *Einstein on the Beach* (1976), created the stage set for a theatre production of *Orlando* which was performed in Berlin (1989), Paris (1993, with Isabelle Huppert in the title role), England (1996) and Taiwan (2009). The first backdrop is, appropriately enough, a closed curtain, an image of a childish, closed world. Here there is little scope for a new identity.[69]

THE SLEEPING ADOLESCENT The adolescent who emerges after we have read the first part of *Orlando,* mainly evokes the image of a youth with an identity that is still dormant. That coincides with what Blos calls early adolescence, that is characterised by a "free floating object libido" (1966, 75). That picture is consistent with allegory of the poetic adolescent.

Youth as we encounter it in *Orlando* is typified by a receptive attitude. He is portrayed with outer beauty and a (still) hidden, all-inclusive inner world. The adolescent is a mystery. We can only guess what he thinks and feels. We

69 Roman Jakobson's work helps to differentiate the everyday world from the poetic. Jan van Luxemburg, Mieke Bal and Willem Weststeijn emphasise how ordinary language dominates the referential function. Texts devoted to emotions have an emotional function. Texts devoted to the way something is said primarily have a poetic function (1999, 37). The poetic function can be recognised by the prevalence of conformities and contrasts (equivalence) in metre, sound, syntax and semantics. Jakobson and Jan Mukarovsky introduce the term "aesthetic function", which can be interpreted somewhat more broadly than the poetic function. The aesthetic function need not be accompanied by incongruous syntax. Emphasis on the aesthetic diminishes orientation on practical aims and makes the manner of expression more important than the substantive focus (Van Luxemburg et al. 1999, 39). In my analysis, *Orlando* is an exponent of that aesthetic orientation.

can only judge by the character's attitude and gestures. A kind of inner sleep prevails. He still lacks an identity of his own. The perceptible tension makes us curious about the moment when this identity will awake. Woolf sketches this prenatal stage of adolescence in its untouched, unconscious, shadowy, harmonious state.

The Rhythm of the Text

MEANDERING The text fragment from *Orlando*—after the first word "He"—proceeds in a meandering stream of words: "for… there… could… be". This is a seemingly improvising technique that goes with the subject. The words in the fragment from Woolf's book move, diverge and continue their way along a different line. It is a steady, almost jazzy narrative style, comprising a rhythmical, rhyming undercurrent on which words travel like small boats. The current has a slow, musing rhythm without any clear ending. Reading not only means listening to the utterances, but also to the regular rhythm that propels the words. Reading is listening. It asks us to move with it and not interfere. If you wish to follow the stream, you ask questions. Such questions from the reader form signposts for the choice of the moment when a fragment can reveal itself.

—for there could be..

When you actively ask questions, you advance in the network of utterances that develops by degrees into an imaginative reality. Accordingly, pen-stroke by pen-stroke, the young poet emerges as a possibility. The words "there could be" refer to possibilities, not certainties.

The representation takes shape. In this case, it greatly resembles a late-impressionist painting. A colourful interplay unfolds: the attractive boy comes to life, with a subtle inter- and intra-systematic dynamic (Blos 1966, 75). The regular ictuses and rests evolve over time. The accompanying punctuation, rhymes, alliterations and rhythms form a logical, cohesive whole. Woolf composes a well-balanced cohesive text with words and pauses based on an unequivocal view of youth.

In this way language becomes a picture, after the model of Jacques Lacan's imaginary order. According to Lacan, the "imaginary order" is the first stage of development in which a child identifies itself totally with its surroundings. In this stage, the child equates itself with "the other". It results in a situation of simultaneous identification and alienation (Mooij 1987, 80). The world is transparent, but also elusive. The imaginary order is an artistically lyrical world and, according to Lacan, a natural world. The Self and the Other are still in the same cocoon. The world is still not divided and has more feminine than masculine features. Roland Barthes calls this world "sticky" (2002, 25).

This brings to mind the late-renaissance world of Shakespeare, the somnolent Victorian world of Burne-Jones' paintings, and even post-impressionists like Vanessa Bell and Duncan Grant. The beauty of the imaginary order extends to the old world that contains the seeds of the new world. This artistically lyrical world is a natural one and has animistic features from which a new culture can flourish. The serene arias of Dowland's castrati sound in the background. The scenography is consistent with a peaceful landscape of rolling, green hills. Purcell's compositions for woodwinds accompany the young adolescent's movements. Musical sounds arise to the rhythm of the words. Sandy Powell's costumes and Ben van Os' splendid banquets (in Sally Potter's film version of *Orlando*) both fit perfectly in the total composition.

THE MYSTERIOUS ADOLESCENT The poetic adolescent now acquires mysterious characteristics—not surprising in a world between waking and sleeping. In *Process and Reality* (1978, originally published 1929), Alfred North Whitehead described the defining aspects of the mysterious world. The endless mysterious space reveals the world of an adolescent living in ignorance, innocence and serenity. Sometimes he speaks in riddles, in invisible numbers. But he is usually silent. That silence is comparable with the long pauses and ictuses of a psalm. The adolescent finds himself in a world with no set duration or dimensions. The fact that it is partly still unconsciously experienced explains the mystical reality.[70]

70 The mystical world of Whitehead is explained by Hent de Vries in *Philosophy and the Turn to Religion* (1999) as a process theology. It is an "ontology of the event". Whitehead's fragmented universe is marked by dynamics, with spirituality as a form of genesis. It is a world of a monad among other monads, in ever-changing positions, which, in an unknowable and infinite world, through countless experiences, establishes its place within the whole. What characterises the universe of the mathematician Whitehead is a consistent and coherent logical system. His speculative philosophy serves to disclose. Mystery provides deeper insight.

The Poetic Monologue

MONOLOGUE The following phrase reads like a river, a natural sequence of words up to: "slicing at the head of a Moor". Each word seems to take its place in the flow. Logical realities *and* illogical realities unfold. Orlando, who, after I had seen Sally Potter's film, acquired Tilda Swinton's face for me, is the source of those words. He presents himself as an exponent of the (ever changing) world of the Elizabethan court.

...was in the act of slicing at the head of a Moor...

The undercurrent is an internal monologue, with the narrator, as a character, sustaining the intervals surrounding these signs. The punctuation introduces the interval, which plays an important part in the narrative style. The punctuation serves as the drummer of a band: the punctuation marks show what it is about and indicate where the reader can or must enter a new area. In this way, the comma, the full stop and the semicolon open up an infinite space.

Yra van Dijk devoted a thesis to this blank as an interval (*Leegte, leegte die ademt*, 2006). The blank is the carrier of the thought. The blank, the space of the blank, is the basis of the stream of consciousness. It is the equivalent of the black, the carrier of *chiaroscuro* in Caravaggio. So I see black as the basis of speech and white as the basis of silence. The blank is the empty white book. It is sleep. Speaking letters fill the blank space and thus represent awakening.

Awakening, the reality of the word on a white/blank page is very prominent in *The Waves* and *To the Lighthouse*. The blank behind the words, the sea present throughout the work, forms the background to the awakening landscape. The words resemble the waves in an ocean. They follow, one after the other. They are different, but belong together. Each wave, each word is a rising, a reiterating ictus in the poetry. These ictuses are followed by brief moments in which everything falls silent: a descent and a pause, an interval, followed by a new wave.

> And in me too the wave rises. It swells; it arches its back. I am aware once more of a new desire, something rising beneath me like the proud horse whose rider first spurs and then pulls him back. What enemy do we now perceive advancing against us, you whom I ride now, as we stand pawing this stretch of pavement? It is death. Death is the enemy. It is death against whom I ride with my spear couched and my hair flying back like a young man's, like Percival's, when he galloped in India. Against you I will fling myself, unvanquished and unyielding, O Death! (1992, 228)

The linear stream of signs proceeds in sequences. The interval, the smallest melody, secretly resounds with the rest. It provides silent moments in Woolf's sea, as if something is about to happen. The words suddenly fan out. The reader can taste them. The peaceful background gives them a transparent element. It is as if you can see effortlessly down to the sea bed and watch the plants swaying, and then you are surprised by a fragment of monologue.[71]

Stéphane Mallarmé's *L'après-midi d'un faune* also shows the natural stream of awakening as described in the above paragraphs: a ritual dance of awakening. Debussy set Mallarmé's poem to music, danced by Nijinsky and painted by Fry. It is one of the highlights of modernism. The poem begins as follows:

> Ces nymphes, je les veux perpétuer.
> Si clair,
> Leur incarnat léger, qu'il voltige dans l'air Assoupi
> de sommeils touffus.
> Aimai-je un rêve? (Mallarmé 1992, 35)

Mallarmé's world is filled with wraithlike figures which briefly appear and disappear. They appear, one by one, clad in rich costumes. The frequent references to the costumes is not entirely arbitrary. Mallarmé (like Woolf) loved fashion, not so much as a form of expression, but more as context. Fashion creates the character, not the other way round. Every garment a character wears gives him a different identity. Every character who is then in his surroundings, gives him a different context, thus altering his identity as well.

Sandy Powell, who—like Tilda Swinton—worked a great deal with Derek Jarman, designed the costumes for Sally Potter's film version of *Orlando*. Every dress and every cloak is highly expressive. However, most important is the overall picture that is created: the constant movement, as with the dresses that featured in Mallarmé's fashion magazine *La Dernière Mode*.[72]

71 The language in *The Waves* (1992, originally published 1931), Woolf's seventh novel, is rhythmical. The work has nine parts, which correspond with the daily movement of the sun in the sky. The key focus is the development of the identities of several friends. When they reach the age of twenty-five, they look back to the tragedy and beauty of their youth. By then Percival has died in India, aged twenty-two. He represents the mystery of eternal youth. The novel consists of soliloquies by the characters for an unaddressed audience. So the book not only alludes to the form of a poem, but also of a play. Woolf calls it a play-poem stemming from the desire to fathom her "mystical feelings". The form is largely derived from Shakespeare, who uses monologue a great deal. Bernard, one of the protagonists in *The Waves*, says that "rhythm is the main thing in writing". Woolf herself said that she based the book more on rhythm than on plot. In 1933 she wrote in hindsight in her diary that writing *Orlando* led her to write *The Waves*. See Hussey 1995, 348–62.

72 For Mallarmé and fashion, see Furbank and Cain, 2004. In his essays Mallarmé distinguishes between *la parole immédiate* and *la parole essentielle*. The former relates to ordinary language, whereas the latter relates to poetic language. With the latter, Mallarmé is referring to a language in which sounds, associations and symbols assert themselves. He sees poetic linguistic usage as the language of one's inner self. The awakening of the inner self is an awakening of the poetic.

THE NATURAL ADOLESCENT The world of the poetic adolescent is a flowing universe and is entirely natural in character. Woolf describes Orlando as someone possessing "strength, grace, romance, folly, poetry and youth" (1998, 24). The adolescent still has no self-awareness, but is part of nature. He is the sleepwalker—sometimes silent and sometimes dancing—who acts, eats, drinks and lives.

This adolescent would seem to experience everything almost automatically—the surroundings do not see the adolescent as "something different". Even animals approach Orlando. What applies to nature also applies to cultural space. Culture annexes him, in this story as the queen's catamite. He does not lead, has no place of his own. He follows, but does not mind. Culture is his natural state. Here he may develop.

The Synaesthetic Effect

...under the moon in the barbarian fields of Africa...

SYNAESTHESIA The reading of the text is likely to produce the pleasant experience of a river that branches out.

The synaesthetic experience is present throughout the book: sometimes underground, sometimes on the surface. When Orlando first meets his beloved Sasha, he describes the impression she makes on him synaesthetically: "A melon, an emerald, a fox in the snow" (1998, 37). In his animistic world everything seems to be animated. Every object seems to have acquired the status of a subject. Accordingly, the Elizabethan world resembles Shakespeare's paradisiacal forest. Every element is part of a greater whole. Every word has the same importance. It is not a world of contrasts, but a system of loving relations.

These synaesthetic experiences bring me to Roland Barthes' description of love: the other side of sleep. The following fragment from *A Lover's Discourse* is illustrative: "In the loving calm of your arms" (1990, 105). Barthes describes how the embrace of one's loved one and the rocking of a baby in its mother's arms represent the same feeling. For him, the similarity lies mainly in surrender, which applies for love and sleep alike—or nature and mystery. Caravaggio's *chiaroscuro* is thinking in activity. Woolf's "stream of consciousness" is thinking in passivity.

Love is characterised by organic cohesion, creates tension and arouses sympathy. Romantic relationships are shaped in such a way that the listener is tempted to identify with them. In this game of identification, the internal focaliser is the intermediary that follows movements on both sides. He converses with the reader and says: "Can you see what they are doing to him?" In romantic reality everything is unique, but is also interconnected.[73]

73 Figures of speech are the framework of *Fragments d'un discours amoureux* (1977), published in English as *A Lover's Discourse: Fragments* (1990). Barthes uses several examples to arrive in a possible world. I also work with figures of speech. My study, if it had been a cinematographic narration, might well be called 'The Language of Youth'. The nine art works I discuss form a montage of scenes out of adolescence. Barthes' *A Lover's Discourse* is constructed around terms like "contacts", "mad" and "monstrous". 'The Language of Youth' would comprise terms like "hero", "lover" and "poet".

THE ADOLESCENT AS A LOVER The poetic adolescent lives on the basis of surrendering to love, with the lover as a symbol of surrender to vital, natural forces. In this case, surrender for me means: opening yourself to what happens to you, a feeling, a thought or an occurrence. Then there is little difference between the external and the internal world. The adolescent is impulsive; he reacts and improvises. Love and friendship are very closely connected. According to Peter Blos, that frequently results in a far-reaching idealisation of a friend (1966, 77).

...the gigantic house of the Lord...

The unity of lovers does have separate parts. The lovers, who have become intertwined like branches, grow through and over each other, not guided from a centre, but at the mercy of circumstances. The adolescent casts doubt on boundaries. His movements are akin to the boundless "barbarian fields of Africa".

The Beat as an Ordering Principle

BEAT Despite all the movement, the text maintains its calmness and cohesion thanks to the rich panoramas—as, for instance, the "gigantic house of the lord". Such words form the images with which language organises itself. Wealth, love, nature, English prosperity and glory: all are interconnected.

The setting in this text is the stable factor. The beat and setting both provide a balanced timing of rests and ictuses. The aesthetic of Orlando and his surroundings transport us at a regular pace past locations like Charing Cross, the dome of St. Paul's Cathedral, moving along with the background music.

The narrator's subtle arabesques are enacted against this décor. You feel as if you are in a painting in which you keep seeing one colour merge into another, without knowing exactly where the dividing line is.

THE AESTHETIC ADOLESCENT Woolf's thinking about the beauty of youth and the poetic adolescent becomes increasingly tangible in conjunction with concrete images like "the gigantic house of the lord". The adolescent who is able to escape thanks to an aesthetic answer to the tragedy of life, makes himself heard. His aesthetic is expressed in a receptive state, such as sleep; mystery, natural innocence and love play important roles in this.

The adolescent proves, while searching and playing, to be in a "state of indeterminacy" (Schiller 2009, 67). This aesthetic focus is more unconscious than conscious. He is not the centre, but a small piece of a partially tragic, partially romantic universe. He finds himself in an enormous, invisible reality, a dream world that coincides with the gigantic house.

Lastly

Art can help us when we reflect on important cultural issues. After all, art is a form of thinking that we can read and from which we can learn—if we have a relevant question. Fry calls fiction "an implicit form of knowledge" (Banfield 2000, 52).

In the caravaggesque world, the theme of homo biologicus arose: the adolescent's confrontation with the physical process of aging, which became apparent when we looked at *David with the Head of Goliath*. It involves a polar, confronting, diagonal and descending way of thinking with an underlying ontology of death.

In the Woolfian world we have ended up with homo poeticus. Nabokov, in *Speak, Memory* (1989, originally published 1951) argues that homo poeticus precedes homo sapiens. Here, in the world of the psyche, we hear the other story of youth. We enter the world of the subjective experience of beauty. In that context, Woolf stresses a free, evolutionary, harmonious, horizontal, improvising and, in particular, continuing way of thinking: a positive ontology of life.

Woolf's *Orlando* becomes a pastoral elegy in this way of thinking. In this first part, the adolescent is described in terms of childish innocence, which is usually protected. Everything is attuned to it: relations with the Court, his budding relationship with Sasha, the escape in the night from the safety of the castle. All these scenes are described with a light, sketchy undertone.

This world is exemplified by a fairy-tale, charming beauty. Unity of self and the other still exists; the imaginary world of the child is still untouched. Woolf teaches us that an adolescent like Orlando belongs in an invisible, platonic world of ideas. Orlando is a child; he does not yet see the world for what it is. Not that he has turned away, but rather he does not yet consciously turn towards the world. We learn about an adolescent living in a world of almost unconscious, emotional experiences: emotions, impulses and sometimes thoughts. This is the world of the "unthought known" where the "true self" has not yet reached maturity—that comes about when one enters into object relations (Bollas 1987, 280). The self senses the conscious and, to some extent, the unconscious. However, for Orlando this reality is not yet an interlocutor. He is locked away in his own realm of thought. Contact between the inner and outer world is only intimated by the narrator.

The lyrical language of the adolescent resembles a recitation, a singsong melody. The voice moves through space in a free state" (Schiller 2009, 75). The described adolescent is still a relatively restrained figure in time and space. The world in which he finds himself is characterised by continuity, solidarity, "the force of nature" and "legislation of reason" (76).

The beauty of youth can be heard everywhere. The liberating game we call beauty is uttered by the acousmetre, sung by the youth as if in a ballad and that follows him playfully—like a cameraman. We see a composite picture of a beloved, a mystical and natural young person.

The poetic monologue results from a stream of consciousness, still largely invisible, in a world of conscious/unconscious fragments and continuity. The intermezzos that comment on the surroundings, like the landscape, the air, the castle or London city, are part of it.

The countless, individual images per reading minute are so close together that a concatenated ensemble comes about; a world of unity that can be divided into atoms. It is the world of Hypnos, from which the narrator's voice can be heard.

"For there could be no doubt of his sex, though the fashion of the time did something to disguise it..."

4

Woolf: Morpheus

Alterity as Contiguous Space

A Changing Point of View

Orlando, as a budding poet, not only has the character of Hypnos, but also of Morpheus, the god of dreams. Orlando represents the dreamy youth. The calm and steady rhythm of sleep in the first part changes in the second part to the strange, self-willed rhythm of dreams. The ebb of sleep and the flow of dream alternate. The young man, a semi-woken dream figure, slowly matures, although, in his/her heart, he/she remains the sleepy adolescent of the past.

In the first two chapters we saw the exterior of the adolescent: his face, his legs, his garments. A traditional adolescent appeared, of almost childishly simple, balanced beauty—a reference to a positive ontology of youth. However, Orlando's language is one of change. He arrives in a dynamic heterogeneity. The tempo changes. The point of view changes. The set rhythm is interrupted by a series of syncopations. The doors and windows of the monads open to "undemarcated, contiguous regions" (Russell). The inception is already apparent in the first fragment, with sentences like "no doubt ... sex". The text falters. The letters pursue a converse mode of reasoning. I hear a different line, a divergent rhythm.

A contrasting rhythm of maturation develops and coincides with a process of gender-bending, which is introduced as an option. It raises the question whether there can indeed be any doubt concerning his sex. The word "disguise" in the following sentence completes that idea. The first sentence second-guesses what later takes place: "Orlando had become a woman—there is no denying it." After which Orlando does indeed appear in female guise, "He stood upright ... he was a woman" (Woolf 1998, 134). The young man has become a woman.

The other female, perspective is apparent in the organisation of the text. Part one still has the one-sided primacy of everyday reality. The emphasis is on the organised outer world. The arrangement of part two need not necessarily be linked to the content, but focuses on the poetic form. The emphasis is increasingly on the inner world. The rhythm of the subject is pivotal. The object world follows. This is reflected in the description of the transformation from man to woman, or the description of Orlando's melancholic immersion in nature, in which his experience is more important than the description of nature. A poetic, rhythmical, detailed and ever-more complex series of sentences replaces a relatively simple plot (Woolf 1998, 137–38).

Orlando is now in the world of dreams. In the essay "At the Other's Play: To Dream" Bollas states: "I regard the dream as a fiction constructed by a unique aesthetic: the transformation of the subject into his thought, specifically, the placing of the self into an allegory of desire and dread that is fashioned by the ego" (1987, 64).

Bollas sees dream as an aesthetic space. The world of the

dream provides scope to doubt gender and to change one's clothes at one's own discretion. One self can appear alongside another. Parallel worlds become visible. Present and past, man and woman, young and old, and 'upper' world and underworld can intermingle in dreams.

According to Bollas, dream is pre-eminently "a place for this interplay of self and other" (1987, 68). The simply shining identity of the child becomes entangled in a game with the alterity of the young adult. The dream tells the story of the unconscious, awakening identity. Bollas describes the concomitant dream experience as losing oneself in the dramatic experience—the theatre—of another. This scope for alterity provides the foundations for the world of polyphony.

Bollas differentiates between the aesthetic principles and scientific and practical principles. The language of dreams is mainly sustained by the ever-changing dream setting: the surroundings, the décor or the thought. Images have a surrealist character. The mise-en-scène, more than the characters, expresses the thought (1987, 75).[74]

THE OTHER ADOLESCENT The poetic adolescent enters the territory of the other. The self expands and appears as a woman. "He" becomes "she". Orlando becomes a woman.

The adolescent has cautiously awoken. He steps outside the genderless demarcation of childhood, possibly unconsciously. The adjoining area is dominated by a thought process in which the woman plays a significant role. The unity of the fairytale, somnolent world where a culturally acquired and cohesive androgynous identity still exists, crumbles and reveals an as yet unknown "self". Here, a dreamy, associative way of thinking develops. In terms of identity development, there is a transition between continuity of thought and discontinuity of thought. The adolescent interrupts the

74 In *The Shadow of the Object*, Bollas addresses the enriching, transgressive interplay. Dream complies with aesthetic laws. The image of youth developing in that linguistic game is, among other things, that of the aesthetic adolescent. He is a dreamer who lands in a rhizomatic reality. Bollas argues that dream-aesthetic is based on a poetic play of forms. The adolescent as a dreamer is characterised by a poetic thought process. Freud compares dreams with literary texts in the territory of 'the Other'. The setting of the dream ties in with that of joke and fantasy (Bollas 1987, 66–67).

chronological, historical demarcation. "His" thinking as a stream of consciousness reveals itself in the relinquishment of similarity and the accessing of related, but also differing and contiguous areas.

The Effect of Syncopations

SYNCOPATIONS Thinking in alterity, the language of the young poet, is manifested as a counter-current. The stream of consciousness has a synchronic counter-movement. From the first "no", Orlando changes, but this transformation chiefly continues from Chapter 3, as if it were syncopation. The clause concerning Orlando's "sex" and the "fashion of the time" anticipates it.

Syncopation is a rhythm that is contrary to the regular metrical accent. It is often used in the jazz that emerged in the 1920s—the time when *Orlando* was published. Syncopation accentuates unexpected places. Sometime the accent will be on the second or fourth beat, rather than the first or third. A short beat may also be inserted.

...no...

The narrative style that is evinced goes with the development in which the set beat is disrupted and swing begins. The calm, tedious rhythm of monotonous love and sleep is obsolete. "Yes" changes into "no". "No" changes back to "yes" and back again to "no". This process generates a stream of words in which one improvisation follows another.

Dreams represent a deepening force that affects the life flow. Bollas speaks of "a remarkable rendezvous between the two domains of existence, our conscious coordination of lived experience involving perception and integration of the observed, and our unconscious reading of life" (1987, 52). Dream affects life and so has constant vitality. The dream figure is one that grows and blossoms. The narrator describes how Orlando arrives in an area that "deepen[s] those feelings which she had had as a man" (154). Orlando is always entering new territories, in which every new geographical relocation can serve as a metaphor for a mental reorientation in time and space, and a rhythmical antiphrasis—a syncopation.

Julia Kristeva posits in *La révolution du language poétique* (1974) that poetic language interrupts logical and linear thinking. This poetic language allows space for non-linear, timeless and emotional processes that dominated literature from the end of the nineteenth century, with the story no longer proceeding according to a set pattern.

The story parts are arranged side by side, as different elements, and the reader can relate them to one another in varying ways. The coercive mechanism of time that was dominant in the previous discussion of the tragedy of youth is breached in the aesthetic world. Poetic reality has fresh combinations, relations, associations and possibilities, and is fundamentally positive and hopeful.

The aspects of sound then prevail over the content, and the narrative style supersedes the pattern of thought. The language which Kristeva refers to is constantly in the throes of breaking through a "fascist state of mind". Language loses the compelling, uniformly prescriptive character of a language that eliminates all differences/contradictions/dichotomies (Bollas 2003, 200).[75]

75 In "The Adolescent Novel" Kristeva posits that adolescence is an age-less concept. For her, adolescence is "less a developmental stage than an open psychic structure" (1995, 136). She does not consider the frequent occurrence of adolescence in fiction as entirely positive. It can also be a compensating mechanism. The "imaginary activities" surrounding adolescence have little to do with the epistemological contribution I focus on in the ABL process. Fiction is the compensation for an absent reality: the absence of an actual rite of passage is compensated in a book, a film of a painting.

doubt.

Ambiguous References

IRONY The story of the young poet is also characterised by autonomous word fragments which sometimes go along with the flow and sometimes go against it, as independent word pictures. Each word creates an indexical reality—of which the word "doubt" is an example.

It represents an environment of its own. The word "doubt" from the first fragment (even though used here in the negative) takes a particular tone, because it can negate all that has gone before with a stroke of the pen. It is as if someone tells a story and then says there are doubts as to its legitimacy. Accordingly, the text can be deprived of its legitimacy with one word, and end up in a new, uncertain context.

The word "doubt" has an ironic quality that already anticipates post-poetic thinking. Woolf does that quite often, sometimes with a militant undertone, thus undermining all form of display and authority. Something that starts as a question mark concerning Orlando's gender, is further elaborated in the encounter with Greene, but especially in the chapter "Orlando on Her Return to England".

Woolf directs more and more attention to the ironic undertone, particularly in the second part of *Orlando*—even to the extent that it could be described as satire. The dispute between Pope, Swift and Orlando, with the foolish Duke Harry in the background, is a good example. The new enlightened thinkers cross swords. They protest in their salon against the antiquated culture of aristocracy.

At the level of the meta-text, the critics are self-important nincompoops, engrossed in their masculine pose. "What are we?" asks Orlando, "Ages to come will never cast a thought on me or on Mr Pope either" (196). The critic is unmasked. The naïve, but also sincerely rebelling Orlando can now see through the contrasting world of appearances that contrasts with himself: the small talk, the unconvincing cheeriness.

The text also alludes to Caravaggio's tragedy of the night. During the day, Orlando makes her 'polite' rounds, like an employee obediently going to work. At night, Orlando changes clothes. She vanishes into the local bars, as she did in Elizabeth's day.

Finally, the ironic thing is the conflict between the chronology of the series of events and the diachrony of the psychological activity. Orlando's diachronically structured psyche mainly reveals itself in the second part. During the process of reaching adulthood, Orlando increasingly becomes an experiencing and exploring subject, rather than an object of perception. The growing structure in separate fragments matches this. On the whole, the external setting is a chronological reality. The internal setting, of the subject and the dream, is far more a diachronic reality.[76]

76 Diachrony relates to a form of nomadic thinking. This internal reality is grouped around themes. The thematic reality does not progress straightforwardly. It consists of a series of separate fragments that are forged together to generate a particular meaning. The material is extremely subjective and also suited to a different arrangement. The chief theme addressed in the second part is woman's marginal position in Western society. However, Woolf does not construct a synchronic reality. Diachronic reality still retains a primarily chaotic structure. The principle of alertness prevails: Orlando mainly knows what she does not want and not yet what she does want.

Robert Wilson made twenty-two drawings (1989) with the theme of Woolf's *Orlando*—the sketches mentioned earlier were for a stage set. Here we see a minimalist portrayal of Orlando's transformation process. The drawings are reminiscent of film stills, resembling windows behind which the various pictures of the adolescent are presented. They form doors behind which the story is enacted. The series is divided into three parts corresponding approximately with the breakdown in my analysis: sleep (identity), dream (alterity) and fantasy (performativity).

The first series—sleep—contains dark sketches and you are struck by the fact that it is difficult for light to penetrate. Now and then it does break through a few fixed points. It is striking that the light is presented horizontally, vertically and, in steps, geometrically.

The second series—dream—starts with a large opening and takes the spectator into another, light space. The background is permanently light. In the foreground, objects can be discerned now and then which temporarily take the light away from the area behind. There are small geometric windows: little figures giving, with the slight contrast, the ensemble something dreamlike. They emphasise that all elements do in fact belong to the same space.

The third series—fantasy—is the most painterly. These images evoke the idea of "waves of light", of clouds and sea. The interplay of the clouds is somewhat mysterious, because it contrasts with the rest of the work with its free geometric arrangement.[77]

THE NOMADIC ADOLESCENT The poetic adolescent travels through a dream world and is, fundamentally, a nomad. The driving force behind that journeying is a healthy scepticism about existence. Adolescents like Orlando live on the border—a border-like space.

The adolescent's world is no longer clearly circumscribed. The adolescent as a subject finds himself in a space-time in which worlds intermingle. One sound continues where the previous one finished, like an improvisation that is not deliberately planned, but occurs purely on the basis of hearing. Yet the previous sound echoes on. More and more figures appear within the space. This space is not a unity but a plurality; its organisation is not centripetal but centrifugal. Inge Boer, in "No-Man's-Land? Deserts and the Politics of Space" (2006), describes this world as a factually uncertain space. It is the world of Orlando travelling through the desert. She has left England behind, but her future is uncertain; she still has no destination. The centre has disappeared. The only set point is the resting-place in the evening (Lutters 2009, 125).

Orlando's world expands rather than contracts. The adolescent is a universe. His psyche consists of numerous celestial bodies that appear as sub-personalities, each tracing its

77 Wilson's work depicts in abstract images how the thinking of Woolf's *Orlando* is structured. In 1989 Wilson made a series of twenty-two drawings for a stage set for a production of *Orlando* in an adaptation by Darryl Pinckney which was performed in Berlin on 11 November 1989. The drawings were then on show in the Annemarie Verna Galerie in Zürich, from the end of 1989 to the beginning of 1990. In the catalogue, Darryl Pinckney describes the first part as "disciplined" and "formal". The second part is defined by "marks" and "spots", part three is "very painterly", "chromatic" and composed of "free projections". Wilson proves with this to be capable of "visually reading" Woolf (with Miele Bal's analysis of Proust in mind).

own course through space; sometimes they harmonise, but sometimes they clash. However, clashes are not the finish but the start; they trigger a new train of thought and start a new system.

Lastly

The poetic rhythm of the words, sentences, punctuation and paragraphs—the rhythm of wind and waves—has taken me into a new possible world of the adolescent. It is the story in which Orlando gradually comes to life. The quiet world of the 'forefathers' from the first part, Orlando's provisional identity, is punctured.

We arrive in a world that Virginia Woolf describes as a "crowded dance of modern life" (1993, ix). The adolescent is in the world of Morpheus, the territory of the other, the unseen, a game with the intra-subjective, congruent realities. The aesthetic and mystical world of continuity comes to an end. Unpredictable, explosive, improvising, rebellious, nomadic thinking sets in.

This new world is characterised by thinking in contiguity. It is the story of a subject that tells his own story via a number of characters and events. Parallel worlds provide sufficient space and time so that ever-new elements can be added. The configuration of those elements causes new figures to come about continuously.

This world of Woolf's is constantly presenting us with puzzles. Something is touched upon, but not completed. Mysteries and suspense exist everywhere. The cards are shuffled time and again, and a new game starts. There are identified areas, but "in-between areas" as well in which the reader and the narrator are situated.

Woolf creates a diachronic world in which parallel areas become visible. Time is more than just a unity. It also breaks up into parts which are interconnected and at the same time are always somewhat different. A-thinking, associating (not reasoning) is, according to Bollas in *The Mystery of Things,* the driving force, the source of new knowledge. The intangible, endless horizon is a fairytale world in an aesthetically unconsciousness, where things can always be different and where you learn to be different.[78]

78 A-thinking can generate extensive analysis. Bollas refers in *The Mystery of Things* to this analysis as a combination of the matriarchal and patriarchal order. The former produces the dream reality proceeding from an unconscious place. The patriarchal order exists concurrently and involves a permanent process of creative interventions (2001, 42). In the end, every analyser makes his own truth (37). Bollas' process of free association fits in the picture of a parabola. This is a knowledge process based on observation, destruction and creation. Knowledge begins with an initial awareness, and goes on, via a process of destruction, to finish in the free word. In that sense, ABL is a process of construction, deconstruction and reconstruction.

He—for there
could be no
doubt ... who
had slain him

5

Woolf: Phantasos

Infinite Time

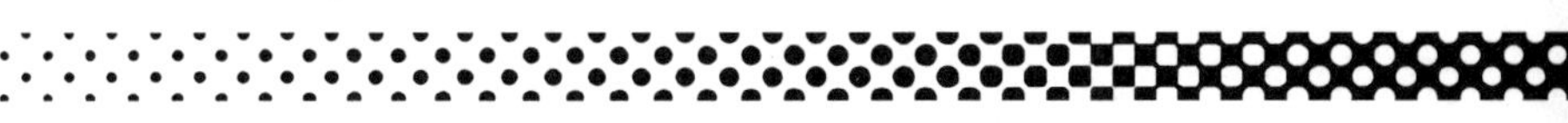

Introduction

In conclusion, by way of our dialogue with Woolf's language and the worlds behind that language, the high-spirited young poet Orlando, becomes a creative Phantasos. Phantasos, the brother of Morpheus and son of Hypnos, is the Greek god of fantasy. "What a phantasmagoria the mind is," Orlando exclaims (Woolf 1998, 169).

Dream moves into fantasy. Now the "I" does not exist in the not-yet reality of the dream, but forms a fictive principle, after Locke and Hume.

Woolf refines the idea that maturation, creativity and the development of self-confidence go together. In her case, identity as a fictive principle means that the reality of a metaphysical essence does not exist. Identity is a positive, dynamic, culturally determined product of imagination—the result of the creative spirit that is defined by cultural factors. Similarly, with this theory of the stages of life, one can say that adolescence is a construct, a fantasy and a cultural given.

Woolf tells about the human psyche, as a free, self-designable space. Intra-subjective reality becomes a complex reality. Life is (like) a dream. And thus dreams become reality. Physical reality is of co-ordinate importance; you are what you think you are.

The last two chapters of *Orlando* describe the path from sleep, via dream, to fantasy. Orlando meets the man of her dreams. A man who, like her...is fantasy? Is reality? Accordingly, fantasy becomes the aesthetician's answer to the tragedy of existence.

The world we now enter gradually goes beyond the linear form. Where Shakespeare's world is still characterised by the word, nineteenth-century linguistic usage is characterised by phrases, as Gertrude Stein explains in her lecture "What is English Literature?" ("the phrases, the emotion of phrases, the explaining in phrases" [2004, 53]). Thinking in phrases that clarify or explain the preceding phrases, also defines Woolf's written style.

He ... him.

However, in *Orlando* Woolf also cautiously attempts to find a new, twentieth-century way of thinking that Stein describes as thinking and writing in paragraphs. For the writer, words or phrases are no longer enough, he/she also includes a cinematographic framework. Whenever you read something, you see and hear complex oxymorons. There is no caesura in the space. The sentence has become part of a scene.

Fact and fiction, space and time, protagonist and supporting actor: everything is mixed up and is interrelated. Tangled configurations result. We have now entered an area known in poetry as free verse, which was already apparent in Rosalind's language. Now, free thought is the only guiding principle and it is only possible to establish retrospectively the strictly individual meaning of a text.[79]

79 Stein and Woolf are rooted in the same tradition: at the interface of thinking in phrases and paragraphs. Nevertheless, there is a difference. Stein inclines more to the twentieth-century world of paragraphs. Woolf to the nineteenth-century world of phrases.

MELODY The narrator sketches the young poet's life as a complex, but finished melody: a cohesive whole of sounds and rests. The rhythmical, explosive, linear stream of words that develops by degrees becomes part of a greater whole. The melody differentiates itself from the rhythm as a whimsical eruption against the coercion of the beat. The melody is the stream of life. It turns the separate parts into a whole. The whole has a beginning and an end, with accents and rests.

Woolf is perfectly aware of the possibilities of the blank space. The narrator also points out "a great blank here" (1998, 242). Woolf suggests that what is not said is, in fact, the most important. These are the unspoken, contiguous spaces. In fact, the text is merely a first step towards a process of thinking. It emphasises what the literary object, as a speaking object, has actually been trying to say from the start: the reader is the owner of the text. It is up to the person filling in the blank space to determine what melody will come about: the creative reader, as a *homo faber,* goes his own way from here on.

THE ADOLESCENT AS A POET The poetic adolescent changes from a receptive mystic, by way of a nomadic rebel, into a poet and performer, with fiction forming the overarching term. The space between the avalanche of words becomes visible. The adolescent no longer dreams. He awakes; not rationally, but in the imagination.

In the story *The Beauty of Youth,* the adolescent reaches the peak of his abilities. To achieve it, he has had to make a U-turn in his thinking. Thinking, the stream that started in the limited object world, ends in the infinite subject world. Fiction forms the basis for his identity. His biological and his cultural determinacy are part of the infinite amount of material available to the adolescent.

Language as Performance

Every letter relating to the young poet requires a living, literary performance. It could be the voice of a third part. Also, the performer could be a voice in the reader's head. Language is an act. The words of the opening fragment, "Perhaps his grandfather", acquire a range of meanings. The language of the object is no longer only the writer's word. Literature as a form of thinking becomes a spoken text that largely depends on the reader's interpretation.

A performance is a new kind of art and a new kind of thinking. The perspective of the reader and the listener is decisive. It is not only a matter of right or wrong, but also of personal taste. The chosen text fragment in the centre panel of the triptych works entirely differently when spoken by a man or a woman. Depending on whether you read the text aloud in silence, or against a musical background, will have quite a different effect. Twenty percent of a text's meaning is, in my view, determined by the content. The other eighty percent of the meaning derives from the context.

...perhaps his grandfather...

THE ADOLESCENT AS A PERFORMER Dick Hebdige emphasises in *Hiding in the Light* how the poetic adolescent emerges as a performer. It is all about style. In the first triptych, with Pedriali, Caravaggio and Kassovitz, we got to know the tragic adolescent. That adolescent was based on the "youth is trouble" approach to style. The triptych with Shakespeare, Woolf and Vinterberg extends to the metaphor "youth is fun". The adolescent is the young Lord Byron, whose thoughts, but actions too, are based on a well-considered concept. He is not only the artist, but also the producer. Not only the composer, but also the musician. Not only the designer, but also the model. He adapts his behaviour, his contacts, his clothing, his language and his expenditure to the underlying concept. In this possible world, beauty becomes freestyle poetry.[80]

80 Hebdige pays a great deal of attention to adolescence as an aesthetic phenomenon. Adolescence is now about the secrets of being young, of taste, popular culture, living on the borderline and on the other side. Hebdige describes how this world coincides with a post-modern setting filled with "vital strategies". He mentions a world that is typified by a "more playful, less authorative, less authority-bound tone" (1988, 225). It is a positive systeem of "soft thinking" expressing itself in a creative stream of hypotheses, play-situations and complex forms. It is the world of Lyotard, who constantly focuses on "the opening up of institutional and discursive spaces within which more fluid and plural social and sexual identities may develop" (226).

Words as a Generative Force

Judith Butler's ideas, formulated in *Gender Trouble* (2007), largely coincide with Virginia's Woolf's thinking. Butler defines "performativity" as the way in which someone may and can create his own subject-orientated reality. The formation of that reality is not a matter of finding the original "me", but rather discovering alterity. Only then does the construction of a fictive identity follow, in the artistic process of self-realisation.

Butler talks about identity as a creative and generative process. After which it is important to live the identity, by continually repeating it. It is an iterative process in which the identity can develop into a consistent, congruent and personal style. In that way, identity acquires a narrative logic. Gradual shifts may sometimes emerge, until a particular goal is achieved.

...sex...
something...
slicing...
shape...save...
save...sunken...
cheeks...
strand...
struck...
started...
swung...slain...

THE ADOLESCENT AS A QUEER Woolf's poetic adolescent might be seen as a 'queer', interpreted as a way of thinking outside the box. A positive development towards freedom is taking place. The concept of freedom that underlies *The Beauty of Youth* is open, transgender and constructs an identity as desired.

Woolf describes an adventurous, strange, exotic world, where the poetic adolescent cultivates himself. In terms of the body, Hebdige says: "the body can be decorated, and enhanced like a cherished object" (2007, 31). The body is a reflection of a stylistic interpretation. It is the world of Ziggy Stardust (David Bowie) and Lady Gaga. The decorated body is the manifestation of the awakened young adult.

Lastly

The analysis of *Orlando* has added a new angle to the series of answers to the question about what adolescence is.

Woolf's language is a series of permanently evolving variations: an endless, living figure. Substantively, it also has an organic structure. Man 'germinates', grows and blossoms. He is constantly changing. Woolf's story conforms with a narrative tradition which, assuming art is part of culture, permeates the whole of social life. The narrative tradition that is based on a negative ontology—as described earlier—appears to be the direct opposite.

Caravaggio, with his work, says in effect that Man, so also the adolescent, is a captive. Decline is a fact. The baroque epistemology is a biologically determined 'thinking-in-regression'. Woolf's modernist epistemology and ontology is a psychologically determined 'thinking-in-progression', a message of consolation and hope in a dark world. In this way, poetic beauty becomes the answer to the desolation of the scientific view of the world.

Have aesthetics and life conquered tragedy and death? Does Woolf's Orlando conquer Caravaggio's David? Has free verse offered the solution? The answer is "no!" Appearances are deceptive. In the end, Orlando is also a tragic, mortal figure. In that sense, the answer to the question concerning the adolescent shows that the ostensibly romantic victory of the aesthetic is a Pyrrhic victory, and that tragic death reigns, despite temporary optimism.

Unconscious death cannot be overcome. At most, we achieve a romantic moment of postponement. The connection between tragedy and poetry is ultimately repeated. Aesthetic is a moment of postponement and not victory over death. For a while, the beauty of the adolescent gives the feeling that he or she is invincible. In the end, the adolescent loses out.

It's the time of the season
When love runs high
In this time, give it to me easy
And let me try, with pleasured hands
To take you and the sun to promised lands
To show you everyone
It's the time of the season for loving.

6

Reprise: Vinterberg

The Rhetoric of Life

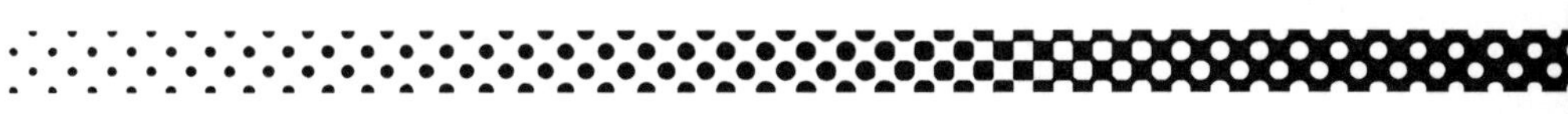

One has already to know (or be able to do) something before one can ask what something is called.
—Ludwig Wittgenstein (2009, 18)

Introduction

I am still standing in front of the second triptych. I take a step to the right and am now in front of the third panel (fig. III.6.1). I read the text of The Zombies from the title song of Thomas Vinterberg's film *Dear Wendy* (2005). With its cult status, it can be considered a twenty-first-century anthropological document. This is, as it were, the sequel to the allegory of the tragic adolescent, in a story that seeks to abolish tragedy: that of the poetic adolescent.

Bearing in mind Peter Brooks' remark that an unequivocal, culturally "sacred" master plot has disappeared and numerous stories have come about in its stead (1992, 6), a new allegorical story emerges here: Vinterberg's *Dear Wendy*. It is a film that creates, rather than represents, reality.

III.6.1 Thomas Vinterberg, *Dear Wendy* (film still), 2005

Dear Wendy is consistent with Woolf's thinking in a stream of consciousness, but takes place in a contemporary setting. Vinterberg sketches a playful picture of a group of boys in a beaten-up old mining town. "It's the time of the season," text from the film soundtrack, forms a good backing. "Something is about to happen…"[81]

Hayden White observes that both fiction and non-fiction can be divided into genres which nurture possible worlds. Also, he considers the romantic genre to be an important variant.

In *Metahistory* (2010, originally published 1973) White argues that this form of "emplotment", with its "poetic sensibility and critical self-consciousness", has been on the rise since the first half of the nineteenth century (Novalis). He is referring to the world of poetry. Orpheus plays his lyre, thus even beguiling Hades. A subcultural framework develops, with the elitist dandy and the idealistic hippie taking over from the sceptical hip-hopper. The attention shifts from biology to psychology.

The romantic approach can be seen as a theory of life, which also featured in the analysis of Woolf. I shall tell the next story of youth against this background, based on three themes:

1. *Biography*: youth as a process of development, conceived as part of a cohesive life flow. Events are not counterposed, but grow from a common source.
2. *Organic connections*: youth as a dream world—a loving, romantic life-world in which elements are organically interconnected.
3. *Epiphany*: youth as a path to the sublime; a living creative force that seeks, in a positive, upward movement, to transcend death, on the way to perfection.

81 The way in which Vinterberg films is a form of visual poetry. His camera assumes a "listening" attitude. Objects, actors and surroundings "utter"; the camera records. The director then plays with the material, just like a writer with his observations. Freud writes in that context in "Creative writers and Day-Dreaming" of 1907: "The creative writer does the same as the child at play. He creates a world of phantasy which he takes very seriously […]" (1959, 143). Vinterberg even swore a 'vow of chastity' at Dogma 95 which amounted to him, as the subject, allowing the object to speak, instead of imposing his own opinion.

THE CONTEMPORARY ADOLESCENT This new adolescent is a poetic figure. The tragic heroes disappear. We are ushered into René Boomkens' postmodern city. He describes it as an anti-mythological cultural landscape. Survival is not easy. The city presents a tough reality in which the only attainable perspective is about less, not more.[82]

The Plot

In this story we see the world as we know it from newspapers, magazines and our own experiences. It is ostensibly a quiet world that explodes, slowly but surely.

The décor is a desolate American mining town. Richard lives there with his father and their housekeeper, Clarabelle. His father works in the mine. Richard is not suited to be a miner, he works in a shop. Clarabelle is the only one who gives him affection.

On the day Richard encounters Wendy, something changes in these dreary, lonely surroundings. Wendy is a small, girl's gun, which he originally bought as a birthday present for Sebastian, Clarabelle's grandson. Yet Richard decides to give Sebastian a book: Oscar Wilde's *The Picture of Dorian Gray*, though the last twenty pages are missing.

From then on, Richard and "his" Wendy are inseparable. At night he goes with Stevie, who also owns a gun, to practise shooting in a mineshaft. The two decide to involve all the town's losers in their conspiracy. They form a club: The Dandies, a non-violent gang. The group even has a manifesto based on pacifism.

One day Sebastian appears in the mineshaft. He is familiar with real life and the harsh reality of guns. His relationship

82 Boomkens carries out extensive research into the globalised and urbanised world in which we live. In his anthropology of the city, chaos reigns, but that chaos also takes on an unusual character which Boomkens describes in *De nieuwe wanorde: Globalisering en het einde van de maakbare samenleving* as "everyday metaphysics" (2006, 296). In this world, revolution and renewal are no longer options. Boomkens in fact defends the importance of continuity—continuism—with which the awareness of identity, in all openness and variability, can be linked continuously with the surrounding queerness, chaos and disarray. Continuism is a living principle and is consistent with the worlds of Shakespeare, Woolf and Vinterberg.

with Richard resembles that between Cain and Abel. A climate of polarisation and recklessness develops. Recklessly, The Dandies decide to deploy their weapons to help Clarabelle overcome her fear of walking in the street. This results in an unintentional confrontation with the police in which, one by one, The Dandies die.

THE ADOLESCENT AS A DANDY The story of *Youth and Beauty* tells of the struggle to escape the captivity, the monotony of life. It is a quest for freedom—not by confronting reality as in *La Haine*, but by creating an alternative reality. In this, the adolescent emerges as a dandy.[83]

83 In *Reading for the Plot: Design and Intentions in Narrative* (1992, originally published 1984), Peter Brooks explains how a story's plot grips the reader. "Plotting", he says, is "the activity of shaping"; it is "the dynamic aspect of narrative"; it is what "makes us read forward," "the unfolding of the narrative". It is "the promise of progress towards meaning" (1984, *xiii*).

A New Flow of Words

Guy Debord criticised in *Society of the Spectacle* (1983, originally published 1967) the precarious world in which young people have to find their way. He describes everyday reality as a Brechtian world in which Man has become alienated from himself. The world is reduced to spectacle and show, and we are mere spectators. Economy and culture are an extension of each other. Quantity is what counts. Quality is meaningless. Everything is now an economic commodity. The beauty of art is no longer the prerogative. The economic value it represents is what matters. Consumptive patterns prevail. Man has become a production factor. He is no longer a live figure. He may not be different. Individual actions are undesirable. Man has become a cog in a machine.[84]

84 Debord was one of the founders of situationism. He wanted to combine poetry and music in the urban landscape. Debord's three elements (urban landscape, poetry and music) are also found in *Dear Wendy*. Vinterberg and Debord are both critical of society. The Dandies stand for what Debord describes: the convergence of theoretical criticism, social practice and poetic knowledge.

It's the time of the season...

Plot Points and Other References

Vinterberg describes defiant youth. "With pleasured hands" they want to change the sleepy town into a dream world. The adolescent wakes up and pursues the discovery of the gun and the subsequent conspiracy. Here, the gun is a surrogate ego. The love between the members of the club and the discovery of a sublimated self trigger a stream of developments.

The Dandies go in search of the promised land. Initially it bears a vague resemblance to a hidden world. During the day, the Dandies live their usual lives, but in their subterranean temple, in the twilight zone, they show their true selves. For instance, they turn up in hip clothes. The abandoned mineshaft forms a world of romantic isolation, a kind of dream. It is a world where love and ideals can exist.

Henri Lefebvre sketches a world that can serve as a model for *Dear Wendy*. In his three-volume work *Critique of Everyday Life* (1947–81), he describes how creative force can be the answer to the static world of matter and form.

According to Lefebvre, poetry serves to arouse the hidden desire for freedom. Like Debord, he advocates a life of practical poetry. The city should be an "aesthetic polis" (Sanders 1989, 70), with its own language: that of the lettrists, an aesthetic movement that believes that every thought can be reduced to a letter (a sign). The lettrists are opposed to the coercive, semantic grip of the word. Each letter represents its own reality.[85]

Lefebvre's defiant poetry can already be detected in Rimbaud's life and work. He creates an insidiously spreading process in which dying does not hinder life, but serves it. Change is the immanent nature. Standstill comes from outside. That view can also be found in the work of Deleuze.[86]

85 René Sanders' *Beweging tegen de schijn: De situationisten, een avant-garde* (1989) describes the spread of a movement that does not pursue innovation in art, but its abolition, the creation of space for a revolutionary political changeover paving the way for a free and independent aesthetic culture. Sanders sketches the path of existentialism, by way of situationism to postmodernism (14). He underlines the work of Lefebvre, who—in preparation for situationism—unites existence philosophy and social criticism. He also draws attention to the connection between the situationists and postmodern philosophers like Deleuze, Guattari, Lyotard and Baudrillard.

86 Lefebvre's practical poetry also returns in the process of ABL. In part 2, Lefebvre quotes from his *Critique of Everyday Life* a comment by Picasso: "First of all I find something, then I start to search for it" (2008, 143). This statement gives an idea of the dialectic character of thinking/learning. Excessive attention to logic makes thinking inflexible, which conflicts with its essence. An excess of logic "presupposes the object without knowing it." It formalises, quantifies and ignores the subjective character. Indexical, contiguous thinking generates the unexpected. It is a form of thinking that touches on poetry.

...with
pleasured
hands...
to promised
lands...

Pictures as Carriers of the Text

The text of the soundtrack revolves around the word "loving". Even killing is seen as a way of making love. It is a form of pacifism with clear, sexual allusions. However, in this story there is an absolute ban on overstepping the mystical boundary: "the regulations are that the most important thing for a Dandy is never to show off his partner, whatever the provocation. We carry them as moral supports. And that's the most important thing. They may be carried, but never brandished. That would be the worst thing of all."

The sexually inspired taboo creates tension. Contravention of the law is inevitable. The postponed moment of wish fulfilment is the moment of downfall. The activation of the guns marks the end. The phallic allusion is unequivocal. The bullets penetrate the Dandies when confrontation with the police transpires, as if this were a sexual act.

Vinterberg sketches the moment of death as a moment of ultimate gratification. The sublimated spirit is released from an irksome body. Death is a moment of deliverance.

It's the time of the season for loving...

Lastly

So much for the second triptych. So far I have engaged in a dialogue with text and image: the museum function (Caravaggio), the library function (Woolf), the cinema function (Ray) and the advanced education function, collaborate—entirely in keeping with the views of Damisch, Bal and Van Alphen, who see the visual arts, literature and film as relevant forms of thinking.

As I was reading, I discovered Woolfian thinking in this second triptych—the story of eternal life, Elysium. Woolf thinks romantically, with beauty forming an important element.

It is the world of creation, poetry, the striving for perfection, harmony and life. Death would appear to have been conquered in a "rhetoric of life".

The two side panels of Shakespeare and Vinterberg express a similar idea. Rosalind marries her beloved Orlando in the end, and Richard experiences the moment of dying as sexual gratification. However, from the very start, there are also cracks in the triptych. The romantic spell is broken.

In the third triptych we see how tragedy surfaces again. It would seem possible for the poetic-romantic world to continue its existence in isolation. It is a reality that is unable to resist the intersubjective, tragic-ironic force of relativisation.

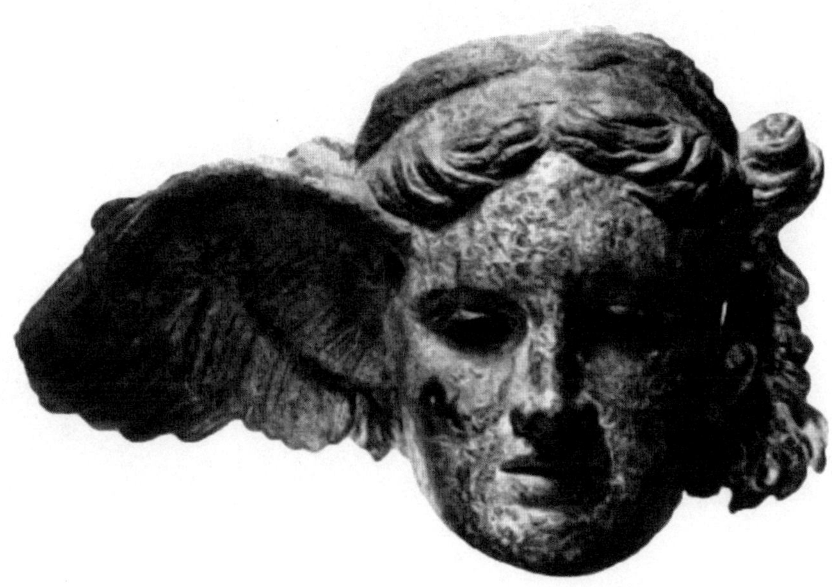

III.6.2 Bronze head of Hypnos found near Civitella d'Arno, Italy, first or second century AD

IV

The Game of Youth

Concerning Film

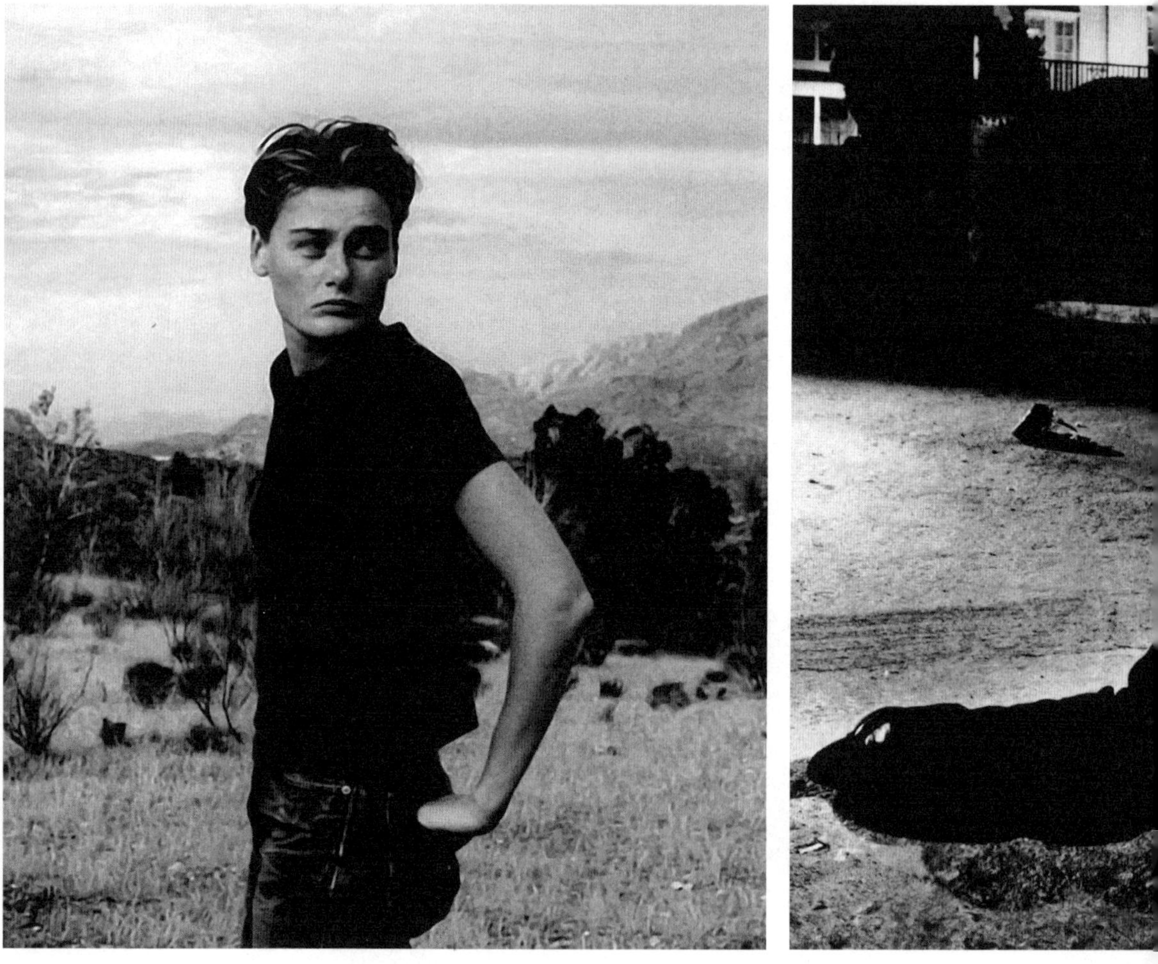

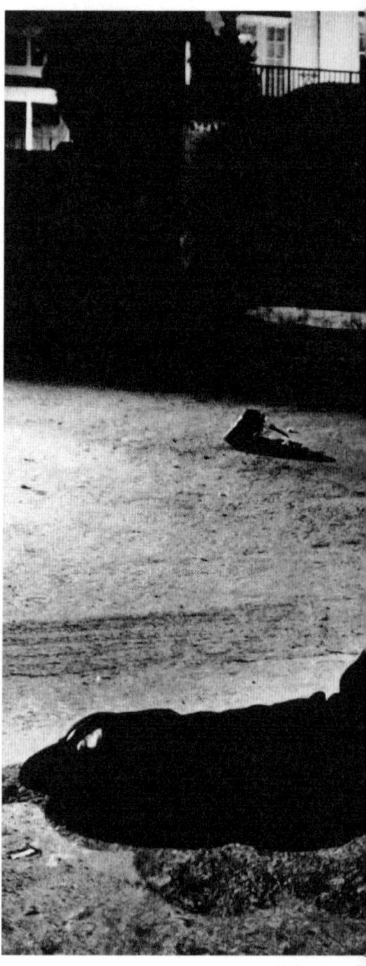

IV.1.1 Triptych: Hazekamp—Ray—Jarmusch

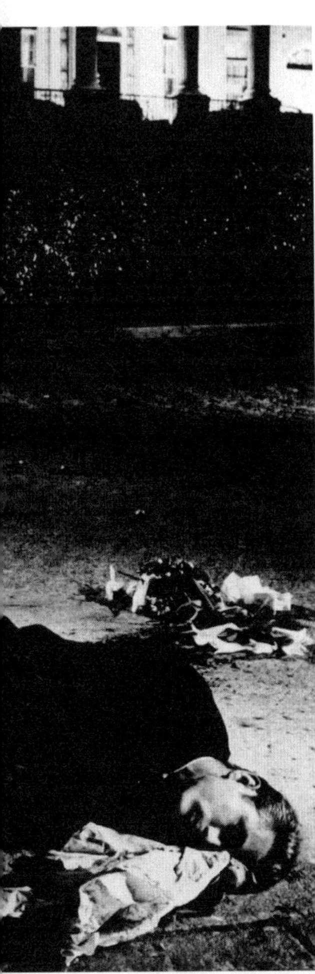

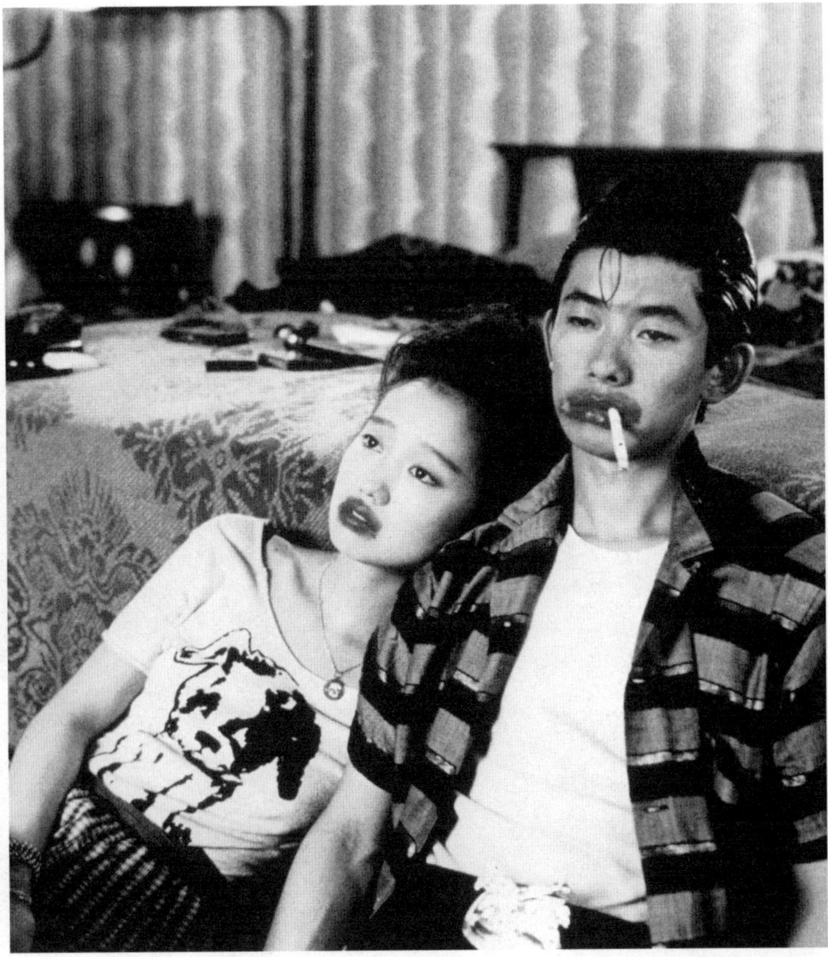

Thinking in dialogues

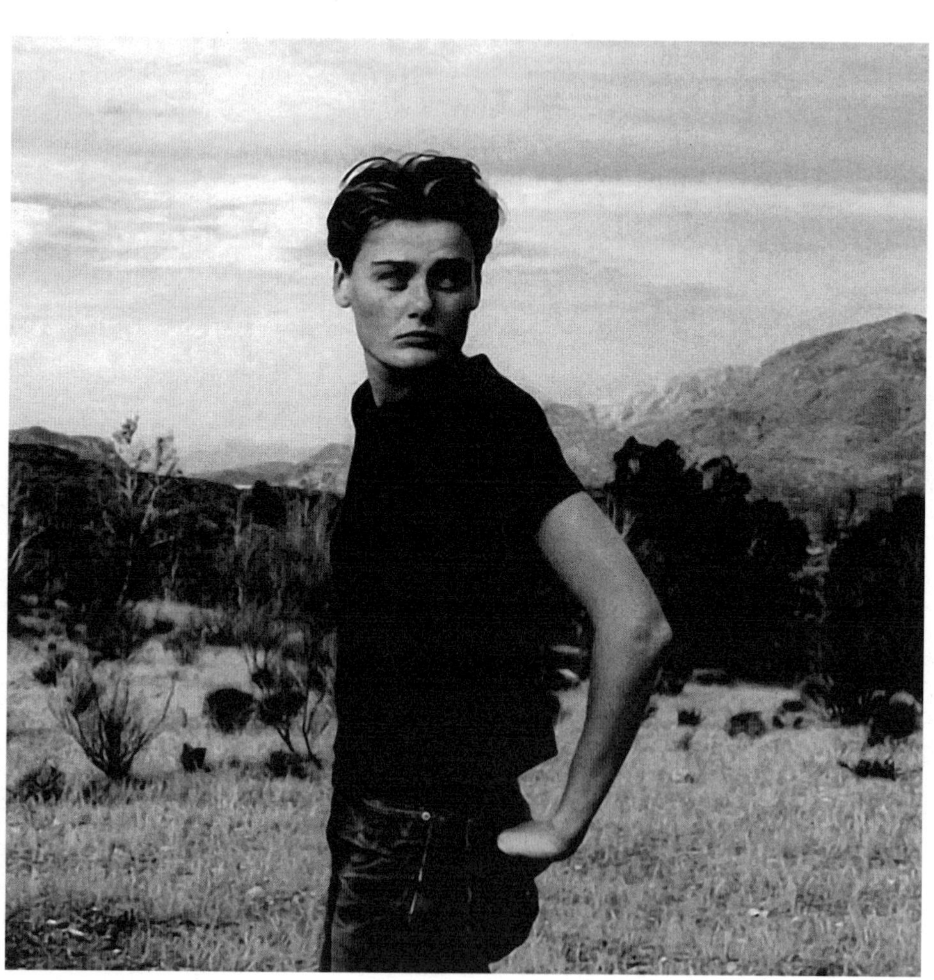

1

Exposition: Risk Hazekamp

Introduction

Meanwhile, the process of ABL has produced two encounters with art works as sources of knowledge. The first triptych had a painting at its centre, the second a fragment of literary text. The third triptych, with which we now enter into a dialogue, has a film fragment at its centre.

This third triptych is called *The Game of Youth*. All parts of the Art-Based Learning process are addressed: ABL as a solitary process, as a dialogical process and now also as a fictive and creative process.

During this study I have, therefore, always aimed at revealing the story of the adolescent as three triptychs. Ideally, the study could serve as a catalogue for a real-life exhibition of the three triptychs. A short résumé:

Triptych I: *Adolescence and the rhetoric of death.* The structure is tragic. Caravaggio's *chiaroscuro* emphasises the form. David is the tragic hero, a protagonist in the world of the object. The metaphors used: Eros, Chronos and Thanatos. The rhetoric of death was already in evidence in

IV.1.2 Risk Hazekamp, *Jack off Jimmy*, 2001

ancient Greece and has lasted until the present.

Triptych 2: *Adolescence and the rhetoric of life.* The structure is poetic, with Woolf's stream of consciousness as the main thought form and Orlando as the aesthetic hero. We enter the world of the subject. The foremost metaphors: Hypnos, Morpheus and Phantasos. The rhetoric of life is a narrative style that peaked in Modernism. We see how, within this approach, an attempt is made to overturn the rhetoric of death—ultimately without success.

Triptych 3: We already anticipate what is to come: *Adolescence and the rhetoric of play.* The structure is ironic. We are entering the post-modern world. After Caravaggio's hero and Woolf's poet, we now encounter a defiant clown. Can he defeat the dreaded death? This third triptych consists of three images, proceeding from present to past.

The first image in the left-hand panel shows a recent picture of the adolescent. *Jack off Jimmy* is by the photographer, Risk Hazekamp. It is an allusion to a film with James Dean, who will return in the centrepiece—that centre panel shows the opening shot from *Rebel Without a Cause* (1955) by Nicholas Ray, with James Dean as Jim Stark. The right-hand panel is a pivotal image from *Mystery Train* by Jim Jarmusch (fig. IV.1.1).

The line of thought I now pursue starts with a photo by Risk Hazekamp (fig. IV.1.2). Why did I choose a photographer when the centrepiece of this triptych relates to a film? The answer is simple: a film consists of photos (stills). So Hazekamp's photos fit into a cinematographic approach to reality. Art manifests itself as a form of thinking that takes place along three lines:

1. *Complexity*. A discontinuous world without essence emerges. A carnivalesque world reveals itself in complex dialogues.
2. *Dialogue*. The adolescent is characterised by the quest for a language of his own and nominalist Babel-like confusion. According to Bakhtin, this can all be found in Fyodor Dostoyevsky's work.
3. *Humour*. The characters humorously comment time and again on the world around them. Implicit stylistic features and reversals with subtle satire. A light, casual answer to the gloomy story of the tragic adolescent and the grandiloquent story of the poetic adolescent. Stories of which parents—those who live in memories—and teachers—those who live in education—are scarcely aware. The world as a private and comical scene, to which one's contemporaries are mainly the ones who know the access code.

THE COMPLEX ADOLESCENT The playful complexity of youth appears. It is the adolescent who lives partly in an as yet unknown future. He fits in a world ranging from David Bowie to Tracey Emin. Films go beyond traditional cinematographic thinking. The approach is more consistent with eclectic, new, moving, ever-editable, digital cinematographic thinking. The new way of thinking is based on fragmentation and complexity. The result is a radical form of freedom and autonomy.

Photography as Cinematography of Interruptions

DISCONTINUITY Risk Hazekamp's intriguing photos of young people portray the next step in the contingent world of the adolescent. I have chosen *Jack off Jimmy* (2001), a rewrite of the picture of James Dean in his last film *Giant*. These photos are from the series in which Hazekamp presents herself as an androgynous James Dean. The series put her on the map as one of the Netherlands' most promising photographers.

What does the photo tell? The story of *Jack off Jimmy* starts with the breathtaking scenery of the desert, the mountains, the steppe-like vegetation. In the middle of the photo we see a young man. If you look more closely, you see it is a young woman. She has her hands in her back pockets, has short hair and is wearing jeans.

Hazekamp's young woman plays with the audience. The photo does not explain. There is emptiness. The spectator does not know why the woman is standing precisely there and in that way. Is she one of the sorcerers out of the hell of Dante's *Divina Commedia* whose faces are back to front, because they are not looking to the future, but to the past? What does she see? Hazekamp queries the context without actually specifying it.

The contextual void with which we are repeatedly confronted occasions discontinuity. The highly characteristic, ongoing series of images of serial thinking (as found in Woolf) ceases. For a moment there is nothing. The spectator must take up the thread himself. The reader is challenged to continue where the image finishes. Accordingly, Hazekamp immediately appeals to your imagination. You are invited to create a picture of your own. In addition, you realise that every form of thinking is based on fiction.

In this way, Hazekamp develops a cinematographic photography of interruptions. Every photo is a film fragment. Every photo is like a paragraph. The image stops and freezes. Tension mounts. The spectator wants to go on, but gets no more answers. The photo does not reach further than a still. The spectator has to complete the film himself. The world of technology becomes a world of fantasy.

Hazekamp's world is one of ontological uncertainty. It is one where tragedy and aesthetics are punctured. Doubt and questions remain. Every question occasions a dialogue within a varying context, in which nothing remains what it was and every discourse is followed by a new discourse. We see a world where reality makes way for fictiveness.

This world full of doubt creates space for mild humour and play. Irony and humour can come about when enchantment is shattered (Rorty 2007, 167). Humour can have a poetic character. Hazekamp's work is an example of such humour.

She is, wrongly, identified with Cindy Sherman. Sherman tends far more towards negative satire. She enters the third space callously. Her *Clowns,* although usually older, have a physically deadly touch. In the same portrait the attempt to abolish tragedy by way of aesthetics declares itself, followed by the attempt to abolish aesthetics. This is a far cry from Hazekamp's mild irony.

Sherman's world is a tragic, negative variant of irony: satire. The well-considered dark background with its romantic lighting accentuates that style. You could consider Sherman as a twenty-first-century Caravaggio. The *chiaroscuro,* the baroque aspect—not hopeful, but dead—is omnipresent.

THE HUMOUR OF THE ADOLESCENT The adolescent with humour can only come about in an open setting. There, poetry and humour are not far removed from each other. Both are complex processes, by their very nature. Both provide an answer to the tragedy of existence. However, poetry is essentially serious and monological. Humour is funny and communicative. Humour comes about in an imaginary—or not—linguistic exercise, with the individual disengaging from himself. Humour is an unpredictable phenomenon that arises from interaction in an open space. The humorous youth is characterised by a dual involvement: on the one had, the affiliation with the object, but, on the other hand, a certain distance as the result of involvement with something else.

The Surroundings as the Protagonist

SURROUNDINGS Hazekamp's representation "speaks" in a time and space where the character is in fact subservient to the surroundings (fig. IV.1.3). The hills, the stalks and the grass speak their own language. It is a world of invisible beings. Narcissus, Sisyphus and Prometheus, three mythological characters that already reach farther than the art work itself, appear in this complex universe.

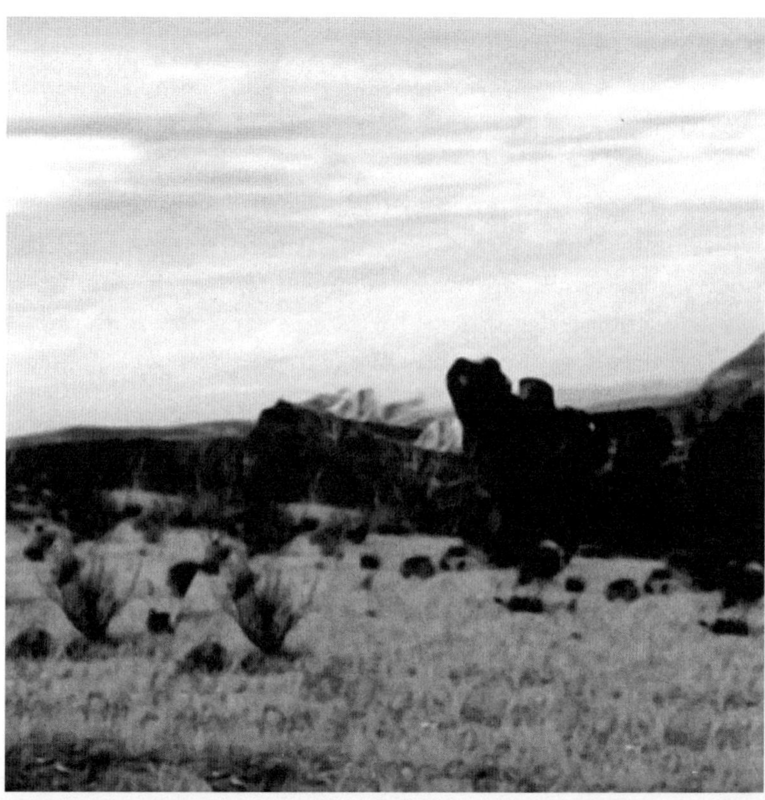

IV.1.3 Risk Hazekamp, *Jack off Jimmy* (detail), 2001

Narcissus stands in the landscape, a solitary figure. He is self-absorbed. There is no refuge whatsoever in the surroundings; no possibility of contact. This narcissistic world is not exactly a world of confusion, but of fixation. It is a form of abandonment, a prison without bars.

Then there is Sisyphus, the wanderer: he is condemned to a pointless task and is barely in contact with his surroundings. You wonder how long this state can last. Is there any development? Will this absurd reality ever end? The absurdity of existence is primarily conveyed in fixation. Photography is a good medium for that. The apparent reality is fixed. Whenever you look, it is the same. No development takes place.

For the third mythological metaphor we have Prometheus, the activist: he is entangled in a performative action within a varying context. It is a positive action, with which the character gives his own meaning to his existence, within the context that is neither the author's nor the spectator's, but one forming an intersubjective third space, where meaning is constantly changing, depending on the perspective.

Of course, these three mythological characters do not automatically come to mind. I try to understand more about Hazekamp's work by placing it in a possible world. I allow A-thinking to prevail: association and reason are at odds with each other.

I recall Albert Camus' work. His early work reflects a harsh, masculine world of anti-heroes, sketching a highly tragic world view. However, there is some development. Camus punctures his own cynicism. With *The Rebel* (1951), his later, post-war work, occupying an important place. Caligula changes into Sisyphus, who in turn changes in Prometheus.

87 The game with reality is also found in Camus' world. Dostoyevsky gives the basis for the late-modern absurd hero, who is encountered in films of the second half of the 1950s. The English translation of Camus' *L'Homme révolté* is actually *Rebel: An Essay on Man in Revolt.* The absurd hero is a paradoxical figure. He does not sink into tragic futility and does not enter a dreamy aesthetic illusion. The absurd hero recognises the complexity of life: he accepts the tragedy of life without meaning. Yet he succeeds in living through love, to make revolt and art the source of his actions.

The theme of Pandora's box hangs above all this—a carnivalesque future, an incomplete time on the dividing line between tragic and comic. The tragedy is the nightmare of an unchanging past. Poetry turns tragedy into the dream of the sublimated present. However, the world we are now living in is a heterogeneous panorama, with a big, but also hopeful question mark.

The world of irony, a world of words, a world of possibilities, a game between reality and fiction, now has the floor. Text and context are in conversation with each other. We find ourselves in a world of constant reversals which appeals to our creativity and which can still assume any form. Comedy can cancel tragedy.[87]

THE DIALOGIC ADOLESCENT The ironic figure proves to be a dialogic adolescent. He keeps his options open and expresses his doubt. Accordingly, the dialogic adolescent represents an important new viewpoint. He is positioned between two extremes. He represents incompleteness and so has something unsatisfactory. The reverse of doubt is hope. Once aesthetic proves to be based on illusion, the adolescent no longer makes the story of youth and death absolute, but relative.

The way in which this adolescent communicates also commands our attention. He is in a permanent process of reversal. Consequently, the adult's relationship with him does not get any easier. He often does not say what he thinks and by no means always means what he says. Satire is characterised by darkness at the end of the tunnel. Yet irony perceives light at the end of the tunnel. The ironic position assumes that there is development, and that will increase in the dialogue with the reality of freedom and autonomy of the adolescent.

The adolescent has changed from a monological into a fundamentally dialectic being. He questions, qualifies, comments and communicates, the aim being to understand his reality. Fact and fiction have the same status in this process. The adolescent simultaneously conducts a dialogue with himself, with the text and with the other. He can be both a man and a woman. He can describe himself or the other. Every point of view tells something else. The adolescent lives in an unfinished time. He remains open, not coercive in his structure and so amenable to change.

Erich Auerbach describes in *Mimesis: The Representation of Reality in Western Literature* (2003, originally published 1953) how literature interprets reality. In the last chapter, relating to Virginia Woolf's *To the Lighthouse,* he describes a process which he characterises in terms of a "multiple consciousness" (549). This world of reflections approaches Winnicott's and Bollas' third space. It is a place where every form of fixation is converted into its opposite. Here, the adolescent appears as a tragi-comic figure.[88]

88 Auerbach describes a process which greatly resembles the method of Art-Based Learning. In his introduction to *Mimesis*, Edward Saïd characterises Auerbach's approach as follows: Auerbach "explicitly rejects a rigid scheme" (in Auerbach 2003, xxxi) and "always comes back to the text" (xxii). Auerbach allows the work to speak, but at the same time pursues his own thoughts.

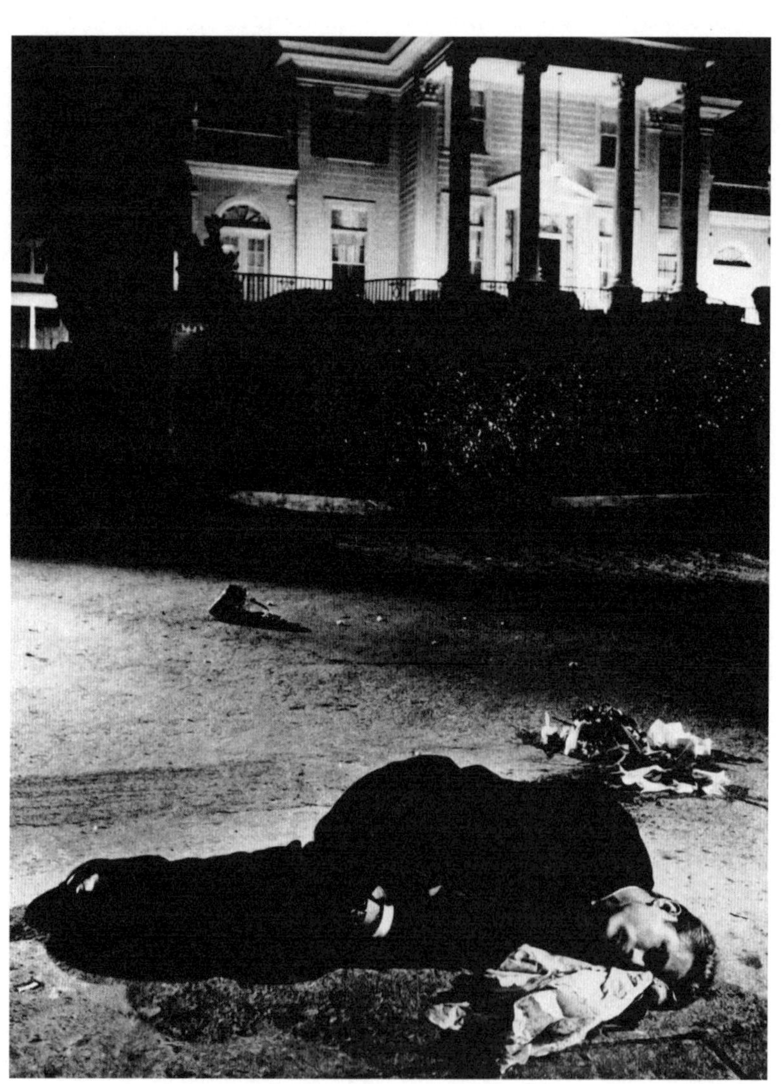

2

Continuing Impact: Nicholas Ray

Introduction

After the side panel, it is time to probe the topic of this triptych, *The Game of Youth*. Nicholas Ray's cinematographic thinking in the centre panel provides an avenue. It is a form of thinking that came about in the late-modern period, one of different perspectives, dialogues and processes of intersubjective identity formation. As in the cases of Caravaggio and Woolf, Ray is not a random choice. The three artists belong in a specific spectrum of relevant thinkers.

With Ray, we encounter a story that further refines our knowledge of youth. I shall concentrate on the starting fragment, for the same reasons I also discussed regarding Woolf's work. What does the teen idol James Dean—as the character Jim Stark—tell about adolescence?

In the opening scene we meet a confused young man (fig. IV.2.1). He is lying on the ground, presumably drunk. "Plain drunkenness", as a policemen remarks later at the police station. The boy is playing with a wind-up toy. The camera features him in full view. The character does not

IV.2.1 Nicholas Ray, *Rebel Without a Cause* (film still), 1955 look at you. For me, the adolescent rapidly evolves to a following level: from hero to poet to what Bakhtin calls a "tragic clown".[89]

89 The opening shot of *Rebel Without a Cause* has been frequently and widely discussed. The whole film is summed up in one image. According to Timothy Jacobs, the film is about "youth's search for truth" (1992, 43). Jacobs says about this opening scene: "Jim Stark lies drunk on the street, in foetal position. Note the toy monkey, which shortly before, he had protectively covered with an old newspaper. James Dean was skilful at improvising scenes like this" (37).

The film opens on a night at Easter. Jim Stark has moved to Los Angeles with his parents. On that very first evening he lands in the police station. A girl—Judith—who has run away from home, is sitting there, and Plato, a scared boy.

Next day Jim goes to school. There is a lesson in the planetarium. A film is shown about the cosmos that makes it clear how small and unimportant we all are compared with the vast universe. Jim tries to make contact, demonstratively, with his fellow pupils, but is jeered at. Outdoors, it escalates into a knife fight between Buzz, the leader of the group, and Jim. Jim wins, but is challenged to a chicken run.

Jim tries to talk to his father, but he does not really react, so that evening Jim goes to the cliff where the race is to be held. Judith and Plato are there too. When the race starts, the cars tear towards the cliff. The first to jump out is "chicken". However, Buzz gets caught in the his car door and plunges into the precipice.

Judith, Jim and later on Plato too, flee to an abandoned house. Buzz's gang track them down. When Jim and Judith creep away together, Plato feels he has been left in the lurch by the couple of lovers, and, with his gun, runs away to the planetarium—after having shot one of Buzz's friends in panic. When the police arrive, they surround the planetarium.
Jim manages to persuade Plato to give himself up, but only after he has removed the bullets from the gun on the sly.
In the end, Plato emerges, threateningly waving the (empty) gun, and is shot dead by the police.

Jim has removed his mask and bends over the body of Plato, who was more like a younger brother to him than a friend. Jim's father, who initially thinks his son is dead, suddenly realises how often he has been absent. He supports his son and makes it clear he will be there for him from then on.[90]

THE MULTICOLOURED ADOLESCENT Ray's multicoloured adolescent is made up of fragments. This confronts us with a form of thinking in passages. This adolescent is a small part of the picture of the adolescent as a whole; he has no definitive form. Judith, Plato, Buzz and Jim constitute small stories, each portraying an aspect of the adolescent. The promethean adolescent is without essence. His strength lies in the acceptance that he transforms with every fragment, in time and space. And so he is fundamentally historical.

The various perspectives can be reproduced, by means of techniques from novels—monologues, dialogues and descriptions. Woolf seeks to eliminate the tragedy of adolescence. Ray tries not to eliminate the introvert, sublimated *monologue intérieur.* Like Dostoyevsky he presents the adolescent as an open, social phenomenon.

The adolescent is the reflection of an involvement with the world of the multiform, carnivalesque, profane, commonplace. With every individual perspective, new specific answers emerge. The actual force of the film is not monological, but dialogical thinking: the permanent interaction between the tragic, the poetic and the comic, from which—precisely in what is *not* said—the final picture comes about.

Films, like novels, comprise a jumble of perspectives that intercommunicate. There is no all-embracing perspective. Nothing is certain. The world of irony is characterised by a combination of fundamental, ontological doubt, engagement, small stories and hope.

90 The fact that *Rebel Without a Cause* takes place at Easter sparks an association with Dante's *Divina Commedia*. After all, Dante's journey through hell, purgatory and paradise took place round Easter. The timing and the structure of the text relate directly to Jesus' Passion. It is the story of the protagonist's judgement, suffering and redemption. This structure is actually found quite often in films of the 1950s: think of Elia Kazan's *On the Waterfront* (1954) and Alfred Hitchcock's *I Confess* (1953).

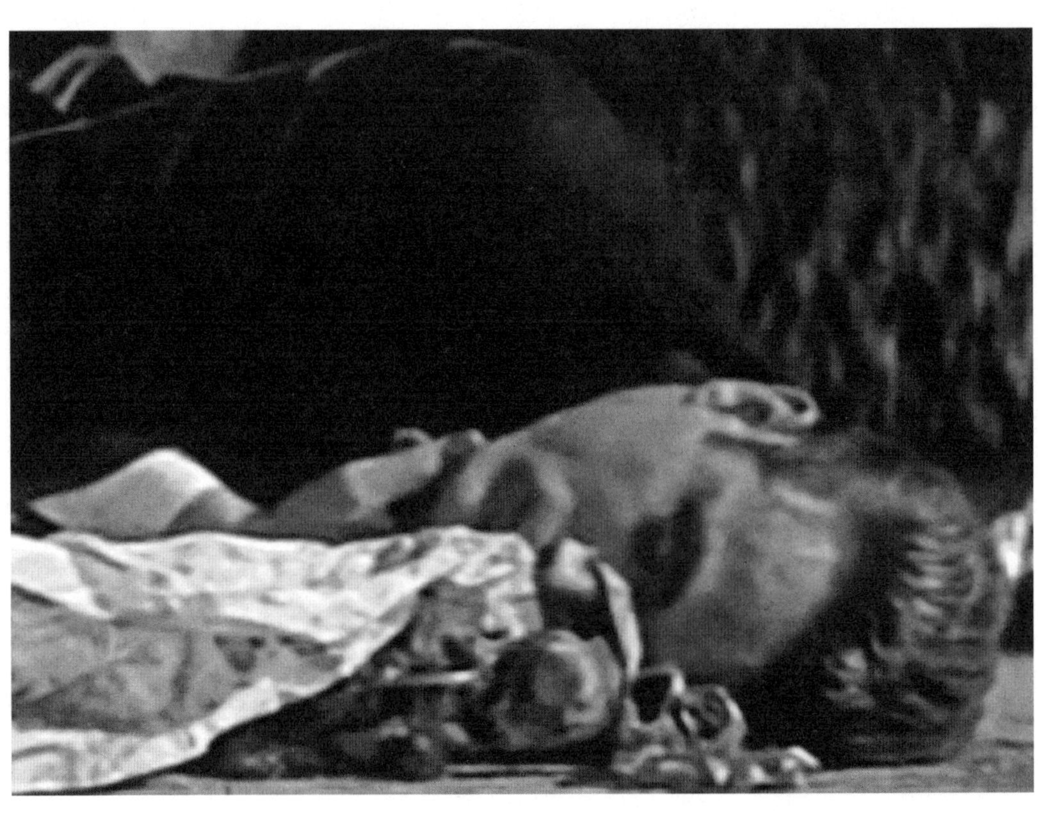

3

Ray: Narcissus

The Loneliness of Youth

A Game with Paradoxical Images

Jim Stark is lying on the ground. If the eye of the camera works like a mirror, he speaks the language of Narcissus. Both character and actor reveal their vulnerability. Are we looking at self-pity or despair? At all events, Jim is connected with one of the other characters, who is dealt with extensively later on, and is nicknamed Plato.

Plato, who is not visible in the opening shot, resounds everywhere: "Nobody can help me", in his own words. He is completely caught up in himself, an enlargement of a facet of Jim Stark. Plato demonstrates fatal powerlessness. He is the tragic all-time low, the illusion of an illusion. However, doubt, the hallmark of irony, now sets thinking in motion again. That motion is not based on the repetitive stationariness that was addressed with Hazekamp's photo. Plato represents, from a different viewpoint, a new beginning.

Nicholas Ray continues to challenge you to keep looking further. After the death, he opens a path to renewal. Plato's death at the end of the film symbolises in Jim Stark's inner

IV.3.1 Nicholas Ray, *Rebel Without a Cause* (detail of film still), 1955

world the death of the old, but also the hope of a new beginning.

Depending on which perspective you choose, the opening shot can be termed paradoxical. The protagonist speaks, lying on the ground. He could well be hanging over a pool of water, as in the classical depiction of Narcissus. He is at the centre of the picture, is looking down, at the toy that is smaller than he is (fig. IV.3.1). What can he see? I cannot look into Jim Stark's mind. Yet his half-illuminated face speaks volumes. The diagonal line tells the tragic story of a forsaken young man.

It is a different picture if we add the director, as the narrating party, to the story. The primary dialogue changes direction. Jim Stark and the toy disappear into the background. Nicholas Ray and James Dean become interlocutors.

The dialogue with the context suddenly means that the protagonist is no longer focused solely on the other as apparent in the toy. He turns the attention to himself. The spell is broken. The game begins. Jim Stark becomes James Dean. James Dean says: "Am I doing it right? Am I lying in the right place?" Again, the subtitle now becomes: "Who is speaking?"

The worlds of *East of Eden* (1955), *Rebel Without a Cause* (1955) and *Giant* (1956) tie in with Sigmund Freud's "On Narcissism: An Introduction" (1985, originally published 1914). Freud describes how the libido and vitality of the narcissist are geared primarily to the ego. He is far less interested in the object of love. His love circles round what he sees, what occupies him and what he cannot let go.

Dick Poutain and David Robins indicate that we are in a world where the protagonist "does not gaze at others, but appears to others; [he] does not gaze but wishes to be gazed at."

Freud goes further into the tragedy of narcissism by drawing attention to its erotic, but also aggressive character. The adolescent is a tragic figure. He is abandoned and experiences pain. This suffering can also lead to destructive and self-destructive behaviour. The despair of the narcissist contains an element of threat and is constantly on the verge of erupting.

However, narcissism also has an ironic aspect, because tragedy continuously turns into the opposite. At one time, the narcissistic adolescent is in an abyss, in the world of the trivial. At another time, he believes he is in the world of the gods and of the sublime. The ironic world is a contingent world in which nothing is fixed. We even find this in the painting of Narcissus (1600) attributed in 1645 to Caravaggio. There is a tragic element, but at the same time a comic antipode.[91]

91 The lacanian psychoanalyst Dylan Evans describes in *An Introductory Dictionary of Lacanian Psychoanalysis* (1996) how Lacan, in *Remarks on Psychic Causality* (1946), emphasises the dualistic nature of narcissism. He sees narcissism as an effective and destructive phenomenon. The child achieves self-awareness by way of his mirror image. The erotic aspect is a consequence of the attraction of the mirror image in the mirror stage. The aggressive aspect stems from the conflict between the wholeness of the mirror image and the fragmented nature of the subject (Evans 1996, 120). The mirror image in the mirror stage is not, by definition, what the child sees in a mirror. Another person can also serve as a mirror. The first images can form on that basis, images that ultimately lead to an autonomous identity within the symbolic order.

Alienation through Sounds

Ray reinforces the idea of the paradoxical adolescent with a series of alienating sounds. He plays a chaotic, jazzy recording, with Miles Davis' *Birth of the Cool* (1950) in mind (fig. IV.3.2). The sounds tend to raise questions rather than answer them. The questions produce desperate thoughts. They go very well with Jim Stark's appearance. He is silent. He is in a void. He looks at the object in the foreground and allows his thoughts to wander freely.

The film viewer identifies with the camera and can merely guess at the protagonist's thoughts. The camera is a researcher. The facial expression prompts us, but there is no certainty. The inaccessible leading character, with furrowed brow and open mouth, keeps us in suspense. He speaks in riddles. He might well be thinking something entirely different than he implies. Is he wearing a mask? Is this misleading? Or am I, the spectator, doing him an injustice with this association?

It helps if we think of François Rabelais' comical world. In this possible world, a conflicting, grotesque, cacophony of sounds prevails, as Mikhail Bakhtin points out in *Rabelais and his World* (1984). Rabelais' stories present a masquerade filled with unexpected events. What's more, he is standing with one foot in the coarse Middle Ages and the other in the stylised Renaissance, thus crossing two worlds: that of 'lowbrow' and that of 'highbrow' culture.

Rabelais is a libertarian border-crosser, and that is precisely what makes him special. He belongs on the one hand to the cultivated world—that thin veneer that came about in the Renaissance and, as his language reveals, intrigues him. On the other hand, he belongs in the world below that, where the giants Gargantua and his son Pantagruel belong. This is a world filled with lust, sexual urges and violence. Rabelais' humour keeps the two worlds intact, not giving preference to either. The novel is a third space. There, the different

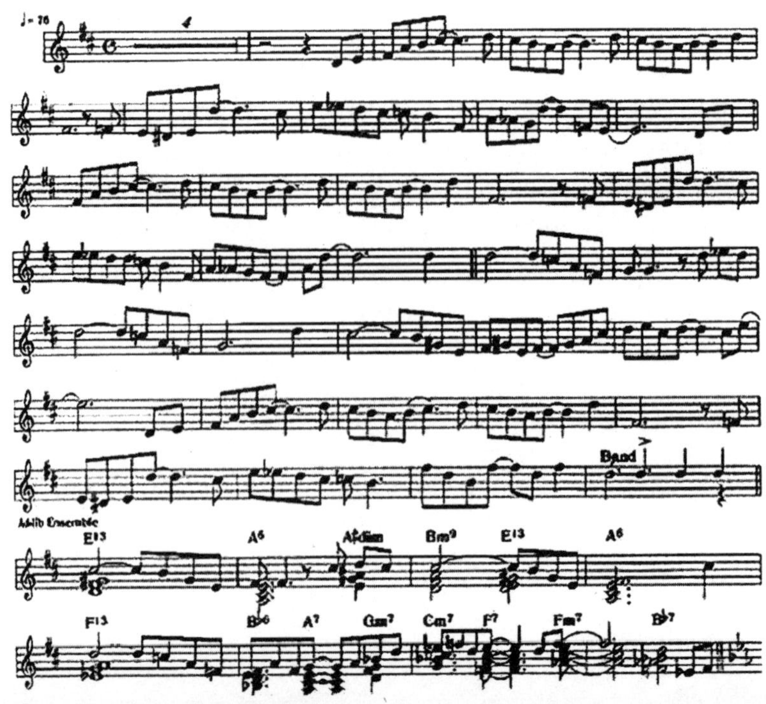

IV.3.2 Jazz in musical notation

worlds are involved in a dialogue. The novel presents so much intertextual space that every word can have the opposite meaning. It reveals the cruel, yet fervently impassioned game of nature. It reveals the high-minded, as well as the grandiloquent being.

Rabelais' humour helps us to appreciate the film director's point of view. Is this the winning answer (for now), after the tragedy and poetry of existence? Is this what Milan Kundera, an admirer of Rabelais, meant with *The Unbearable Lightness of Being* (1983)? Is this the ability to love, from a certain distance, the complex world around us, in its perfect imperfection? Is this the love of and solidarity with the endearing phenomenon "Man", as expressed by Rorty?[92]

THE CONFUSED ADOLESCENT The Ray-dian adolescent is confused. The film director and the novelist show us an overpowering reality, in which it is not always easy to fend for oneself. The ironist is "cool" and, despite despair, has found a way to relate to reality. Irony, to an amazing extent, is set against a backdrop of the big city, as a metaphor for a complex world in which the individual is trying to find his place. The reality of Tokyo and Los Angeles shows that every from of generalisation is ridiculously superfluous. The world is out of control. Every individual forms a unique story.

Can the story, which has a completely original character and a fundamentally open end, still be regarded as a form of thinking? Now, art seems the only relevant way of thinking—does that mean that open and creative thinking replaces closed, logical thinking?[93]

92 In *Encounter* (2009), Kundera posits that Rabelais is the genius of the non-serious. He abhors the extent to which Rabelais is stripped of the carnivalesque and opposes all moralising teaching. He defends the immature individual about whom nobody knows how he will develop. Rabelais' novel is an example of a world of infinite possibilities. In this context, I should like to stress once more how Art-Based Learning is not only a method, but also a didactic approach to "the immature". It is didacticism with an open character—which has far-reaching consequences for teaching practice.

93 Poutain and Robins indicate how the youth has started to think ironically. The adolescent behaves in a cool way. Irony and cool are in fact related. Poutain and Robins, in *Cool Rules: Anatomy of an Attitude*, describe irony as "an essential component of cool" (2000, 158). Cool is an idea that emerged in the 1950s and 60s. Its legacy is still in evidence. Cool "wishes to be gazed at" (116) and is characterised by "amorality and unpredictability" (118). It is a world of "intense passion" (119).

Details as Carriers of Meaning

Every detail is a carrier of meaning. The clothing a character wears is the armour into which he has been poured. Clothing has its own language. A dress makes a woman of someone, a headscarf makes her a Muslim woman. Also, clothing is conditional on the surroundings. The illustration show how small differences can be and how important it is to allow the work to speak.

Jim Stark wears appropriate clothes. Smart, but that is not all. What does the suit tell? What do you, as a spectator, relate to it? He wears traditional black and white: the colours of the orderly, imperishable world. But how are things underneath? Is everything all right? A little later Jim shouts: "You are tearing me apart!" to his quarrelling parents. Is conformism not just a façade concealing considerable problems?

The creases in the suit are perhaps more important than the suit itself. Perhaps the scrap of paper on the ground says that it is impossible for smartness (the suit) to be maintained (fig. IV.3.3). In that sense, the paper represents Jim's state of

IV.3.3 Nicholas Ray, *Rebel Without a Cause* (detail of film still), 1955

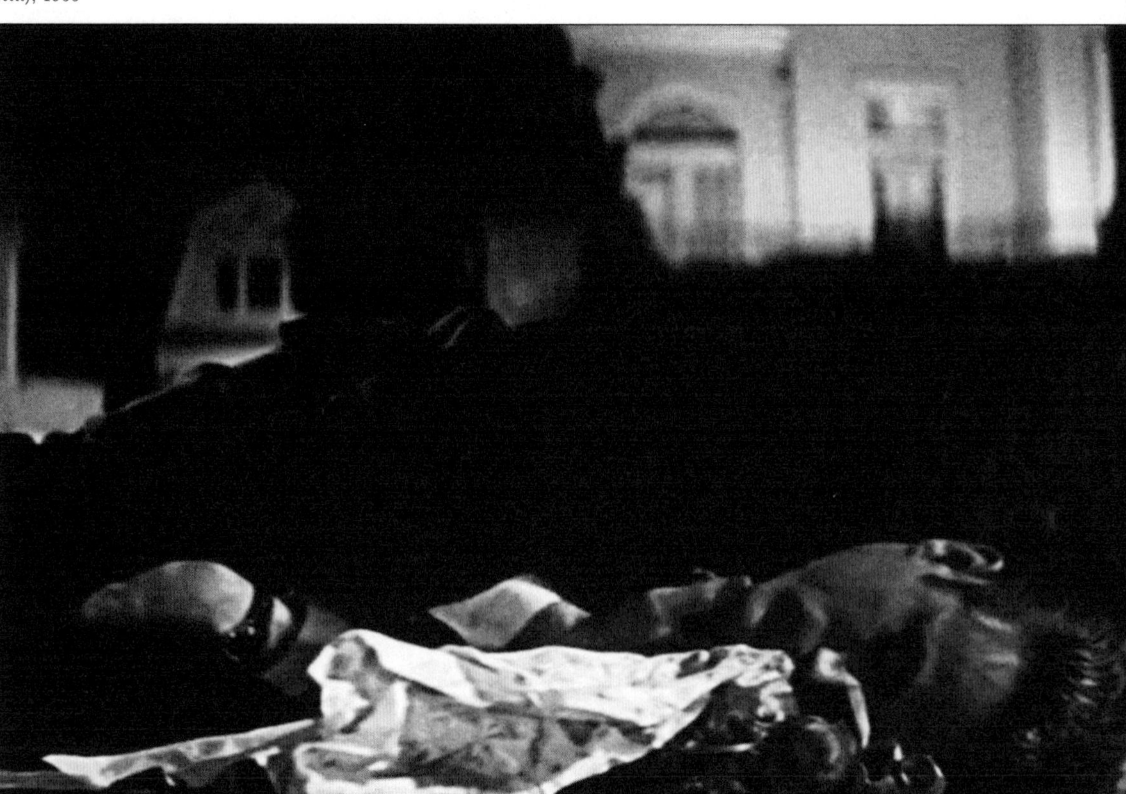

mind, the representation of what is going on in his head. A game develops, between the suit and the paper that is supported by countless attributes: music, colours, rapid, shallow dialogues, varying styles of dress, cars in all makes and sizes.

Jim Stark's fragmented world, filled with reversals, resembles the world in James Purdy's strange Bildungsroman, *Malcolm* (1959). Purdy sketches a world of bizarre encounters. The adult world is one where sham is more the rule than the exception. It is a poetic-ironic world. Malcolm walks through it with an open mind, seemingly naïve, like Orlando. And Malcolm and Orlando are similar in more ways than one.

The character of Malcolm is a symbol of Purdy's dialogical thinking. He does not see through all the pretence: he achieves a *dialogue extérieure*. He even manages in unsettling and inspiring his surroundings with his astute observations. He is not an introvert dreamer, but understands the social impact of the word. Malcolm may be narcissistic, but he is also an extravert. In his comments, he reveals contradictions. Sometimes it may be a matter of unimportant issues that are relatively easy to solve. Sometimes it is a matter of a harrowing reality. In this context, the reversal of the roles of young and old is interesting. The pupil and his teacher swap places. The coming generation teaches the former generation what the future should look like. Malcolm dies, not yet having reached the age of twenty, of love and excessive alcohol consumption—his hair snowy white.[94]

THE ARTICULATE ADOLESCENT The articulate adolescent emerges. He is situated at the centre of the action and does not hesitate to speak out. He is like Marlon Brando in *The Wild One* (1954): a cheeky, provoking, assertive gang leader. This adolescent resembles Ray's Inuk (Anthony

94 Purdy's Malcolm reads and lives the world around him. Susan Sontag describes in the essay "Writing as Reading" how you can develop your own view of the word by reading and writing. With respect to writing she says: "Writing is [...] a series of permissions you give yourself to be expressive in certain ways. To invent. To leap. To fly. To fall. To find your own characteristic way of narrating and insisting; that is, to find your own inner freedom" (2000). Purdy's universe is an argument for freedom. He outlines a world where reality is based on imagination.

Quinn) in *The Savage Innocents* (1960). Inuk the Eskimo lives in his own world: a sincere, but also egocentric world, where every word seems to have the opposite meaning. It is a world where a garment as a sign of civilisation implies uncivilised rather than civilised behaviour.

Jim Stark is like Bob Dylan: the depiction of the ironic answer of youth to the tragedy and poetry of existence. It was not for nothing that in his album *Self Portrait* (1970) Dylan wrote a tribute to Quinn's interpretation of Inuk the Eskimo.

In Dialogue with the Surroundings

The film speaks its own language. The background of the fragment is filled with white houses, which, in their stateliness and verticality, contrast with the foreground (fig. IV.3.4). Now Ray answers the question about adolescence with imposing décors. You can see this in all his films: *Johnny Guitar* (1954), *The Savage Innocents* (1960) and *55 Days at Peking* (1963). However, these large décors are not the main

IV.3.4 Nicholas Ray, *Rebel Without a Cause* (detail of film still), 1955

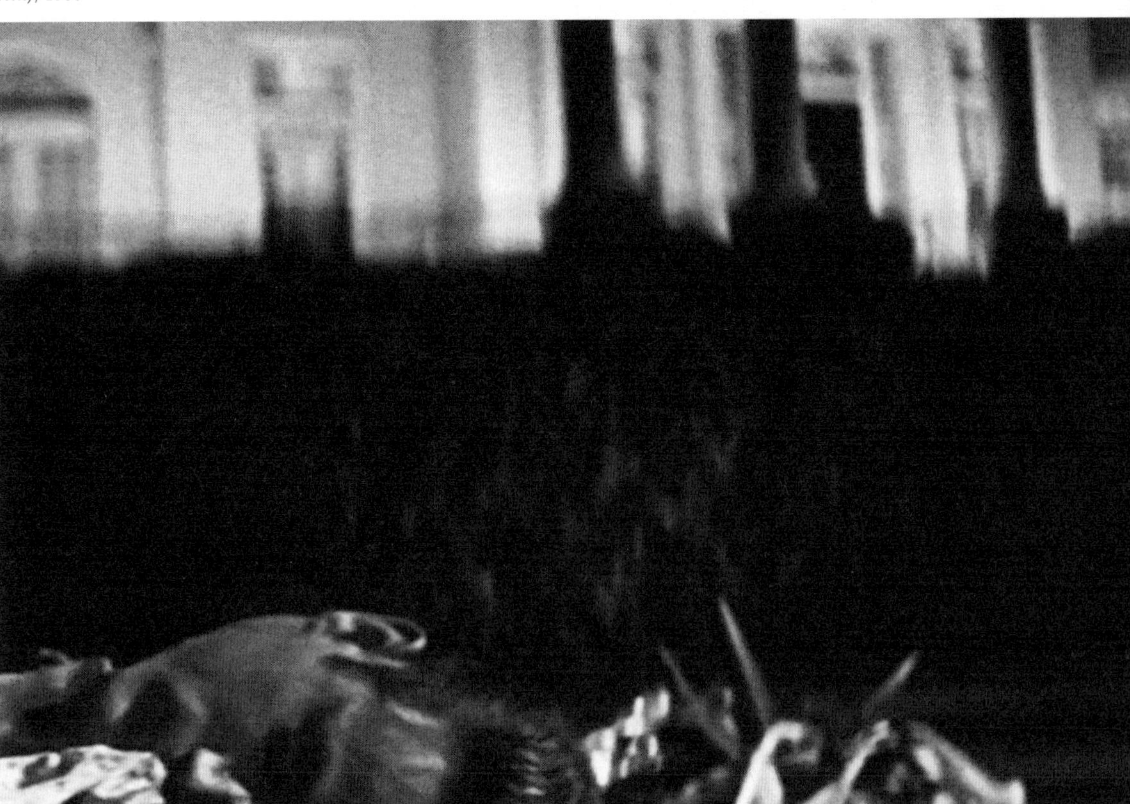

character of the narrative, as they are in tragedy or aesthetic reality.

The conversation generally puts the finger on the immensely lonely, withdrawn and self-enclosed theatrical world facing the inept little Narcissus. In this world, Jim Stark is the protagonist. Just like the central figure in James Dean's favourite book: *The Little Prince* by Saint-Exupéry, he has fallen to Earth and knows more than the biggest among us.

The overwhelming locations keep recurring in the film. They form an environment that seems to continue to ask questions, thus compelling the introvert individual to make comments. The planetarium featuring in the film offers the experience of the vast cosmos that makes a tremendous impression. This cosmos is commented on repeatedly to avoid being at its mercy. Below the cliff where the race is held, an enormous, untameable abyss gapes. The old house where Jim and Judy seek refuge refers to a parental home that, in this way, they explore together.

THE VAIN ADOLESCENT The narcissistic adolescent is a vain figure. He is a living paradox. He is situated above and outside society. He is confused, articulate, speaks a language in which you are never sure what he means, is unassailable and only understandable to a very limited extent. His surroundings do not understand him either. Narcissism is a phenomenon that was highlighted after the Second World War. In addition, film is often the medium with which to portray narcissism, and comment on it at the same time.

Nicholas Ray describes the loneliness of youth. However, with his kind of portraiture he also provides ironic commentary, thus preluding a promethean adolescent. The adolescent we see here is a narcissistic character who is trapped in himself. Yet there is hope—hope that was absent in the absolute tragedy in Caravaggio's philosophy, and even in Woolf's poetic way of thinking.

It is a small toy in the foreground that speaks: the small monkey that looks bigger than Jim Stark (fig. IV.4.1). Jim looks at it in fascination. It is as if the little monkey knows a secret that goes unnoticed by the self-absorbed adolescent.

The small monkey turns the world around. It signals, like Risk Hazekamp (who is more like the monkey than James Dean in that respect), something that is still not visible and thus contains a promise. It represents a world in colour and sees something that the self-obsessed Jim Stark has not yet seen, but gradually seems to discover.

It is precisely that combination of tragic narcissism, loving, poetic thinking and ironic lightness that has made the collaboration between Nichols Ray and James Dean one of the most productive in film history, by revealing the adolescent in all his complexity.

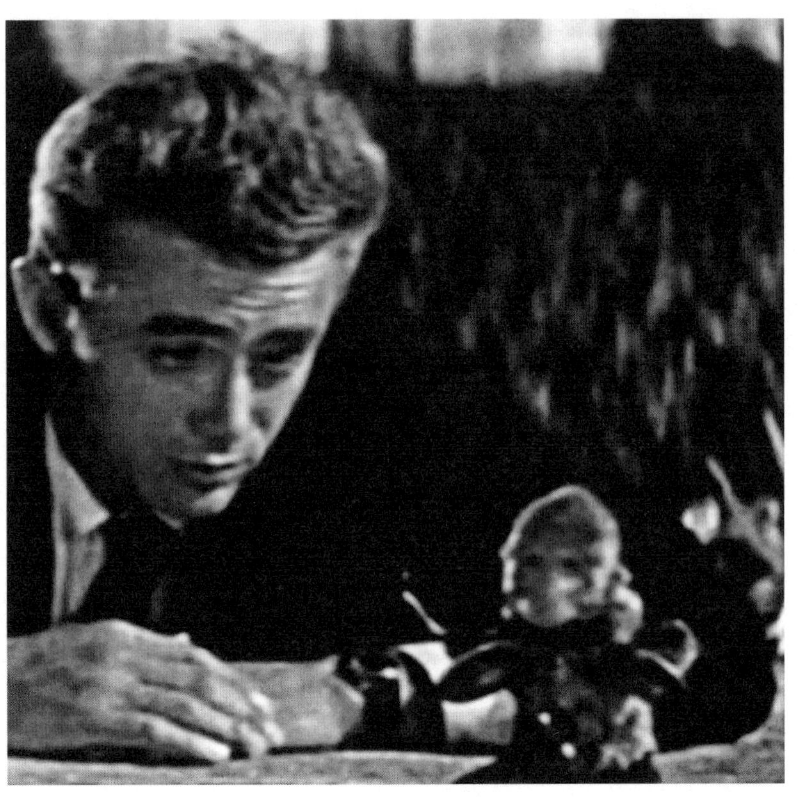

4
Ray: Sisyphus
The Absurdity of Youth

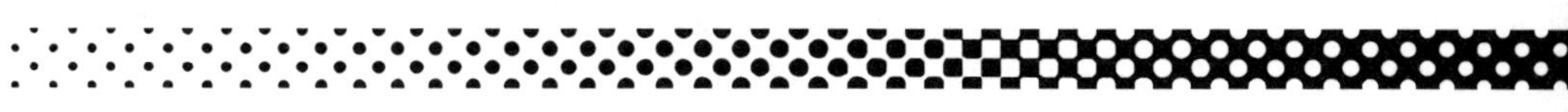

The Effect of the Foreground

Absurdity speaks where triviality comes to the fore. Narcissism speaks in exaggerated dimensions. In a fantasy reality, the small toy can also be the Judy character. The spectator sees the toy move in a world without a final goal.

The toy is engaged in an absurd dialogue and does not see Jim, the spectator. It looks ahead, without seeing anything. It tells about the vain attempt to make contact with the other. We are wind-up machines in a meaningless masquerade. We have no idea who winds us up.

An alienating, Kafkaesque world comes about. It has no feeling but, at most, arouses it. It is a world in which the subject understands nothing of his surroundings. The toy can be operated as long as it lasts. Then it stops. As a small, insignificant and laughable item, it is not in contact with the spectators.

IV.4.1 Nicholas Ray, *Rebel Without a Cause* (detail of film still), 1955

Ray films, with considerable use of shadows, a game of light and dark (fig. IV.4.2). However, there is a difference between Caravaggio's shadows and Ray's. Judy and Jim, Ray's protagonists, do not do battle with the shadows. They leave them for what they are. The shadows are more of a décor than an opponent.

The imposing décor of the empty house is not an area to escape from, but a place to live. The cliff fascinates the characters. The planetarium at the start and the end (Griffith Observatory in L.A.) offers an overwhelming experience. The décors talk: they advance on the spectator and form the organising principle. They offer a context that supports the protagonist, as do the dialogues.

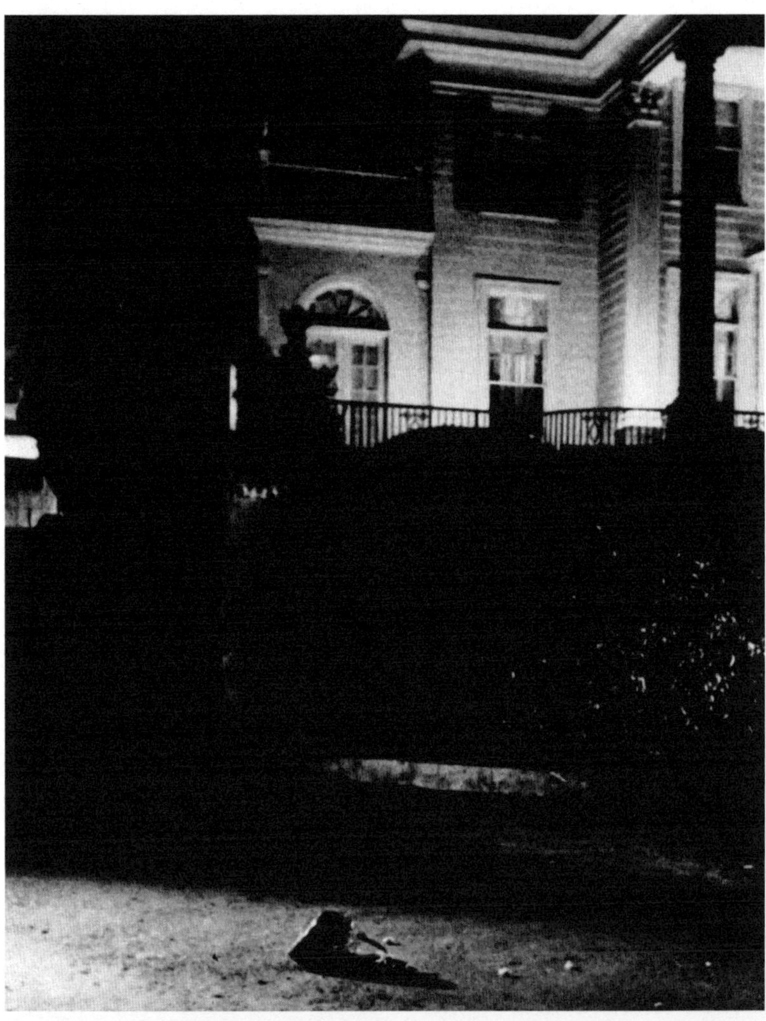

IV.4.2 Nicholas Ray, *Rebel Without a Cause* (detail of film still), 1955

When I elaborate on the effect of these dialogues, I come to J.D. Salinger. He describes in *The Catcher in the Rye* (1951) a shadowy world of youth. The seventeen-year old Holden Caulfield is locked in a nihilistic worldview. The drama of life at the boarding school has made way for a pointlessly drawn-out existence in which one day differs little from another, and there is little hope of improvement. Caulfield's world is dismal.

In a paradoxical sense, the emphasis placed on dialogues in the novel actually reveals the impossibility of communication. The search for meaning and the requests to the teachers for answers, only make it clearer that there are no answers.

Salinger shows that the battle is over. The fictional character Caulfield criticises the wrongs that take place around us. So the meaning of Caulfield's story lies mainly in the description of the negative circumstances, which the character cannot influence.[95]

95 From the very start, Salinger's *The Catcher in the Rye* has a critical tone. 'If you really want to hear about it, the first thing you'll probably want to know is where I was born and what my lousy childhood was like, and how my parents were occupied and all before they had me, and all that David Copperfield kind of crap, but I don't feel like going into it, if you want to know the truth. In the first place, my parents would have about two hemorrhages apiece if I told anything pretty personal about them' (1951). Incidentally, not everyone interprets Salinger's critical approach negatively. Kenneth Slawenski emphasises in *J.D. Salinger: A Life*, how Salinger embraced D.T. Suzuki's Zen Buddhism at this specific time (2010, 190). From that point of view, Holden Caulfield's course is that of dropping everything that does not matter.

THE SATIRICAL ADOLESCENT The scenes that have been described lead me to the satirical adolescent. He denounces social conditions and is an enlarged version of Peter Pan: a sarcastic figure. He becomes a Till Eulenspiegel. He spits the establishment in the face, though it does not help; the establishment does not change as a result.

In his film *Rebel Without a Cause*, Ray paints an adolescent who has become the victim of an environment that gives him no chance to develop into a strong personality. The tragic hero may have become a regal warrior, a poetic adolescent or a cultured poet, but the adolescent addressed here is a street clown.

Poetry cannot give him the answer. The only answer he still has to the tragedy of existence and the awareness of death (that is inherent in life) is a form of acceptance of the negative. Consequently, what happens to him is at all events bearable.

Here, Camus' *The Myth of Sisyphus* can be identified: a state in which things might change for the (anti) hero, but not develop. Jim is flanked by Plato and Judy. Judy (Nathalie Wood) in particular evinces considerable cynicism, especially when she is with Buzz. "I'll never get close to anybody," she says in the opening scene at the police station. Judy lives in a world of pretence, a materialist world of ostentation, pointless and absurd, aimless.

The narcissist still has an interest in himself, but that too has vanished here. A wry smile, a sarcastic, self-mocking undertone, a critical remark and a series of curses and tirades are all that remain. It is a mirror of a world without hope.

Ray's perspectivist world opens a new time and space. Here, all time and space seems like a world that no longer wishes to exist, but does so regardless. Gertrude Stein tells how—after the words and phrases—a world of paragraphs starts. Characters and décors from this film are the paragraphs to which Stein refers. The absurd, which also crops up here, leads to a crisis without end. It is characterised by the fact that there is no cause and effect. Jim is a prisoner in a meaningless intermediate state.

Ray achieves this effect by giving his characters no logical objective. There is no apparent reason why a character is where he is. Nor do his actions appear to have any effect. We see the world of Sisyphus: a world you cannot influence, that repeats itself and leaves the spectator with a feeling of boredom.

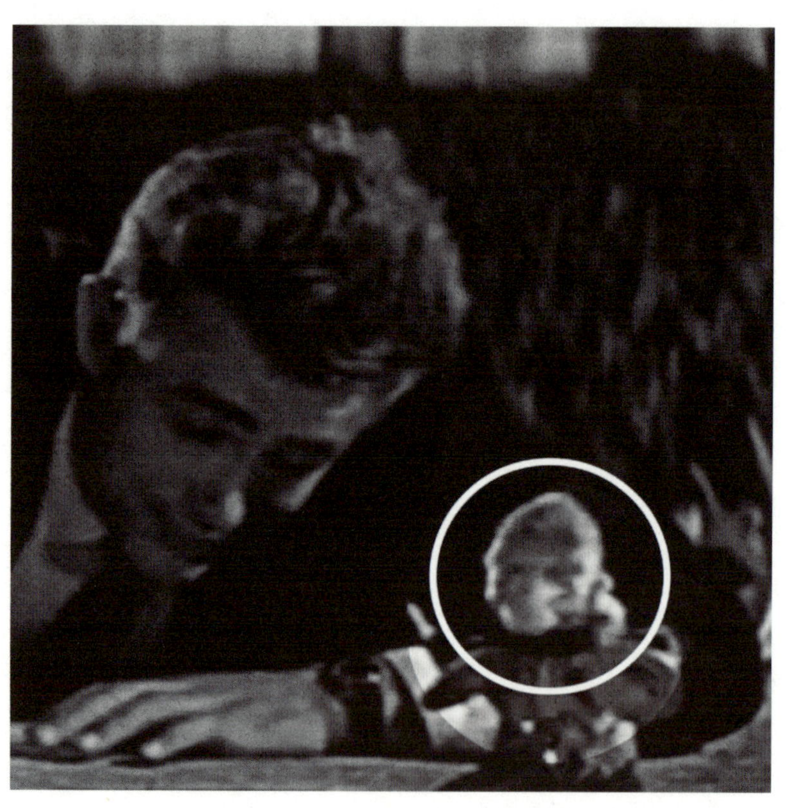

5

Ray: Prometheus

Youth as Hope

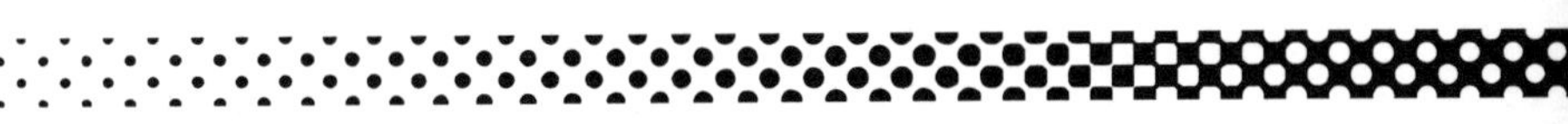

The Functionality of Colours

You could reduce every centre panel to a colour that tells its own story: black, white and red. Black is the colour of Caravaggio's tragic story of the adolescent, in the game of shadows. White is the colour of Woolf's poetic story of the adolescent. Red is the colour of Ray's ironic story of the adolescent.

The suit jacket, which can still be seen in the opening shot, is exchanged in the course of the story for a bright red jacket, with which Plato is covered when he dies. The red of the jacket is already in evidence in the opening shot, in the toy's hat (fig. IV.5.1).

Now, the central metaphor is that of Prometheus, the rebellious young god. Ray's promethean style is like a red rag to a bull. Jim Stark gains in significance in contrast with the others. His red stands out against the blue-black of the surroundings: Prometheus as an answer to Narcissus and Sisyphus. Red is also found with the other characters.

IV.5.1 Nicholas Ray, *Rebel Without a Cause* (detail of film still), 1955

Bakhtin's world is one of many sounds and colours and opens the way to the perspectivist world view of the novel. Bakhtin uses the term heteroglossia, the coexistence of different types of speech, which he derives from the work of Dostoyevsky. In that way, Bakhtin offsets narcissism and absurdism.

The world he describes comes about because the central forces diminish. This can be seen as a social, but also an individual state. According to Tzvetan Todorov, in *Mikhail Bakhtin: The Dialogical Principle* (1984), polyphony, the opposite of poetic monophony, is an expression of intersubjective diversity. With its diversity, the novel wins a new world. The different languages that exist side by side in principle, are positioned together in this world of heteroglossia in an intertextual connection (Todorov 1984, 60). The novel is born between the various dialogical utterances that are part of this intertextual network. In this way the novel differs fundamentally from poetry.

Poetry unfolds between utterance and word, and is primarily a complex aesthetic reality (64). Prose unfolds between the various actors and their utterances. In the world that emerges, the dialectic of nature evolves into the dialogue of culture. The individual meaning is interrupted. Meaning comes about in the social relationship between "me" and "you".

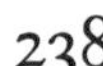

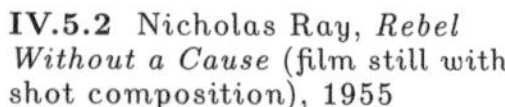

IV.5.2 Nicholas Ray, *Rebel Without a Cause* (film still with shot composition), 1955

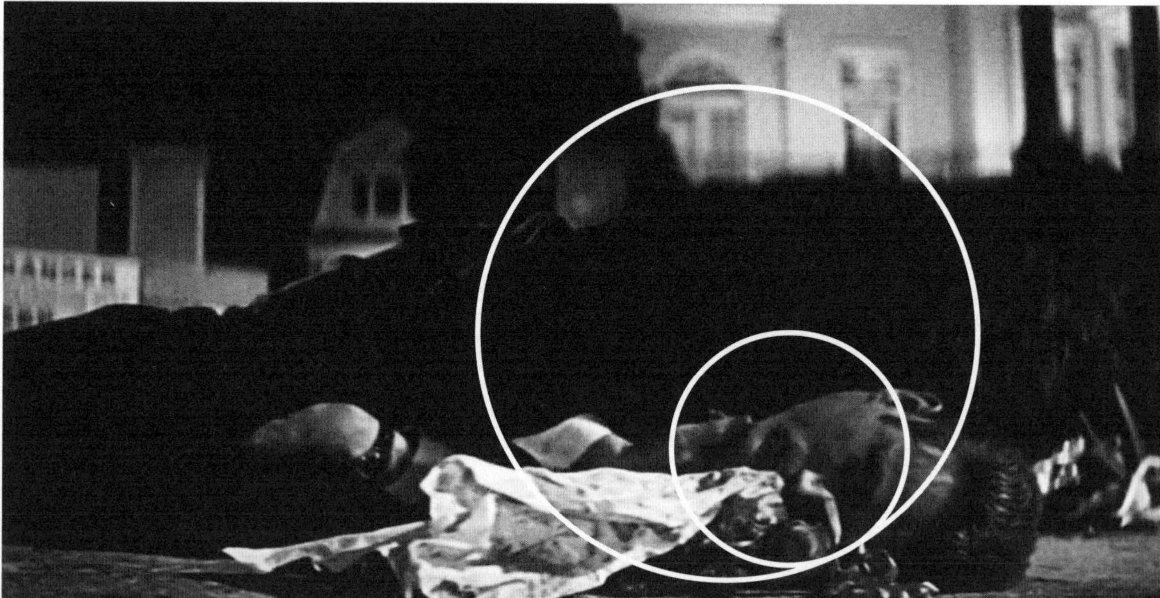

The inversion of the perspective that results is also responsible for humour. This light form of humour neutralises tragedy and deprives it of its severity. Humour is geared more to the other than to the "me"; this explains why there is less humour in poetry than in prose.[96]

THE HUMOROUS ADOLESCENT The promethean adolescent is a humorous adolescent, like the character of Tereza in Kundera's *The Unbearable Lightness of Being*. Time and again she looks at reality from a different, future-orientated perspective, thus repeatedly surprising the gloomy Tomas. This humorous adolescent has a constant dialogue with the other. She tries to make the other happy. A phenomenon becomes a new phenomenon because she takes another look at it. This adolescent resembles a lively harlequin and offers hope.

Changing Viewpoints

Ray's thinking in perspective is supported by camera movements. Jim Stark is Bakhtin's "wise fool" (2003, 150). He does not allow himself to be governed by a senseless manoeuvre. He chooses his own way, outside the peer group. He does not join in the other's game, but devises his own.

The changing viewpoints provide ever-new information. The still I examine here via ABL is completely different from Dean's viewpoint via the toy in the foreground or the camera recording the story. Every new perspective generates a different story line.

Jim Stark tells a story of sympathy. The toy tells an adventurous and possibly naïve story. The perspective of the camera is 'dismantling'—as if Jim is portrayed as James Dean in the end.

96 Todorov deals extensively with Bakhtin's dialogical principle which is defining for this third narrative about the adolescent. The dialogue form can be described as a heterogeneous chronotope with a pronounced movement towards the periphery, an ongoing conversation with the other, an intertextual relation between present and past, a complex exchange between the various participants and an interaction in which each verbal utterance also contains its social context (the discourse).

The absence of an all-inclusive perspective guides me towards the world sketched by Richard Rorty. It is one of multiformity, of heterogeneous thinking. Some will describe this world as weak, because there is no one, clear principle. On the other hand, it offers a guarantee against the cruelty that is often the result of the desire to dominate rather than tolerate others. Here, love can rival cruelty.

Rorty's possible world is a creative reality—a world where something new is always developing or being made. It is a relative world, fundamentally uncertain, but having the advantage that we are given enough space. Something can be added to whatever is unfinished. Freedom in this world is a valuable asset. By contrast, cruelty implies that you begrudge the other his freedom and you enter another's space.

THE LIBERTARIAN ADOLESCENT Thus the libertarian adolescent comes about. He sees the community as a space full of possibilities in which he can express himself freely. This not only takes the form of expression of an individual desire, as can still be the case with the performative adolescent (addressed in the story of the poetic adolescent). The significance of this young Prometheus is now also situated outside him. The libertarian adolescent is cool. He does voluntary work for Greenpeace, Amnesty International or the WWFN. Such adolescents play with reality in order to create space.

Lastly

This third, long look at the picture of Jim Stark calls to mind Prometheus: the recalcitrant Titan who rebels against (parental) authority. This is Jim Stark speaking, the protagonist between Plato and Judy. Ray treats his actors with affection. The camera slowly rolls towards them. It is the world in which Plato and Judy are conquered. Jim is living in an uncertain universe. In that respect, he does not differ from Plato and Judy. However, they become trapped in themselves and do not stand a chance without Jim's help.

Jim's strength is that he does not focus on himself, but on the other. He is anti- cruelty. This is demonstrated nicely in the way he covers the toy from the first scene with a paper blanket. Jim represents a positive, existentialist, ironic and libertarian way of thinking. He goes beyond the framework of his own world and enters a world where the old may be infringed and where the future gets a new chance. It is the world of hope: hope that had vanished with tragedy, and in poetry had retreated outside reality.

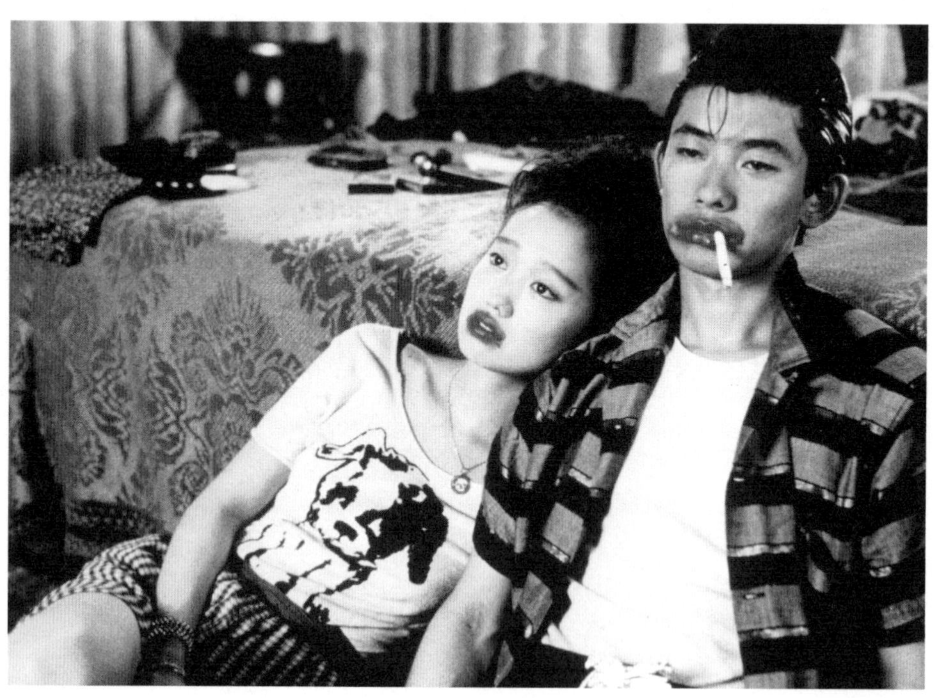

6

Reprise: Jarmusch

The Rhetoric of Play

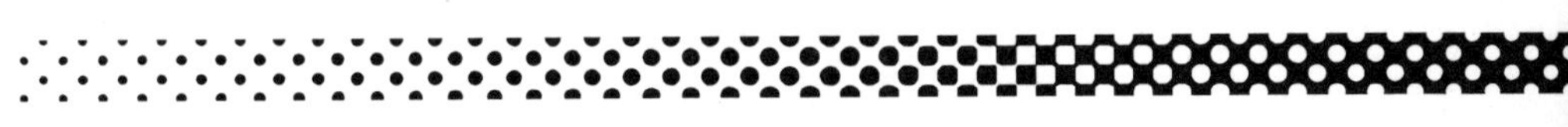

Introduction

What does adolescence mean now? Having arrived at the third panel, I want to examine what Jim Jarmusch's film *Mystery Train* (1989) can tell me. In the previous panel, the Ray-dian game formed the undertone of contemporary, ironic youth culture. It is art that morphs into ethnography. This "past in the present" helps what is contemporary to develop. In *Mediated: How the Media Shapes Your World and the Way you Live in It* (2005), the anthropologist Thomas de Zengotita describes how images that are repeated time and again in the media shape reality.

I shall describe this third ironic version of youth as a "multi-person world" rather than a "one person world" (Doležel) using a fragment from Jim Jarmusch's film *Mystery Train*: a depiction of a Japanese couple watching television in Memphis (fig. IV.6.1). Bearing in mind that films create realities, this film brings about a contemporary social reality. I am now referring to subcultural thinking, in which complexity, dialogue and humour are at the fore.

IV.6.1 Jim Jarmusch, *Mystery Train* (film still), 1989

The rhetoric of the game mainly revolves around a mixture of toughness and fundamental doubt. This rhetoric stands for a final disengagement from all essentialist thinking. It is the acknowledgement of doubt on which the uncertainty of youth is based. However, philosophers like Rorty stress that doubt can have the opposite effect. It can create space for what Foucault describes as a new, hopeful "practice for freedom".[97]

97 Foucault explored freedom by concentrating on exclusion mechanisms (particularly in the earlier work) and freedom practices (particularly in the later work). He also examined Greek-Hellenic culture. You could say my method of ABL and Foucault's work are related, in that knowledge is considered categorically as fiction in both cases. In "Writing starting from an experience", Foucault remarks: "Who has ever thought to make anything other than fiction?" (2004, 174) Foucault sees art as a kind of thinking.

SUMMARY *Mystery Train* is a story in three parts. This structure demonstrates that reality can no longer be summarised from one perspective, but looks different depending on how it is approached.

Part 1: *Far from Yokoyama. Mystery Train* starts with the arrival of a young Japanese couple at Memphis railway station. After a two-day train journey they have reached the place where music icons like Elvis Presley and Jerry Lee Lewis grew up. Memphis looks desolate. Mitsuko and Jun walk through the suburbs and visit the legendary Sun Studios, located in dilapidated, out-of-the-way premises. It is nightfall. They stop in front of a small hotel near the railway and spend the night in room 27. At 2.17 a.m. Elvis Presley's "Blue Moon" is played on the radio. Early in the morning, a gunshot is heard somewhere in the hotel.

Part 2: *A Ghost*: A young Italian girl, Luisa, is taking her dead husband, in his coffin, to the airport. She has to spend the night in Memphis and ends up in a bar, having first visited a newsagent's. There, a man pesters her with an unlikely story about Elvis Presley. In the same hotel as the one where Mitsuko ad Jun are staying, she meets Dee Dee, the sister of the local barber. She has just left her English boyfriend, Johnny. Luisa and Dee Dee decide to take a room together for the night (room 25). That night Elvis Presley's ghost appears around 2.17 a.m., as "Blue Moon" is being played. In the morning, a gunshot is heard.

Part 3: *Lost in Space*. Johnny has just been fired from his job and has lost his girlfriend. He has a revolver and waves it recklessly round in the bar. His "brother-in-law" and a friend take him away. They buy some booze in a liquor store, after which Johnny shoots the store owner. In the car—it is 2.17 a.m.—"Blue Moon" is playing. As they flee, they seek refuge in the hotel, which is owned by a brother-in-law of one of the friends. They get the worst room: number 22. There, Johnny tries to kill himself and, in his attempt, shoots the so-called brother-in-law in the leg. They take flight.[98]

98 Ludvig Hertzberg has collected in *Jim Jarmusch: Interviews*, a number of interesting interviews with Jarmusch, including one by Luc Sante entitled "Mystery Man" (1989). In the interview, one of the subjects discussed is *Mystery Train*. Jarmusch refers to Nicholas Ray, with whom he worked intensively. Ray's use of colours is remarkable. He paints like Kandinsky and in *Johnny Guitar* and *Rebel Without a Cause*, deliberately made use of certain colours (Hertzberg 2001, 95). In an interview with Cathleen McGuigan, "Shot by Shot: *Mystery Train*" (1990), Jamusch's use of colour in *Mystery Train* is described as a "cool palette", because he does not use yellows and oranges (Hertzberg 2001, 101). Jarmusch says of the way he directs actors: "I like the differences" (96).

Characters

Jarmusch's thinking in complex, carnivalesque figures containing a form of alienation, corresponds with an aspect of youth in the Western world. We see two young people, but the red lips stand out, giving the picture something clownish (fig. IV.6.2).

The boy at the centre of the picture represents a tragic clown. He looks sorrowful, his eyes cast down, a cigarette in the corner of his mouth, his shoulders drooping. Nothing is cheerful. His face radiates boredom. The girl on his left tells a different story. She stares ahead dreamily. She makes no connection with the world around her, but she does with a world within her.

The only things connecting the two young people's lives are time and place. One wonders whether their relationship is more than a casual encounter in a contingent universe. Perhaps, after this shared journey, they will bid each other farewell and never see each other again.

The world of youth has become a complex, alienating, virtual one where the characters are no longer in control, but are part of a postmodern, fantasy landscape, "a light-hearted game in which style and genres are sometimes (irreverently) mixed" (Verstraten 2004, 18). We also encounter a similar landscape, for instance in Quentin Tarantino's *Kill Bill* (2003–4), David Lynch's *Mulholland Drive* (2001), and *Sin City* (2005) by Robert Rodriguez. The subject experiences himself as a small element of a larger universe—unlike the tragic poetic adolescent, who still considers himself to be the centre of the universe.

Time and again, this complex reality presents emerging, roaming characters. It responds to the principle of the crime story: "wrong time, wrong place." The fact that you are the victim is inexplicable here. The world you live in is determined by coincidence.

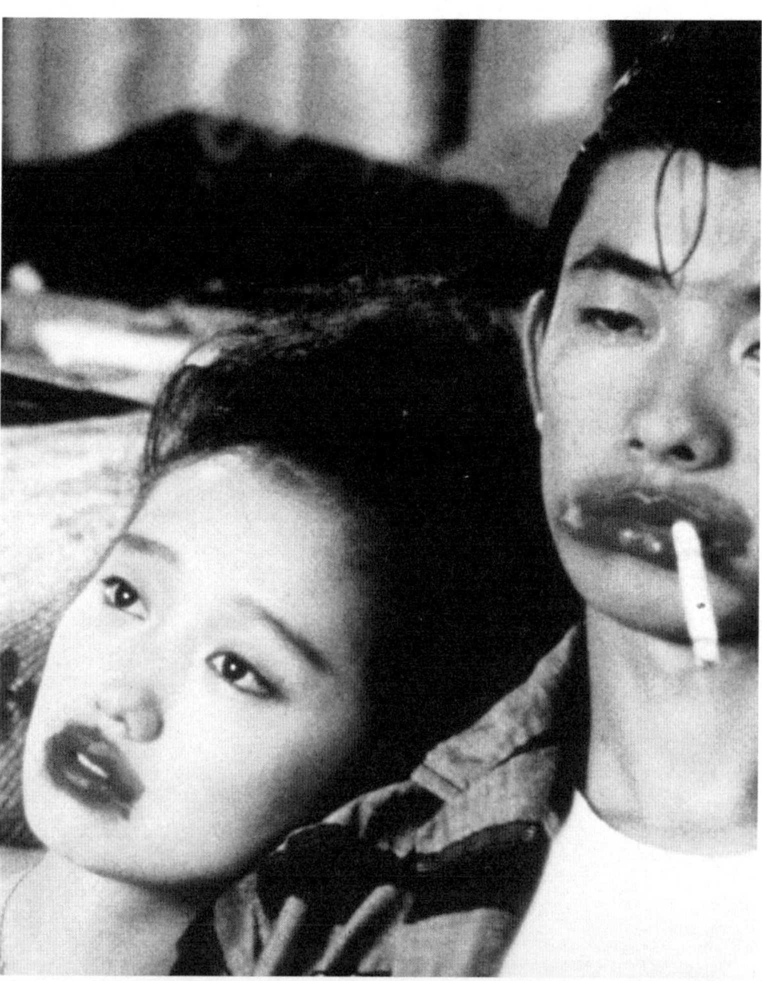

IV.6.2 Jim Jarmusch, *Mystery Train* (detail of film still), 1989

Here, chance is an active concept, an established fact that enables us to act fittingly. Every occurrence poses the question whether we are passing into a new space-time—a new continuum in which new patterns apply.

This world of perspectives is not a continuous stream. Here, discontinuity is the general principle. There are short, ever-different stories. It is the world of Godard's Nouvelle Vague. This world dismantles the dream of gods and creates a new kind of hero: one who is not in control of the situation but, time and again, responds to it creatively.[99]

99 In his *Handboek filmnarratologie* (2006), Verstraten connects up the complex worlds of Tarantino and Jarmusch. The films are full of allusions, which are often unnamed and are based on the spectator's "(visual) erudition" and "knowledge of handed-down narrative structures" (168). This typifies what Mieke Bal refers to in her foreword to Verstraten's book as the "post-post-structuralist era" (10).

THE SMART ADOLESCENT The ironic adolescent is a smart adolescent, who is mainly notable for his astuteness, not for his strength or sensitivity. He uses his intelligence to interpret situations and new ways. He is a snooper. He is unconventional, creative and independent, conforming with the idea of the new Generation Y, also known as the Einstein Generation. He resembles a creation of Marcel Duchamp; he is an innovator and cares nothing for conventions.

The Construction of Non-Dialogues

Jarmusch allows two characters to speak. Their faces reflect an absurd, antisocial reality. They are saying: "What's the point of everything? What can be my impact on a world without a centre?" They mainly portray how it does not work. They do not look at each other. Is it a lack of interest or is it weariness? The still shows the absence of dialogue, thus stressing the importance of dialogue in human relations. The very absence of meaningful words demonstrates how important words are and how absurd life is without them (fig. IV.6.3).

Mitsuko and Jun, both eighteen years old, are travelling together from Japan to the United States. A bold undertaking, you might say. Communication between them has an alienating character. Mitsuko does her utmost to mask disappointment and boredom. The narcissistic Jun makes very little effort, but lets her get on with things. When she asks why he looks so sad, he replies cynically "That's just the way my face is."

The sentimental love songs of celebrities from the fifties like Ray Orbison, Carl Perkins and Elvis Presley, contrast sharply with the lack of mutual affection between the two. They seem to be conversing with a world that consists of nothing other than what is on the tapes they have with them. They are not conversing with the world they inhabit physically.

PSEUDO WORLDS The absurd world of non-dialogues is one of the chief characteristics of Dostoyevsky's and Ray's universes: worlds of pure appearances. Material reality consists of phantoms. We are conversing with shadows that that do not in fact matter. The world of ideas, of great stories, is one with which we no longer have any contact, but it is that world that truly matters. That is where the great images live.

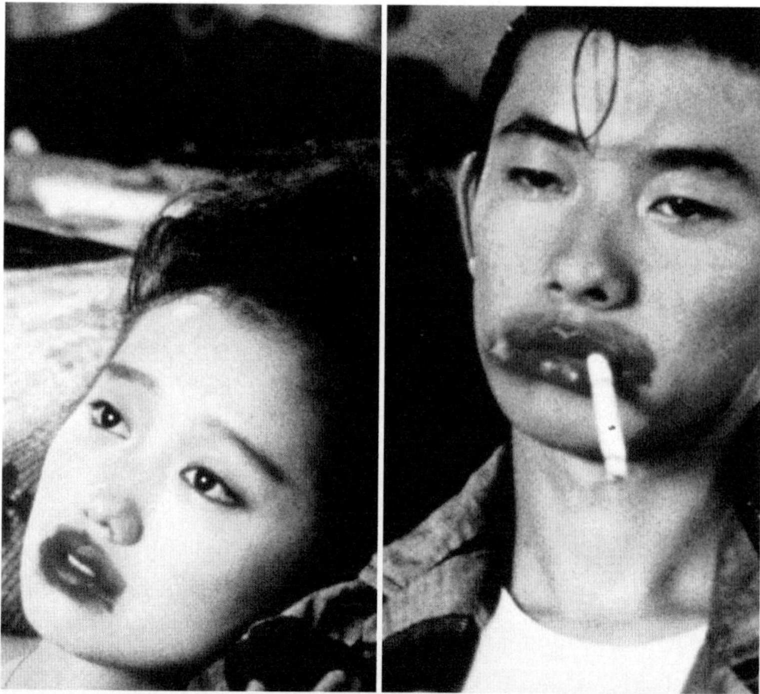

IV.6.3 Jim Jarmusch, *Mystery Train* (detail of film still with vertical line), 1989

The ironic individual argues that even that world of ideas does not exist, but is merely an invented world. Not that for the ironic person, a pragmatist through and through, there are no effective images left.

In the 1989 interview with Luc Sante, Jarmusch describes the Memphis of *Mystery Train* as typifying a period in world history, "the decline of the American empire" (Hertzberg 2001, 93). True contact does not exist (any longer), and America has deteriorated into a dilapidated house in which people cling to phantoms, like the past glory of old films and rock-'n-roll stars (Pilar Blanco and Peeren 2010, 6).[100]

100 G. Bruce Boyer describes America in ruins in *Rebel Style* (2005) by way of actors like Brando, Dean, Clift and Newman. They represent a youth style that is characterised by a fair degree of irony which, since the 1950s, has become a dominant style. I believe that this ironic story of youth which correlates with the tragic and poetic story, can still be heard, though the tone has clearly changed since 9/11.

THE (ANTI) SOCIAL ADOLESCENT In the end, the lack of communication in a world of non-dialogues does offer hope as well. In fact, the antisocial monologues emphasise the importance of dialogue. The absurdity of poetry makes a U-turn. The adolescent does not understand, but dissatisfaction with the not-understanding does stress the necessity of a new way of understanding.

An indexical social world of dialogues is conjured up. Whereas the poetic adolescent is satisfied with his inner world, the ironic adolescent calls for the reversal of a non-social world. He longs for conversation. The outside world is the setting for chance encounters. In that way, contact acquires a somewhat enigmatic character.

The Origin of Humour

Jarmusch's style is one of black comedy. The lipstick-painted faces are situated in a dark, deserted space (fig. IV.6.4). I can hear the voices of Mitsuko ("Elvis...") and Jun ("Carl

Perkins…"), bickering. Are they tragic or amusing figures?

Humour comes about when there are innuendoes—a prime ironic principle. The humorist creates a multiform reality. Every action can acquire a different meaning if described from a different perspective.

The humour of Mitsuko and Jun lies in the innuendo. What they say is not what they mean and what they mean is not what they say. Mitsuko and Jun are constantly kidding themselves and others. And so every action is relative. Their pain is intense, but at the same time a question of time and perspective as well.

Black comedy relates, in its callousness, to the human condition. Why, in all its venom, is it so human? One answer may be found in its taboo-breaking character. Black comedy comments on something that otherwise would not be put into words. Things are said or shown that are normally glossed over or presented more attractively than they are.[101]

THE LAUGHING ADOLESCENT A laughing adolescent emerges as the ultimate manifestation of liberal thinking. The

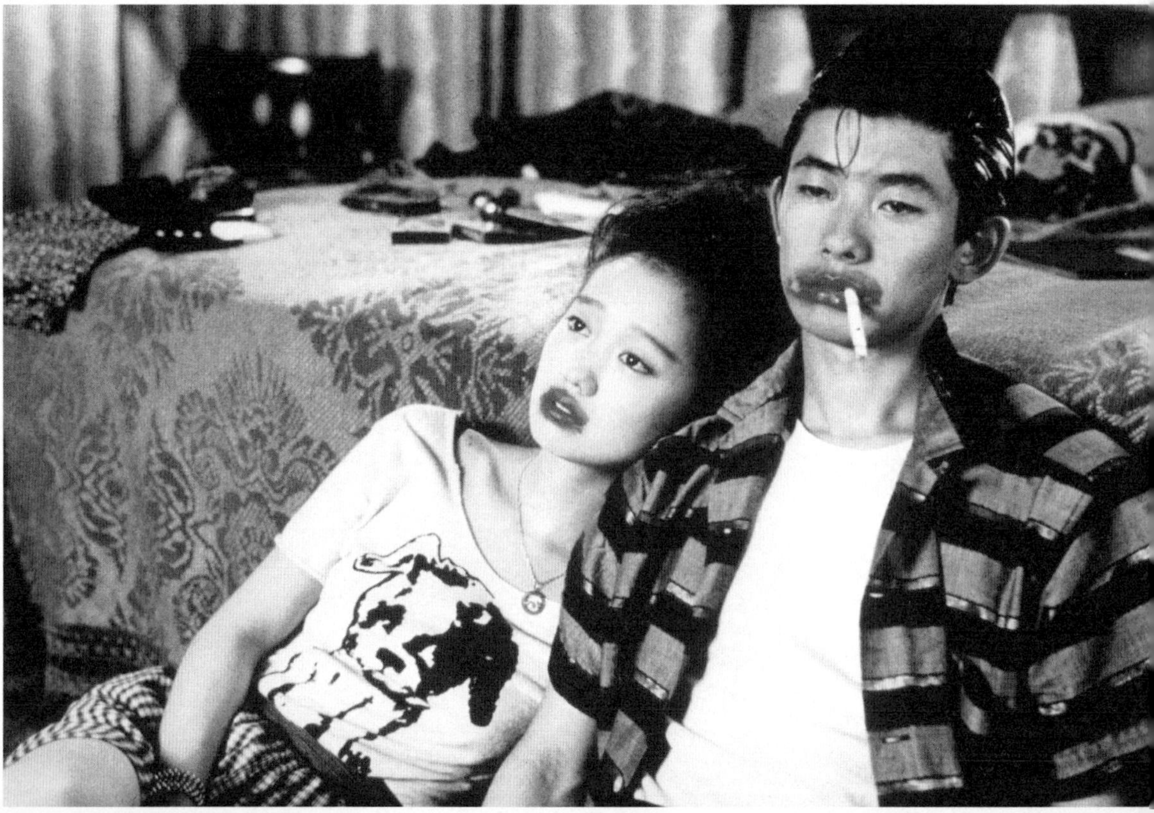

101 Hebdige sees the breaking of a taboo in *Subculture* initially as a dark, solitary action, typical of a youth style that is in keeping with the work of Jean Genet. It is "the idea of style as a form of refusal" (2007, 2). This youth style, which is rooted in tragedy and is searching for a poetic answer, ends in resistance to every form of common sense (136). The lighter ironic form emerges in *Hiding in the Light*. Youth styles stem from metaphors, according to Hebdige. 'Youth-as-trouble' now transforms into 'youth-as-fun'.

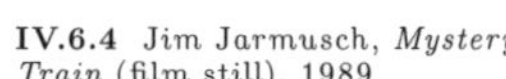

IV.6.4 Jim Jarmusch, *Mystery Train* (film still), 1989

tragic adolescent may have been a captive and the poetic adolescent a dreamer in a prison cell, but the ironic adolescent is an inventive, young and self-confident adolescent, who breaks out of strictly circumscribed reality.

The tragic hip-hopper from the first triptych comes to his end. The dreaming "altie" from the second triptych steps down. The optimistic whiz kid—always searching for a new perspective—steps forward in the third triptych. The allegories of the hero and the poet turn into an allegory of the clown.

The adolescent is the skilful player: innovative and creative. He is not guided by the mechanical laws of the past, but is geared to an as yet unknown future. He has passed beyond shame and laughter—the guardians of the taboo. He is a young Einstein who insinuates, creates space and chooses a doorway to something new. He is travelling.

Time and space have become relative. The contemporary adolescent described here is in an open third space. He is on the way to a new playing field. Life, death: nothing is taboo any more and nothing is automatically impossible. The adolescent becomes the protagonist in a comedy. He creates his own future in words and images, and goes on to give them meaning, with a smile.

Lastly

In this third triptych, art again proves to be a source of knowledge and information. Art is philosophy in words, images and sounds; it is a form of thinking, and so an incentive for thinking. In my process of allowing art works to speak, I began to think in detail about adolescence as a contemporary cultural phenomenon.

I have considered several thought processes, which has resulted in an ethnography of subcultural youth styles: a dialogue between youth and death, the beauty of youth and the game of youth. They have turned out to be stories with underlying rhetorical systems.

The term "rhetoric" as the art of persuasion, might be intensified with the word "dialectic", since, in the end, none of the stories stand alone. Poetic discourse is inconceivable tragic discourse. In irony, in turn, remains unreal without prior poetic awareness.

I take this idea of the dialectic of youth styles to develop a sequel to the story of the semiotician, Dick Hebdige, the ethnographer of subcultural youth styles. I seek to describe ethnography—with its relatively static categories—more in dialectic terms.[102]

102 In *De glimlachende sfinx: Kernvragen in de geschiedenis*, Von der Dunk counters the biased defeatism of the one's own times which, in his view, is an ancient phenomenon. Historiography is, along the lines of Huizinga, the form in which a culture accounts for its past. There is no automatic cohesion—that must be added by the historian (Lorenz 2002, 106). I have deployed ABL to clarify how, within the wealth of one culture, not just one, but several linguistic games concerning youth take place.

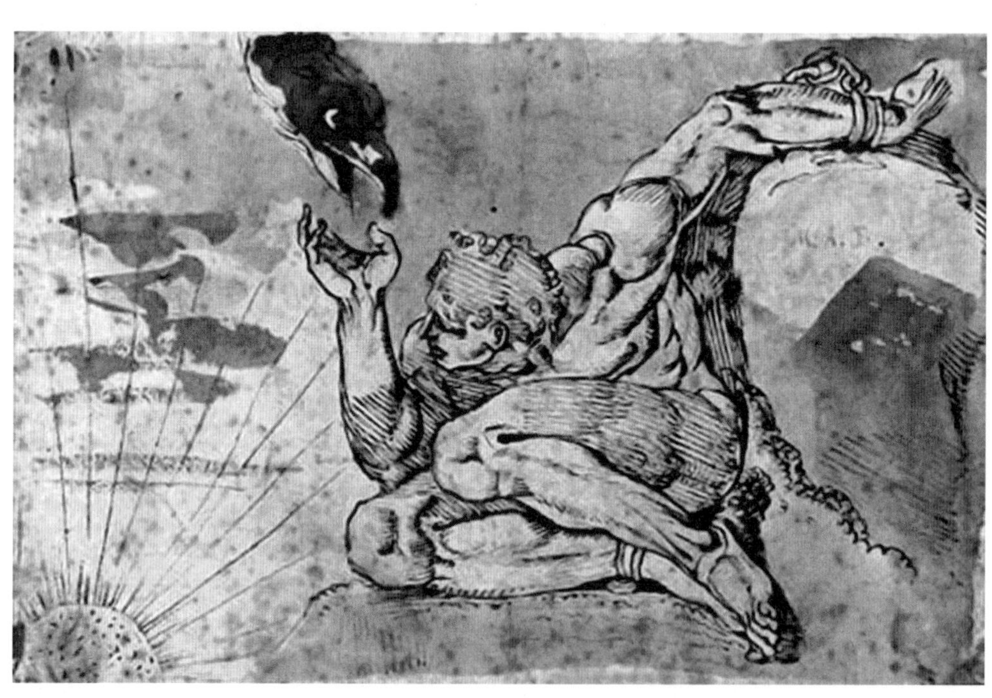

V

Conclusion

In the Shadow of the Art Work

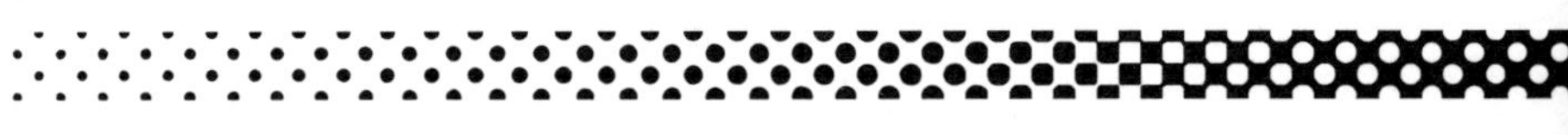

The only advice, indeed, that one person can give another about reading is to take no advice, to follow your own instincts, to use your own reason, to come to your own conclusions.
—Virginia Woolf (1993, 59)

Art-Based Learning

In his introduction to Genette's *Narrative Discourse* (1980), Jonathan Culler remarks that it is not advisable to separate method and content in a study. After all, method and content are interwoven. In my study, the content is what has led to knowledge that is not immediately obvious. Never before have I found out so much about the varying forms of adolescence in fiction. I have tried to show how art is a source of knowledge and, as such, can be used in certain types of education. Accordingly, this study builds on the work of such thinkers on art education as Ernst van Alphen, Hubert Damisch and Mieke Bal. In this context, the important aspects are:

IV.6.5 Henry Fuseli, *Prometheus*, 1770–71

1. *Art-Based Learning as a form of cultural research*: New, extensive insight in cultural language games. "Truth games" concerning the phenomenon of adolescence in the cultural "unthought known".
2. *Art-Based Learning as learning art:* A form of knowledge with art as the source; a way of researching that sees art as a form of writing poetry and thinking.
3. *Art-Based Learning as effective didactics in higher education*: Education, with help from Art-Based Learning, becomes a lively, unorthodox, contemporary "happening"—the lifetime experience to which Elliot Eisner refers.

In *The Arts and the Creation of Mind,* Eisner posits that "the arts can serve as a model for teaching the subjects we usually think of as academic" (2002, 196). Not only is the art work as an object a form of thinking, in his view (cf. Damisch, Van Alphen), but thinking itself is also an artistic, creative process. Eisner argues that we can learn from art, because we: 1) gain experiences outside the "normal" provision of knowledge; 2) experience multiple perspectives; 3) seek deeper understanding in qualitative relations; 4) observe small differences with great effects; 5) learn to think in matter; 6) notice what cannot be said. If one proceeds in this way, a perspective develops that is in keeping with the development of a simple into a complex self, which Bollas sees as the crux of the process of developing a sense of self. The researcher discovers that a problem can have several solutions, that reality is not fixed, that more is to be known than words can express, and that knowledge extends to the domain of intrinsic value. These basic principles are important for anyone wishing to embark on ABL.

The Level of Content

The first level is that of content. Elaborating on Dick Hebdige's work, I have sought, by way of art works, to understand the story of Western youth as a cultural phenomenon. It has become a story of youth styles, which often remain concealed, as seen through the eyes of different artists.

Artists are experts on youth in texts and images within contemporary Western culture. I see my source material as a form of analysis, not as an object of it. In short, this material led me to develop the idea that adolescence in late-modern Western culture is defined in a complex way. Tragedy, poetry and irony cannot be considered separately. With all three, the finiteness of existence repeatedly plays an important role.

Hayden White's genre theory, which he formulates in *Metahistory* (2010) provides a framework for the three triptychs that have been presented. White describes four forms of historical representation. The first ties in with my *Adolescence in fiction: Caravaggio's portrayal of the adolescent* (2006), the second with *The poetic language of adolescence: on the beauty of otherness* (2009) and the third and fourth coincide with *The lost paradise of the adolescent* (1999):

1. the tragic representation
2. the romantic representation
3. the comic representation
4. the ironic representation

The similarity makes it all the more likely that C.S. Lewis was right when he remarked that we think in fiction. Tragedy is sometimes wrongly considered to be closer to the truth than comedy. So, in the end, there is no hierarchy of genres, however tempting the idea might be. "Each of these forms chooses out of real life just those sorts of events it needs" (1992, 80).

The Level of Method

The second level is that of the method. My method has been derived from *Being a Character* by Christopher Bollas. I have sought to translate the achievements of depth psychology into teaching practice. The method I derived from Bollas' work has been highly productive as a theoretical framework. It is a route entailing for me, as both a student and a researcher, a development that can be compared with one progressing from a "simple self" to a "complex self" (Bollas 2003, 27). If I translate it into cultural research, I could describe it as a development of a simple view of culture to a complex view of culture.

1. *The choice of the object*: In this process, coincidence has played an important part, consistent with Bollas' thinking (2003, 30). The realm which then materialised was one of deep experiences (15). "To be dreamed by it" (57) was a process that Bollas correctly compares with an erotic process. "To be played by it" (189) was the precondition for achieving knowledge. Learning becomes a "walkabout" (18) that has led to what Bollas, following on from Lacan, terms a *jouissance* with the self (17).
2. *The game of the object*: The learning process has developed into what Bollas describes as "play work" between the analyst and the analysed (2003, 46). It is a dialectic process in which student and teacher,

researcher and promoter, together create meaning (93). It is also a generation game (275). Vital processes form to a large extent an unconscious game between the subjects involved (190). That is how "mind music" came about (90). In the process of chaos, the necessary cohesion gradually arose in the game (88).

3. *The self as an object*: I have got a better understanding in the area of the "unthought known". It corresponds with what Bollas—like White and Rorty—describes as the ironic position. It is the situation in which my "me" reveals itself in ever-changing ways during the dialectic process between the self and culture as an object (Bollas 2003, 29). There is no more sacred theory, but an "erotics in form" (89). Reality becomes a complex symphony (109). My "fascist state of mind" appears to have been surmounted as far as the subject of my study—the adolescent—is concerned (200). A moment of free experience and speaking comes about (110). For myself, that was the recognition that I did not want only to be a writer, not only a researcher, but above all a teacher.

So ABL is an approach involving reception theory: an approach to art that is based on the reader's or spectator's experience. The method ties in with the work of pioneers like C.S. Lewis with his *An Experiment in Criticism*, but also with that of theorists like Roland Barthes and Ernst van Alphen. The typical thing about this approach is the (inter)-subjective orientation, with which the reader, as an active agent, arrives at an independent and equitable text-related performance. The fact that the subject plays an important role in the process of attributing meaning means that, unsurprisingly, there are quite a few links between reader response criticism and psychoanalysis, and that more traditional critics tend to dismiss the approach as subjectively anarchist.

The Level of Didactics

1. LEARNING FROM THE ART WORK ABL primarily means prioritising an art work as a speaking object, a kind of thinking. This fundamental choice has tremendous impact. You suddenly have to learn that, for now, you are no longer the centre of the universe. In this dialectic model the object—the material art work and the ensemble of concomitant cultural and mental images—has something important to tell. The art work is the teacher and it speaks out, All you have to do is create the intellectual space within which the details can speak.

Living with a question, means inviting the object to move towards you. It may occupy space. It may instruct. It may tell a story. It may give an unconventional answer to your question. It is essential to wait with a process of attribution of meaning. The greatest danger is to generalise too soon. Training is needed to appreciate what is specific, different and unique, and then stop. It is of essential importance to allow the details, the fictitious characters and imaginary spaces to do their work as living realities.

2. LEARNING FROM YOURSELF In the second place, ABL is founded on learning as a complex, individual process. It is important to encourage students to keep on asking questions, in complete freedom. One of the most difficult things is to help them trust themselves. The student learns to explore his own mind, in an expansive process. He does not have to be an expert in the field in question; his attitude is what matters.

I encounter this attitude also in the work of Van Alphen, who describes it as "a poetic reading attitude": a manner of reading in which the art work can speak and can begin its own, original thought process. The chosen question affects your existence; you learn the concomitant process of depth psychology during your studies. Here, asking questions is not a static 'given'. Living with a question means the question is regularly changing. The student often only discovers the real question in the course of his research.

The approach to the "complex self" chosen here assumes that the self comes about in a dialogical, communicative and intersubjective process of developing meaning. Continuing in this vein, Bal and Van Alphen stress that the self is a dynamic cultural reality, rather than a static essentialist fact. This implies for the person who is learning that he must constantly ask himself: "Who am I?" Am I aware of my conditioning? Am I still the same? Do I dare to play with my identity? (Bal 2002, 322).

3. LEARNING FROM THE OTHER ABL is, after all, learning from the other. Bal describes a learning process in *Travelling Concepts in the Humanities* (Bal 2002, 316) that draws on the metaphor of "friendship". This concept—which we also come across in Spivak's *politics of friendship*—is different from Bloom's concept of love and commitment to the truth. Bloom's model eventually creates dependence on the teacher. The new teacher is not a messenger of the gods and no longer has to have a set, hierarchical relationship with his student.

The idea of friendship assumes a model of "intellectual honesty" (Spivak 2006, 6). Teacher and student do not differ fundamentally from each other. The teacher is genuinely interested in the knowledge the student acquires. He deploys his own experience of knowledge within the educational community, which functions as a "third space", a "borderland" or twilight zone, with no owner. This is the place for continuous dialogue. Here, there is no definitive answer. An answer is merely a short pause, followed by a new question.

A teacher should mainly be capable of sustaining the learning process. Spivak refers to changing the teacher's mental habits (2006, 41). His most important didactic task is to ask unexpected, 'out-of-the-box' questions. In the interview "Home", Spivak clarifies this: sometimes you are only aware of your real questions "through the questions asked by other people" (7). The most important questions come about in an intersubjective process.[103]

Is this why in later years Foucault gave more and more interviews? We can already recognise ABL in his analysis of Velázquez' *Las Meninas* at the beginning of *The Order of Things* (2002, originally published 1966). In his later work, interviews were more of a transformative space where knowledge developed.

The images that emerge here are like shadows of an art work: "the shadow of the object as it falls on the ego, leaving some trace of its existence" (Bollas 1987, 3). They are images which, in an intersubjective process of "framing" and "reframing" (Foucault 2002, 136), lead to unexpected humanities-related knowledge.

Consequences

Charles Sanders Peirce argues in "Some Consequences of Four Incapacities" dating from 1868: "Let us not pretend to doubt in philosophy what we do not doubt in our hearts"

103 2.0 learning is mathetics and so a continuation of the work of Jan Amos Comenius (1592–1670). The difference between mathetics and didactics is that the former is geared to the art of independent learning by a creative student. Didactics focuses on the art of learning to teach and assumes a creative teacher. Didactics is suited to the classroom. Mathetics is suited to the atelier, studio or workshop. So mathetics is an educational concept in a third area. Essentially, ABL is mathetics.

(1955, 228). A process of semiosis is set off, with learning-as-a-method becoming what I would like to describe as 'learning-as-a-happening". In this study, I want to show how ABL can generate a dialectic process between teacher, art work and student to enhance an academic discipline like cultural analysis. It is a quest to find the past in the present.

Aristotle saw this sincere search, the field of dialectics, as the opposite of rhetoric. This method can, in Foucault's words, lead to new border experiences. Art-Based Learning is appropriate to the 2.0 learning of a new iPod generation. Borders may be crossed. Study has become an unorthodox process of self-analysis.

In the course of this publication I have seen and recreated art works: the Dino Pedriali, Michelangelo Merisi da Caravaggio, Mathieu Kassovitz triptych, the William Shakespeare, Virginia Woolf and Thomas Vinterberg triptych, and the Risk Hazekamp, Nicholas Ray and Jim Jarmusch triptych. Together they give an impression of the landscape that is home to the adolescent—the adolescent as a tragic hero, an aesthetic poet and an ironic clown.

I open my eyes. It is as if I have woken from a dream. Everything has changed. I notice I have got older. My hair is more grey. My children are now fifteen and sixteen years old. I recognise in them the topic I have been dealing with: adolescence. At the same time, I realise that a metamorphosis in my thinking has taken place. Lifelong learning: the tangible art work has taken the place of a psycho-social phenomenon. Art has become the primary object of research, not adolescence.

Bibliography

Abma, Tineke, and Guy Widdershoven. 2006. *Responsieve methodologie: Interactief onderzoek in de praktijk*. The Hague: Lemma.

Alphen, Ernst van. 1998a. *Francis Bacon and the Loss of Self*. London: Reaktion Books.

———. 1998b. "Het intellectuele museum." *De Witte Raaf* 75 (September–October), 12–13.

———. 2000. *Armando: Shaping Memory*. Rotterdam: NAi Publishers.

———. 2005. *Art in Mind: How Contemporary Images Shape Thought*. Chicago: University of Chicago Press.

Alphen, Ernst van, Lizet Duyvendak, Maaike Meijer, Ben Peperkamp. 1996. *Op poëtische wijze: Handleiding voor het lezen van poëzie*. Bussum: Coutinho.

Ankersmit, Frank. 1983. *Narrative Logic: A Semantic Analysis of the Historian's Language*. The Hague: Nijhoff.

———. 2005. *Sublime Historical Experience*. Stanford, CA: Stanford University Press.

Arendt, Hannah. 1998. *The Human Condition*. 2nd ed. Chicago: University of Chicago Press (orig. pub. 1958).

Aristotle. 1984. *The Complete Works of Aristotle: The Revised Oxford Translation*. 2 vols. Ed. by Jonathan Barnes. New Jersey: Princeton University Press.

Auerbach, Erich. 2003. *Mimesis: The Representation of Reality in Western Literature*. Trans. by Willard Trask. Princeton, NJ: Princeton University Press (orig. pub. 1953).

Bachelard, Gaston. 1988. *The Flame of a Candle*. Dallas Institute Publications (orig. pub. 1961).

———. 1994. *The Poetics of Space*. Boston: Beacon Press (orig. pub. 1958).

Bakhtin, Mikhail. 1984. *Rabelais and His World*. Trans. by Hélène Iswolsky. Bloomington: Indiana University Press (orig. pub. 1965).

———. 2003. *Problems of Dostoevsky's Poetics*. Ed. and trans. by Caryl Emerson. Minneapolis: University of Minnesota Press.

Bal, Mieke. 1990. *Verf en verderf: Lezen in Rembrandt*. Amsterdam: Prometheus.

———. 1996. *Double Exposures: The Subject of Cultural Analysis*. New York and London: Routledge.

———. 1997. *The Mottled Screen: Reading Proust Visually*. Trans. by Anna-Louise Milne. Stanford, CA: Stanford University Press.

———. 1999. *Quoting Caravaggio: Contemporary Art, Preposterous History*. Chicago: University of Chicago Press.

———. 2001a. *Looking In: The Art of Viewing*. Amsterdam: G & B Arts International.

———. 2001b. *Louise Bourgeois' Spider: The Architecture of Art-Writing*. Chicago: University of Chicago Press.

———. 2002. *Travelling Concepts in the Humanities: A Rough Guide*. Toronto: University of Toronto Press.

Banfield, Ann. 2000. *The Phantom Table: Woolf, Fry, Russell and the Epistemology of Modernism*. Cambridge and New York: Cambridge University Press.

Barrett, Terry. 2003. *Interpreting Art: Reflecting, Wondering, and Responding*. New York: McGraw-Hill.

Barthes, Roland. 1974. *S/Z*. New York: Hill and Wang.

———. 1977. "The Death of the Author." *In Image–Music–Text*. Trans by Stephen Heath, 142–48. New York: Hill and Wang (orig. pub. 1977).

———. 1990. *A Lover's Discourse: Fragments*. London: Penguin Books (orig. pub. 1977).

———. 1994. *Roland Barthes by Roland Barthes*. Trans. by Richard Howard. Berkeley and Los Angeles: University of California Press (orig. pub. 1975).

———. 2002. *Uit de taal van een verliefde*. Trans. by Dennis van Broek. Utrecht: IJzer.

Bataille, Georges. 1961. *Tears of Eros*. San Francisco: City Lights Publishers.

Baudrillard, Jean. 1994. *Simulacra and Simulation*. Trans. by Sheila Faria Glaser. Ann Arbor: University of Michigan Press (orig. pub. 1981).

Becker, Ernest. 1973. *The Denial of Death*. New York: Free Press.

Beljon, J.J. 1987. *Ogen open: Grondbeginselen van vormgeving*. Amsterdam: Arbeiderspers.

Benjamin, Walter. 1968. "Theses on the Philosophy of History." In *Illuminations: Essays and Reflections*. Ed. by Hannah Arendt, trans. Harry Zohn, 253–64. New York: Schocken.

———. 1999. "Surrealism: The Last Snapshot of the European Intelligentsia", trans. Edmund Jephcott. In *Walter Benjamin: Selected Writings: Volume 2: 1927–1930*. Ed. by Rodney Livingstone et al. Michael Jennings, Howard Eiland, and Gary Smith, 207–21. Cambridge, MA: Harvard University Press.

Berger, John. 1969. *The Moment of Cubism: And Other Essays*. New York Pantheon Books, 1969.

———. 1972. *Ways of Seeing*. London: Penguin.

———. 1976. *Het moment van het kubisme*. Trans. by Kees Vollemans and Jan Eyking. Nijmegen: SUN.

———. 2009. *About Looking*. London: Bloomsbury (orig. pub. 1992).

Blanchot, Maurice. 1995. *Literature and the Right to Death* (1949). In *The Work of Fire*, 300–44. Trans. by Lydia Davis. Stanford: Stanford University Press.

Blandford, Steve, Berry Keith Grant and Jim Hillier, ed. 2001. *The Film Studies Dictionary*. Oxford and New York: Oxford University Press.

Bloom, Harold. 1997. *The Anxiety of Influence: A Theory of Poetry*. 2nd ed. Oxford and New York: Oxford University Press.

———. 1999. *Shakespeare: The Invention of the Human*. New York: Riverhead.

———. 2002. *Genius: A Mosaic of One Hundred Exemplary Creative Minds*. New York: Warner.

———. 2004. *Where Shall Wisdom Be Found?* New York: Riverhead.

Blos, Peter. 1966. *On Adolescence: A Psychoanalytic Interpretation*. New York: Free Press (orig. pub. 1962).

———. 1985. *Son and Father*. New York: Free Press.

Boer, Inge E. 2006. "No-Man's-Land? Deserts and the Politics of Place." In *Uncertain Territories: Boundaries in Cultural Analysis*. Ed. by Mieke Bal, Bregje van Eekelen and Patricia Spyer, 107–38. Amsterdam: Rodopi.

Bollas, Christopher. 1987. *The Shadow of the Object: Psychoanalysis of the Unthought Known*. London: Free Association Books.

———. 2001. *The Mystery of Things*. London and New York: Routledge.

———. 2003. *Being a Character: Psychoanalysis and Self Experience*. London and New York: Routledge.

———. 2004. *Dark at the End of the Tunnel*. London: Free Association Books.

———. 2009. *The Evocative Object World*. London and New York: Routledge.

Bologna, Ferdinando, and Vincenzo Abbate. 2005. "Caravaggio: The Final Years (1606–1610)." In Cassani and Sapio 2005, 16–48.

Bolz, Norbert, and Willem van Reijen. 1995. *Walter Benjamin*. Trans. by Laimdota Mazzarins. Amherst, NY: Prometheus.

Boomkens, René. 1998. *Een drempelwereld: Moderne ervaring en stedelijke openbaarheid*. Rotterdam: NAi.

———. 2006. *De nieuwe wanorde: Globalisering en het einde van de maakbare samenleving*. Amsterdam: Van Gennep.

Boyer, G. Bruce. 2005. *Rebel Style: Cinematic Heroes of the 1950s*. New York: Assouline.

Brook, Peter. 2003. *Evoking (and Forgetting) Shakespeare*. New York: Theatre Communications Group.

Brooks, Peter. 1977. "Freud's Masterplot." *Yale French Studies* 55/56, 280–300.

———. 1992. *Reading for the Plot: Design and Intention in Narrative*. Cambridge, MA, and London: Harvard University Press (orig. pub. 1984).

Bruner, Jerome. 1986. *Actual Minds, Possible Worlds*. Cambridge, MA, and London: Harvard University Press.

———. 2002. *Making Stories: Law, Literature, Life*. New York: Farrar, Straus and Giroux.

Buck-Morss, Susan. 1989. *The Dialectics of Seeing: Walter Benjamin and the Arcades Project*. Cambridge, MA: MIT Press.

Bull, Duncan. 2006. *Rembrandt/Caravaggio*. exh. cat. Amsterdam (Van Gogh Museum); Zwolle: Waanders.

Burke, Peter. 2004. *Wat is Cultural History*. Oxford: Polity Press.

Butler, Judith. 1993. *Bodies That Matter: On the Discursive Limits of Sex*. New York and London: Routledge.

———. 2000. "Sekse, gender en verlangen." In *Genderturbulentie*. Trans. by Ineke van der Burg and Niels Helsloot, 29–94. Amsterdam: Boom.

———. 2007. *Gender Trouble: Feminism and the Subversion of Identity*. New York and London: Routledge (orig. pub. 1990).

Camus, Albert. 1966. *Caligula, Het misverstand en De rechtvaardigen*. Trans. by Victor van Vriesland et al. Amsterdam: De Bezige Bij (orig. pub. 1944 and 1950).

———. 1956. *The Rebel: An Essay on Man in Revolt*. Trans. by Anthony Bower. New York: Vintage (orig. pub. 1951).

———. 1975. *De mythe van Sisyfus*. Trans. by Anton van der Niet. Amster-

dam: De Bezige Bij (orig. pub. 1942).
———. 1977. *De pest*. Trans. by Willy Corsari. Amsterdam: De Bezige Bij (orig. pub. 1947).
———. 1983. *De vreemdeling*. Trans. by Adriaan Morriën. Amsterdam: De Bezige Bij (orig. pub. 1942).

Cassani, Silvia, and Maria Sapio, ed. 2005. *Caravaggio: The Final Years*. Exh. cat. Trans. by Mark Weir. Naples: Electa.
Cherry, Deborah, ed. 2008. *About Mieke Bal*. Oxford: Blackwell.
Chion, Michel. 1994. *Audio-Vision: Sound on Screen*. Ed. and trans. by Claudia Gorbman. New York: Columbia University Press.
———. 1999. *The Voice in Cinema*. Trans. by Claudia Gorbman. New York: Columbia University Press.
Code, Lorraine. 1991. *What Can She Know? Feminist Theory and the Construction of Knowledge*. Ithaca, NY, and London: Cornell University Press.
Combs, Richard. 1980. "John Cassavetes." In *Cinema: A Critical Dictionary*. 2 vols. Ed. by Richard Roud, 340–47. New York: Viking; London: Secker and Warburg, 1980.
Conrad, Peter. 1999. *De metamorfose van de wereld: De cultuurgeschiedenis van de twintigste eeuw*. Amsterdam: Ambo/Anthos.
Crone, Eveline. 2008. *Het puberende brein: Over de ontwikkeling van de hersenen in de unieke periode van de adolescentie*. Amsterdam: Bert Bakker. English trans. *The Adolescent Brain: Changes in Learning, Decision-making and Social Relations*. London: Routledge, 2016.

Dalton, David. 2001. *James Dean: The Mutant King: A Biography*. Chicago: Chicago Review Press.
Damisch, Hubert. 2001. *Skyline: The Narcissistic City*. Trans. by John Goodman. Stanford: Stanford University Press.
———. 2002. *A Theory of /Cloud/: Toward a History of Painting*. Trans. by Janet Lloyd. Stanford: Stanford University Press.
———. 2007. *A Childhood Memory by Piero della Francesca*. Trans. by John Goodman. Stanford: Stanford University Press.
Dana, John Cotton. 1999. *The New Museum: Selected Writings*. Ed. by William A. Penniston. Washington, DC: American Association of Museums.
Debord, Guy. 1983. *Society of the Spectacle*. Trans. by Ken Knabb. London: Rebel Press (orig. pub. 1967).
Deleuze, Gilles. 1986. *Cinema 1: The Movement-Image*. Trans. by Hugh Tomlinson and Barbara Habberjam. Minneapolis: University of Minnesota Press (orig. pub. 1983).

———. 1989. *Cinema 2: The Time-Image*. Trans. by Hugh Tomlinson and Robert Galeta. Minneapolis: University of Minnesota Press (orig. pub. 1985).

———. 1990. *The Logic of Sense*. Ed. by Constantin V. Boundas. Trans. by Mark Lester and Charles Stivale. New York: Columbia University Press (orig. pub. 1969).

———. 1991. "Coldness and Cruelty." Trans. by Jean McNeil. In *Masochism*, 9–138. New York: Zone Books.

———. 1996. *A Thousand Plateaus: Capitalism and Schizophrenia*. Trans. by Brian Massumi. London: Athlone Press.

———. 2006. *The Fold: Leibniz and the Baroque*. Trans. by Tom Conley. London and New York: Continuum (orig. pub. 1988).

Deleuze, Gilles, and Félix Guattari. 1998. *Rizoom*. Trans. by René Sanders. Utrecht: Spreeuw.

Derrida, Jacques. 2006. *De gave van de dood*. Trans. by Sophia van 't Ende. Kampen: Klement; Kapellen: Pelckmans (orig. pub. 1999).

Dijk, Yra van. 2006. *Leegte, leegte die ademt: Het typografisch wit in de moderne poëzie*. Nijmegen: Vantilt.

Doležel, Lubomír. 1998. *Heterocosmica: Fiction and Possible Worlds*. Baltimore, MD, and London: Johns Hopkins University Press.

Dostojevski, Fjodor. 2006. *De broers Karamazov*. Trans. by Arthur Langeveld. Amsterdam: Van Oorschot (orig. pub. 1880).

Driel, Hans van. 1993. *De Semiosis: De semiotiek van C.S. Peirce in verband gebracht met het verschijnsel film*. Diss. Tilburg: Katholieke Universiteit Brabant.

Dunk, Hermann von der. 2011. *De glimlachende sfinx: Kernvragen in de geschiedenis*. Amsterdam: Bert Bakker.

Durand, Régis. 2006. *Cindy Sherman*. Exh. cat. Paris (Musée de Jeu de Paume).

Eco, Umberto. 2004. *History of Beauty*. New York: Rizzoli.

Eisner, Elliot W. 2002. *The Arts and the Creation of Mind*. New Haven, CT, and London: Yale University Press.

Elferen, Isabella van. 2010. "Haunted by a Melody: Ghosts, Transgression, and Music in Twin Peaks." In *Popular Ghosts: The Haunted Spaces of Everyday Culture*. Ed. María del Pilar Blanco and Esther Peeren, 282–95. London: Continuum, 2010.

Emerson, Ralph Waldo. 1993. *Self-Reliance and Other Essays*. New York: Dover Publications (orig. pub. 1841).

Evans, Dylan. 1996. *An Introductory Dictionary of Lacanian Psychoanalysis*. London: Routledge.

Fish, Stanley. 1980. *Is There a Text in This Class? The Authority of Interpretative Communities*. Cambridge, MA, and London: Harvard University Press.

Foucault, Michel. 1986. "Of Other Spaces." Trans. by Jay Miskowiec. *Diacritics* 16 (1), 22–27 (orig. pub. 1967).

———. 1988. *Madness and Civilization: A History of Insanity in the Age of Reason*. Trans. by Richard Howard. New York: Vintage (orig. pub. 1961).

———. 2002. *The Order of Things: An Archaeology of the Human Sciences*. Trans. by Alan Sheridan. London and New York: Routledge (orig. pub. 1966).

———. 2004. *Breekbare vrijheid: Teksten en interviews*. Ed. by Laurens ten Kate and Aukje van Rooden. Trans. by Rob van den Boorn et al. Amsterdam: Boom/Parrèsia.

Fowler, Catherine. 2009. *Sally Potter*. Urbana and Chicago: University of Illinois Press.

Freud, Sigmund. 1950. *Totem and Taboo: Some Points of Agreement between the Mental Lives of Savages and Neurotics*. Trans. by James Strachey. New York: Norton (orig. pub. 1913).

———. 1959. "Creative Writers and Day-Dreaming (1908; orig. pub. 1907)." In *The Standard Edition of the Psychological Works of Sigmund Freud*, vol. 9. Ed. and trans. by J. Strachey. London: Hogarth Press, 141–54.

———. 1983a. "De schrijver en het fantaseren." In *Sigmund Freud: Cultuur en religie*. Ed. by Hans W. Bakx, trans. Hans W. Bakx et al., 9–25. Meppel: Boom (orig. pub. 1907).

———. 1983b. "Het 'Unheimliche.'" In *Sigmund Freud: Cultuur en religie*. Ed. by Hans W. Bakx, trans. by Hans W. Bakx et al., 153–97. Meppel: Boom (orig. pub. 1919).

———. 1985. "Ter introductie van het narcisme." In *Psychoanalytische theorie*, Vol. 1. Trans. by Thomas Graftdijk and Wilfred Oranje, 25–65. Meppel: Boom (orig. pub. 1914).

——— 1997. *The Interpretation of Dreams*. Ware: Wordsworth (orig. pub. 1900).

Friedländer, Walter. 1974. *Caravaggio Studies*. Princeton, NJ: Princeton University Press (orig. pub. 1955).

Furbank, Philip N., and Alex M. Cain, ed. and trans. 2004. *Mallarmé on Fashion: A Translation of the Fashion Magazine* La Dernière Mode, *with Commentary*. Oxford: Berg.

Gay, Peter. 1991. *Sigmund Freud: Zijn leven en zijn werk*. Trans. by Bert van Rijswijk. Baarn: Tirion.

Genette, Gérard. 1980. *Narrative Discourse: An Essay in Method*. Trans. by Jane E. Lewin. Ithaca, NY: Cornell University Press.

Hall, Stuart, ed. 1997. *Representation: Cultural Representations and Signifying Practices*. London: Sage.

Halpern, Richard. 1997. *Shakespeare among the Moderns*. Ithaca, NY, and London: Cornell University Press.

Harrison, George B. 1991. *Introducing Shakespeare*. Harmondsworth: Penguin.

Hebdige, Dick. 1998. *Hiding in the Light: On Images and Things*. London and New York: Routledge (orig. pub. 1988).

———. 2007. *Subculture: The Meaning of Style*. London and New York: Routledge (orig. pub. 1979).

Hertzberg, Ludvig, ed. 2001. *Jim Jarmusch: Interviews*. Jackson: University of Mississippi Press.

Hibbard, Howard. 1983. *Caravaggio*. London: Thames and Hudson.

Higbee, Will. 2006. *Mathieu Kassovitz*. Manchester: Manchester University Press.

Hughes, Ted. 1993. *Shakespeare and the Goddess of Complete Being*. London: Faber and Faber.

Hume, David. 2010. *Four Dissertations*. Charleston, SC: Nabu Press (orig. pub. 1757).

Hussey, Mark. 1995. *Virginia Woolf A to Z: A Comprehensive Reference for Students, Teachers, and Common Readers to Her Life, Works, and Critical Reception*. New York: Facts on File.

Huyssen, Andreas. 1995. *Twilight Memories: Marking Time in a Culture of Amnesia*. New York and London: Routledge.

Jacobs, Timothy. 1992. *James Dean*. Trans. Write On Productions. Harmelen: Ars Scribendi. Orig. pub. London: Citadel Press, 1992.

Jakobson, Roman. 2004. "Two Aspects of Language." In *Literary Theory: An Anthology*, 2nd ed. Ed. by Julie Rivkin and Michael Ryan, 76–80. Oxford: Blackwell.

Jonge, Piet de. "Looking through the Glass." ‹www.riskhazekamp.nl/lookinguk.php› (accessed 11 November 2011).

Kandinsky, Wassily. 1946. *On the Spiritual in Art*. Trans. H. Rebay. New York: Solomon R. Guggenheim Foundation for the Museum of Non-Objective Painting (orig. pub. 1912).

Kegan, Robert. 1982. *The Evolving Self: Problem and Process in Human Development*. Cambridge, MA, and London: Harvard University Press.

Kermode, Frank. 2002. *The Romantic Image*. London and New York: Routledge (orig. pub. 1957).

Klamer, Arjo. 2011. *In hemelsnaam! Over de economie van overvloed en onbehagen*. Amsterdam: Ten Have.

Kripke, Saul. 1980. *Naming and Necessity*. Cambridge, MA: Harvard University Press.

Kristeva, Julia. 1974. *La révolution du langage poétique*. Paris: Seuil.

———. 1982. *Powers of Horror: An Essay on Abjection*. Trans. by Leon S. Roudiez. New York: Columbia University Press.

———. 1995. "The Adolescent Novel." In *New Maladies of the Soul*. Trans. by Ross Mitchell Guberman, 135–53. New York: Columbia University Press.

Kundera, Milan. 1985. *The Unbearable Lightness of Being*. Trans. by Michael Henry Heim. New York: Harper & Row (orig. pub. 1984).

———. 2010. *Encounter: Essays*. New York: HarperCollins (orig. pub. 2009).

Lakoff, George, and Mark Johnson. 1980. *Metaphors We Live By*. Chicago: Chicago University Press.

———. 1999. *Philosophy in the Flesh: The Embodied Mind and Its Challenge to Western Thought*. New York: Basic Books.

Lavin, Irving. 1980. *Bernini and the Unity of the Visual Arts*. 2 vols. New York: Pierpoint Morgan Library and London: Oxford University Press.

Lefebvre, Henri. 2008. *Critique of Everyday Life*. 3 vols. Trans. by John Moore. London and New York: Verso (orig. pub. 1947–81).

Leibniz, Gottfried Wilhelm. 1908. *The Monadology. In Discourse on Metaphysics, Correspondence with Arnauld and Monadology*. Trans. by George R. Montgomery, 249–72. Chicago: Open Court.

Lewis, C.S. 1992. *An Experiment in Criticism*. Cambridge and New York: Cambridge University Press (orig. pub. 1961).

Lievegoed, Bernard. 1965. *Naar de 21ste eeuw: Anthroposofie en de toekomst van de wereld*. Zeist: Vrij Geestesleven.

Locke, John. 1998. *An Essay Concerning Human Understanding*. London: Penguin (orig. pub. 1690).

Lorenz, Chris. 2002. *De constructie van het verleden: Een inleiding in de theorie van de geschiedenis*. Amsterdam: Boom.

Lutters, Jeroen. 1999. *Het verloren paradijs van de adolescent*. Zeist: Indigo.

———. 2006. *Adolescentie in fictie: Caravaggio's verbeelding van de adolescent*. Utrecht: Agiel.

———. 2009. *De poëtische taal van de adolescent: Over de schoonheid van het anders-zijn*. Antwerp: Garant.

Lutters, Jeroen, and Renée van der Linde. 2008. "Streetwise in Junkcity." Utrecht: DERA.

Luxemburg, Jan van, Mieke Bal and Willem Weststeijn. 1999. *Over literatuur*. Bussum: Coutinho.

Lyotard, Jean-François. 1989. "The Dream-Work Does Not think." Trans. by Mary Lydon. In *The Lyotard Reader*. Ed. by Andrew Benjamin, 19–55. Oxford: Blackwell.

———. 2000. *Het postmoderne weten*. Trans. by Cécile Janssen et al. Kampen: Kok Agora. Published in English as *The Postmodern Condition: A Report on Knowledge*. Trans. Geoff Bennington and Brian Massumi. Manchester: Manchester University Press, 1984 (orig. pub. 1979).

Maguire, Laurie E. 2000. "Feminist Editing and the Body of the Text." In *A Feminist Companion to Shakespeare*. Ed. by Dympna Callaghan, 59–79. Malden, MA, and Oxford: Blackwell.

Mallarmé, Stéphane. 1992. *Poésies*. Paris: Gallimard.

Man, Paul de. 1984. *The Rhetoric of Romanticism*. New York: Columbia University Press.

Manguel, Alberto. 2000. *Reading Pictures: What We Think About When We Look at Art*. New York: Random House.

Marin, Louis. 1995. *To Destroy Painting*. Trans. by Mette Hjord. Chicago: Chicago University Press.

Marini, Maurizio. 1994. "Dino Pedriali: Rappresentazione di anima e di corpo." In *Dino Pedriali*. Ed. by Peter Weiermair, 108–10. Zurich: Stemmle, 1994.

Martelaere, Patricia De. 2001. "Hume over smaak." In *David Hume: Filosoof van de menselijke natuur*. Ed. by Patricia De Martelaere and Willem Lemmens, 166–87. Kapellen: Pelckmans; Kampen: Kok Agora.

McCloud, Scott. 1993. *Understanding Comics: The Invisible Art*. Northampton, MA: Kitchen Sink Press.

Mead, George R.S. 2005. *Vaihinger's Philosophy of the As If*. Whitefish, MT: Kessinger.

Meeuse, Piet. 2003. "Inzoomen, uitzoomen: Notities over kijken en kennen." *Raster* 103, 6–17.

Moi, Toril. 2002. *Sexual/Textual Politics: Feminist Literary Theory*. London and New York: Routledge.

Moir, Alfred. 1989. *Caravaggio*. New York: Harry N. Abrams.

Mooij, Antoine. 1987. *Taal en verlangen: Lacans theorie van de psychoanalyse*. Meppel: Boom.

Mugnai, Massimo. 2005. *Leibniz: Filosoof en mathematicus*. Trans. by Etta Maris. Amsterdam: Veen (originally published as Leibniz: *Vita di un genio tra logica, matematica e filosofia*. Milan: Le Scienze, 2002).

Mul, Jos de. 1990. *Het romantische verlangen in (post)moderne kunst en filosofie*. Kampen: Kok Agora.

———. 2002. *Cyberspace Odyssee*. Kampen: Klement.

———. 2006. *De domesticatie van het noodlot: De wedergeboorte van de tragedie uit de geest van de technologie*. Kampen: Klement.

Nabokov, Vladimir. 1989. *Speak, Memory*. New York: Vintage (orig. pub. 1951).

Neubauer, John. 1992. *The Fin-de-Siecle Culture of Adolescence*. New Haven, CT, and New York: Yale University Press.

Nuijten, Kees. 1999. *Freud en fictie: Literaire genres vanuit psychoanalytisch perspectief*. Amsterdam: Boom.

Pasolini, Pier Paolo. *Heretical Empiricism*. Ed. by Louise K. Barnett; trans. by Ben Lawton and Louise K. Barnett. Bloomington: Indiana University Press, 1988.

———. 2016. *The Street Kids*. Trans. by Ann Goldstein. New York: Europa (orig. pub. 1955).

Pater, Walter H. 2010. *The Renaissance: Studies in Art and Poetry*. Gloucester: Dodo Press (orig. pub. 1873).

Pavel, Thomas G. 1985. *The Poetics of Plot: The Case of English Renaissance Drama*. Minneapolis: University of Minnesota Press.

———. 1986. *Fictional Worlds*. Cambridge, MA: Harvard University Press.

Pedriali, Dino. 1989. *Pier Paolo Pasolini: "Testamento del Corpo"*. Arnhem: Arturist.

Peirce, Charles Sanders. 1955. "Some Consequences of Four Incapacities." In *Philosophical Writings of Peirce*. Ed. by Justus Buchler, 228–50. New York: Dover Publications.

Pensky, Max. 1993. *Melancholy Dialectics: Walter Benjamin and the Play of Mourning*. Amherst: University of Massachusetts Press.

Pilar Blanco, María del, and Esther Peeren, ed. 2010. *Popular Ghosts: The Haunted Spaces of Everyday Culture*. London: Continuum.

Pisters, Patricia. 2002. *Lessen van Hitchcock: Een inleiding in mediatheorie*. Amsterdam: Amsterdam University Press.

Potter, Dennis. 1994. *Potter on Potter*. Ed. by Graham Fuller. London: Faber and Faber.

Poutain, Dick, and David Robins. 2000. *Cool Rules: Anatomy of an Attitude*. London: Reaktion Books.

Puglisi, Catherine. 2000. *Caravaggio*. London: Phaidon Press.

Purdy, James. 1959. *Malcolm*. New York: Pfarrar, Straus and Giroux.

Rajchman, John. 2001. "Introduction." In Gilles Deleuze, *Pure Immanence: Essays on a Life*, 7–22. New York: Zone Books.

Rascaroli, Laura. 2009. *The Personal Camera: Subjective Cinema and the Essay Film*. London: Wallflower Press.

Romein, Ed, Marc Schuilenburg and Sjoerd van Tuinen, eds. 2009. *Deleuze Compendium*. Rotterdam: Boom.

Rorty, Richard. 2007. *Contingentie, ironie en solidariteit*. Trans. by Kees Vuyk and Oscar van den Boogaard. Kampen: Ten Have.

Roud, Richard, ed. 1980. *Cinema: A Critical Dictionary*. 2 vols. New York: Viking; London: Secker and Warburg.

Russell, Bertrand. 2005. *A Critical Exposition of the Philosophy of Leibniz*. London and New York: Routledge (orig. pub. 1900).

———. 2008. *Geschiedenis van de westerse filosofie vanuit de politieke en sociale omstandigheden van de Griekse Oudheid tot in de twintigste eeuw*. Trans. by Rob Limburg and Vivian Franken. Utrecht and Antwerpen: Servire.

Salinger, J.D. 1951. *The Catcher in the Rye*. Boston: Little Brown and Company.

Sanders, René. 1989. *Beweging tegen de schijn: De situationisten, een avant-garde*. Amsterdam: Huis aan de Drie Grachten.

Schiller, Friedrich. 1967. *On the Aesthetic Education of Man in a Series of Letters: In a Series of Letters [by] Friedrich Schiller*. Ed. and trans. by Elizabeth M. Wilkinson and L.A. Willoughby. Oxford: Clarendon Press (orig. pub. 1795).

———. 2009. *Brieven over de esthetische opvoeding van de mens*. Vert. Aart J. Leemhuis. Amsterdam: Octavo (orig. pub. 1795.)

Schwartz, Barth David. 1995. *Pasolini Requiem: Een biografie*. Trans. by Karel van Eerd et al. Amsterdam: Meulenhoff.

Segal, Erich. 2001. *The Death of Comedy*. Cambridge, MA, and London: Harvard University Press.

Sennett, Richard. 2008. *The Craftsman*. New Haven, CT, and London: Yale University Press.

Shakespeare, William. 1985. *Wat u wilt*. Trans. by Gerrit Komrij. Amsterdam: Bert Bakker.

———. 2008. *As You Like It*. In *The Norton Shakespeare*. Ed. by Stephen

Greenblatt, 1615–1785. New York and London: Norton.
Siewert, Senta. 2008. "Soundtracks of Double Occupancy: Sampling Sounds and Cultures in Fatih Akin's Head On." In *Mind the Screen: Media Concepts According to Thomas Elsaesser*. Ed. by Jaap Kooijman, Patricia Pisters and Wanda Strauven, 198–208. Amsterdam: Amsterdam University Press.
Silverman, Kaja. 1996. *The Treshold of the Visible World*. New York and London: Routledge.
Slawenski, Kenneth. 2010. *J.D. Salinger: A Life*. New York: Random House.
Snaith, Anna, ed. 2007. *Virginia Woolf Studies*. New York: Palgrave.
Sontag, Susan. 2000. "Writers on Writing: Directions: Write, Read, Rewrite: Repeat Steps 2 and 3 as Needed." *The New York Times*, 18 December.
Spivak, Gayatri Chakravorty. 2003. *Death of a Discipline*. New York: Columbia University Press.
———, et al. 2006. *Conversations with Gayatri Spivak*. Calcutta: Seagull Books.
Stein, Gertrude. 2004. "What Is English Literature?" In *Look at Me Now and Here I Am: Selected Works, 1911–1945*. Ed. by Patricia Meyerowitz, 31–58. London: Peter Owen.
Steiner, George. 1990. "A Note on Absolute Tragedy." *Literature and Theology* 4 (2), 147–56.
———. 1992. *Tolstoj of Dostojevski: Een oefening in de oude kritiek*. Trans. by Peter Bergsma. Amsterdam: Bert Bakker.
Steinberg, Leo. 1983. *The Sexuality of Christ in Renaissance Art and in Modern Oblivion*. Chicago: University of Chicago Press.
Stevenson, Jack. 2003. *Dogme Uncut: Lars von Trier, Thomas Vinterberg, and the Gang That Took on Hollywood*. Santa Monica: Santa Monica Press.
Stone, James W. 2010. *Crossing Gender in Shakespeare: Feminist Psychoanalysis and the Difference Within*. New York and London: Routledge.

Taylor, John Russell. 1980. "Federico Fellini." In *Cinema: A Critical Dictionary*. 2 vols. Ed. by Richard Roud, 192–93. New York: Viking; London: Secker and Warburg, 1980.
Thurschwell, Pamela. "The Ghost Worlds of Modern Adolescence." In 2010. *Popular Ghosts: The Haunted Spaces of Everyday Culture*. Ed. by María del Pilar Blanco and Esther Peeren, 239–50. London: Continuum, 2010.
Todorov, Tzvetan. 1984. *Mikhail Bakhtin: The Dialogical Principle*.

Trans. by Wlad Godzich. Minneapolis: University of Minnesota Press.
Tompkins, Jane P., ed. 1980. *Reader-Response Criticism: From Formalism to Post-Structuralism*. London and Baltimore, MD: Johns Hopkins University Press.
Treffers, Bert. 1991. *Caravaggio, genie in opdracht: Een kunstenaar en zijn opdrachtgevers in het Rome van rond 1600*. Nijmegen: SUN.

Verstraten, Peter. 2004. *Celluloid echo's: Cinema kruist postmodernisme*. Nijmegen: Vantilt.
———. 2006. *Handboek filmnarratologie*. Nijmegen: Vantilt.
Visser, Ad de. 1990. *Hardop kijken: Een inleiding in de kunstbeschouwing*. Nijmegen: SUN.
Vos, Joeri. 2009. *Orlando: Werkboek*. Arnhem: Toneelgroep Oostpool.
Vries, Hent de. 1999. *Philosophy and the Turn to Religion*. London and Baltimore, MD: Johns Hopkins University Press.

Weiermair, Peter, ed. 1994. *Dino Pedriali*. Zurich: Stemmle.
Westen, Mirjam, ed. 2009. *Rebelle: Art & Feminism, 1969–2009*. Exh. cat. Arnhem: MMKA.
White, Hayden. 2010. *Metahistory: The Historical Imagination in Nineteenth-Century Europe*. London and Baltimore, MD: Johns Hopkins University Press (orig. pub. 1973).
Whitehead, Alfred North. 1978. *Process and Reality: An Essay in Cosmology*. Ed. by David Ray Griffin and Donald W. Sherburne. New York: Free Press (orig. pub. 1929).
Wilson, Robert. 1989. *Orlando: 22 Zeichnungen*. Zurich: Annemarie Verna Galerie.
Winch, Christopher, and John Gingell. 2004. *Philosophy of Education: The Key Concepts*. 2nd ed. London and New York: Routledge.
Winnicott, Donald W. 2005. *Playing and Reality*. 2nd ed. Abingdon and New York: Routledge (orig. pub. 1971).
Winterson, Jeanette. 2008. *The Stone Gods*. London: Penguin.
Wittgenstein, Ludwig. 2009. *Philosophical Investigations*. Trans. by G.E.M. Anscombe, P.M.S. Hacker and Joachim Schulte. Oxford: Blackwell (4th ed., orig. pub. 1953).
Wolfswinkel, Anneke van. 2010. "Fotografie als verleiding." ‹www.riskhazekamp.nl/fotografiealsverleiding.php› (accessed 9 November 2011).
Woolf, Virginia. 1992. *The Waves*. London: Penguin (orig. pub. 1931).
———. 1993. *Selected Essays: Volume 2: The Crowded Dance of Modern Life*. Ed. by Rachel Bowlby. London: Penguin.

———. 1998. *Orlando*. London: Penguin (orig. pub. 1928).
———. 1953. *A Writer's Diary: Being Extracts from the Diary of Virginia Woolf*. San Diego, New York and London: A Harvest Book.
———. 2000. *A Room of One's Own*. London: Penguin (orig. pub. 1929).

Zengotita, Thomas de. 2005. *Mediated: How the Media Shapes Your World and the Way You Live in It*. London: Bloomsbury.

List of Illustrations

Summary

Could not science become fictional? Fiction would proceed from a new intellectual art.
—Roland Barthes (1994, 90)

This design-orientated study looks closely at a new form of tertiary art education: Art-Based Learning (ABL). This is a way of learning not about, but from art. The following three premises summarise this study:

1. ABL is a different form of thinking.
2. ABL constitutes a way of consulting unconventional sources of knowledge.
3. ABL offers an alternative didactic working method geared to teaching arts and culture in higher education.

A Rich Academic Tradition

ABL is set in a rich academic tradition, with art not constituting the finish, but the start of thought. It is an interdisciplinary approach that is important for literary scholars, theologians, philosophers, anthropologists, psychologists, sociologists, film and theatre scholars, (art) historians and other culture scholars.

The ABL 'edifice' is built primarily on the cultural analysis of Mieke Bal, Ernst van Alphen and Hubert Damish. In their work, art is a highly relevant form of thought; a philosophy in words and images. I have sought to transpose this approach into educative practice.

Christopher Bollas' psychoanalytical studies form another interesting cornerstone. His description of the unthought known is compelling and a useful definition of the unconscious—knowing what has not yet been thought. With this, he opens the way to imagination as a valid form of thinking. Thinking and creativity come together.

Dick Hebdige's anthropological studies are the third important cornerstone. His work on the adolescent constitutes a visual anthropological examination, with cultural artefacts triggering the narration of a story about modern youth culture.

A Different Form of Thinking

ABL is a different form of thinking and is arranged in four domains which express the quality of thinking, but emphatically do not produce uniform results. These domains are generally traversed in a specific order. However the educative design is not linear, but concentric, meaning that every aspect can return at every level.

The first domain relates to "the questioning subject". In Haanstra's authentic learning this corresponds with the authentic question of the student seeking insight in a social context. The personal, topical and so relevant question is the start for a valid dialogue with the art work.

The second domain involves "the speaking object". The student comes in contact with the art work that presents itself as a speaking object. It is important that the art work tells its own story, which presupposes from the spectator a listening attitude and an eye for detail.

The third domain pertains to "the possible worlds". The student embarks on association based on what has gone before, and arrives in the realm of the unthought known. Object and subject of perception converge. The art work becomes part of a possible world.

The fourth domain is that of "story-telling". The student has become a reader and writer; reception becomes production; the scholar becomes an artist. He combines acquired experience with the original question and reaches new conclusions.

An Unconventional Source of Knowledge

ABL takes full advantage of unusual sources of cultural knowledge, thus disclosing adolescence as an interdisciplinary domain of study. To that end, I have put together three triptychs. They came about as unthought known.

The title of the first triptych is "The story of youth and death". The adolescent comes across as a warrior-hero. Three art works are examined, with a painting by Caravaggio *David with the Head of Goliath* (c. 1600), as the primary focus. On its left, a photo by Dino Pedriali, *Autoritratto immaginario* (1989) and on its right, a still from Mathieu Kassovitz' film *La Haine* (1995).

The structure of the story of youth and death is a tragic one. Everything centres around the confrontation with mortality. The moment that the endless potential of youth is discovered is at the same time the moment that you realise life is past in a trice.

Unsurprisingly, black is the dominant colour here. Aristotle echoes in the background. Violence in the contemporary adolescent's world becomes understandable.

The second triptych is headed "The story of the beauty of youth". The adolescent emerges as a poet. A literary work, Virginia Woolf's *Orlando* (1928), is the focal point, with a fragment from Shakespeare's play *As You Like It* (1599) on its left and, on its right, a still from Thomas Vinterberg's film *Dear Wendy* (2005).

This story of youth has a poetic structure. It is the story of beauty of 'otherness'. It tells how youth is also a moment in which the adolescent discovers himself in his otherness.

The dominant colour is white. Schiller and Harold Bloom echo in the background. Romance in the contemporary adolescent's world becomes understandable.

The third triptych is called "The game of youth". The adolescent alternately appears as a tragic, poetic and critical clown. The central panel is a film, Nicholas Ray's *Rebel Without a Cause* (1955). On the left side, we see Risk Hazekamp's photo *Jack off Jimmy* (2001); on the right, a still from Jim Jarmusch's film *Mystery Train* (1989).

This story is ironic in structure. The irony of youth turns adolescence into a moment in which nothing is fixed. The adolescent does not say what he means and does not mean what he says. His perspective is ever changing.. Voices sound within him, and without. The most striking colour is red. Bakhtin speaks in the background. The contemporary adolescent's freedom becomes understandable.

A Contemporary Didactic Working Method

ABL is a contemporary didactic working method which can be deployed in art education and the humanities, provided there is a didactic setting that simultaneously stimulates perception, analysis, imagination and conceptualisation. Didactics, the art of teaching, becomes mathetics, the art of learning.

The learning environment requires open-source philosophy. The college or university no longer suffices as a location. The (virtual) museum, cinema, library or theatre are vital for an intellectual dialogue with the art works in question.

The position of the teacher is, of necessity, one of "intellectual friendship" (a term coined by the postcolonial theorist, Gayatri Spivak). The teacher's main task is to ask provoking questions in order to initiate a productive dialogue between student and art work. This applies in all of the individual fields.

The curriculum has been designed to stimulate integral cognitive development. ABL is a process in which the student is encouraged to engage simultaneously in disciplined close reading, clear logical reasoning and free, creative imagination. Each domain yields new information in this ongoing process of knowledge and insight.

As we said, ABL is also suited to the curricula of academies of art, of dance, of drama and of music, particularly in the field of artistic research. It offers a concrete, didactic methodology in which students and teachers can integrate intellectual and artistic schooling—a process that does not end with graduation, since learning from art is a form of éducation permanente.

Index of Person's Names, Art Works, Exhibitions, Organisations

Index of Terms

Acknowledgements

First of all, I would like to thank all those at Valiz Publishers, without whom the translation and editing of this 2012 thesis would not have been possible. I owe a debt of gratitude to Els Brinkman for the editing, Elke Stevens for the editing and indexing, Wendy van Os-Thompson for the editing and translation, Sam de Groot for the design and image editing based on Paul Scheulderman's material, Sarah van Binsbergen for the PR, Till Hormann for the image research, Pia Pol for the production, and the publisher, Astrid Vorstermans.

In addition, this publication would not have come about without support from ArtEZ, University of the Arts. I am especially grateful to Nishant Shah, member of the ArtEZ Board, Carin Rustema, director of the master's programmes, the members of the team of my professorship in Art education as Critical Tactics (AeCT) at ArtEZ, particularly Veronique Steenmetser, who is an invaluable support for the AeCT professorship in the administrative, communication and production field, and Jan Brand, the former publisher of ArtEZ Press who directed me to Valiz.

Moreover, those people at the University of Amsterdam who were involved with the original Dutch publication in 2012 deserve mention: in particular, my thesis supervisor Prof. dr. Mieke Bal, Paul Scheulderman the designer of the original visual material, and Huug van Gompel, the publisher of the original thesis (Garant). Thanks to their contributions at that time we now have a text for an international audience. A text that relates to Art-Based Learning: an approach to education in dialogue with art works that has already gained a foothold in Europe and farther afield.

And 'last but not least' I wish to thank Jantine, Boris, Robin and Jelijn for their unshakeable belief and confidence in my work. Jantine and I are constantly aware that the new generation—that of Boris, Robin and Jelijn—is one that lives in a world without formal borders, where English is now the lingua franca in the arts and sciences, comparable with Latin in the Middle Ages and the Renaissance. It is this new generation's implicit and explicit plea that prompted this undertaking.

About the Author

Jeroen Lutters is an art and culture analyst and educational designer. His critical educational theory concentrates on the central role of the arts and humanities in the contemporary curriculum, the need for artist educators as wandering teachers, the theory and practice of art-based learning, and the development of twenty-first-century educational landscapes. His most recent publications focus on art-based learning, for instance: *The Shadow of the Art Work: The Practice of Art-Based Learning* (Garant, 2012 / Valiz 2019), *Teaching Objects: Studies in Art Based Learning* (ArtEZ Press, 2015), *Ema: Nude on a Staircase: Studies in Art Based Learning* (ArtEZ Press, 2017) and *Cy Twombly's Quattro Stagioni: Studies in Art-Based Learning* (ArtEZ Press, 2018). As an educational designer he participated in several multi-level and interdisciplinary educational designs with a focus on creativity, such as: the Bernard Lievegoed University (Driebergen), Teacher College (Almere and Zwolle), ArtEZ International Research School and International Master Artist Educator (Arnhem), No School (Eindhoven and Zwolle), and Create Space (Arnhem and Nijmegen).

Author: Jeroen Lutters
Editing: Els Brinkman, Jeroen Lutters, Elke Stevens, Wendy van Os-Thompson
Translation Dutch–English: Wendy van Os-Thompson
Proofreading: Els Brinkman
Image editing: Jeroen Lutters, Paul Scheulderman
Index: Elke Stevens
Design: Sam de Groot
Layout assistance: Alexandre De Sousa
Typefaces: Eldorado (William Addison Dwiggins, 1953), Computer Modern (Donald Knuth, 1984), SKI DATA (Tariq Heijboer, 2014)
Printing and binding: Bariet/Ten Brink, Meppel
Publisher: Astrid Vorstermans, Valiz, Amsterdam, ‹www.valiz.nl›

Distribution
NL/BE/LU: Centraal Boekhuis, ‹www.cb.nl›
GB/IE: Anagram Books, ‹www.anagrambooks.com›
Europe/Asia: Idea Books, ‹www.ideabooks.nl›
USA: DAP, ‹www.artbook.com›
Australia: Perimeter, ‹www.perimeterdistribution.com›
Individual orders: ‹www.valiz.nl›

This publication is kindly supported by ArtEZ University of the Arts, ArtEZ International Research School (AIRS) and International Master Artist Educator (IMAE), Art Based Learning Centre (ABLC), Arnhem–Zwolle–Enschede (NL).

ISBN 978-94-92095-66-4
Printed and bound in the EU

vis-à-vis

The vis-à-vis series provides a platform to stimulating and relevant subjects in recent and emerging visual arts, architecture and design. The authors relate to history and art history, to other authors, to recent topics and to the reader. Most are academic researchers. What binds them is a visual way of thinking, an undaunted treatment of the subject matter and a skilful, creative style of writing.

Series design by Sam de Groot, ‹www.samdegroot.nl›.

2015

Sophie Berrebi, *The Shape of Evidence: Contemporary Art and the Document*, ISBN 978-90-78088-98-1

Janneke Wesseling, *De volmaakte beschouwer: De ervaring van het kunstwerk en receptie-esthetica*, ISBN 978-94-92095-09-1 (e-book)

2016

Janneke Wesseling, *Of Sponge, Stone and the Intertwinement with the Here and Now: A Methodology of Artistic Research*, ISBN 78-94-92095-21-3

2017

Janneke Wesseling, *The Perfect Spectator: The Experience of the Art Work and Reception Aesthetics*, ISBN 978-90-80818-50-7

Wouter Davidts, *Triple Bond: Essays on Art, Architecture, and Museums*, ISBN 978-90-78088-49-3

Sandra Kisters, *The Lure of the Biographical: On the (Self-)Representation of Artists*, ISBN 978-94-92095-25-1

Christa-Maria Lerm Hayes (ed.), *Brian O'Doherty/Patrick Ireland: Word, Image and Institutional Critique*, ISBN 978-94-92095-24-4

2018

John Macarthur, Susan Holden, Ashley Paine, Wouter Davidts, *Pavilion Propositions: Nine Points on an Architectural Phenomenon*, ISBN 978-94-92095-50-3

Jeroen Lutters, *The Trade of the Teacher: Visual Thinking with Mieke Bal*, ISBN 978-94-92095-56-5

Ernst van Alphen, *Failed Images: Photography and its Counter-Practices*, ISBN 978-94-92095-45-9

Paul Kempers, *'Het gaat om heel eenvoudige dingen': Jean Leering en de kunst*, ISBN 978-94-92095-07-7

Eva Wittocx, Ann Demeester, Melanie Bühler, *The Transhistorical Museum: Mapping the Field*, ISBN 978-94-92095-52-7

2019

Nathalie Zonnenberg, *Conceptual Art in a Curatorial Perspective: Between Dematerialization and Documentation*, ISBN 978-90-78088-76-9

Wouter Davidts, Susan Holden, Ashley Paine (eds.), *Trading between Architecture and Art: Strategies and Practices of Exchange*, ISBN 978-94-92095-67-1